Stratification and Social Change among Tribals

Stratification and Social Change among Tribals

An Anthropological Study among the Sherdukpens of Arunachal Pradesh

RINCHIN MEGEJEE

Indira Gandhi Rashtriya Manav Sangrahalaya, Bhopal
(National Museum of Mankind)

RAWAT PUBLICATIONS
Jaipur • New Delhi • Bangalore • Guwahati • Kolkata

ISBN 978-81-316-0853-1

Published by
Indira Gandhi Rashtriya Manav Sangrahalaya
Shamla Hills, Bhopal-462013 (Madhya Pradesh)
email: directorigrms@gmail.com

Prem Rawat for **Rawat Publications**
Satyam Apts, Sector 3, Jawahar Nagar, Jaipur 302 004 (India)
Phone: 0141 265 1748 / 7006 Fax: 0141 265 1748
E-mail: info@rawatbooks.com
Website: www.rawatbooks.com

New Delhi Office
4858/24, Ansari Road, Daryaganj, New Delhi 110 002
Phone: 011 2326 3290

Also at *Bangalore, Guwahati* and *Kolkata*

Printed at Chaman Enterprises, New Delhi

Contents

Foreword

This book is a valuable addition to the context of understanding the tribal situation of Arunachal Pradesh; and also for a critical cognition on the nature of inequality or stratification – a reality deeply embedded in the social structure of the tribe under study. Moreover, this is the first publication of a book on Sherdukpens by a Sherdukpen anthropologist which has added implications in the context of new methodological and epistemological discourse. Rinchin Megejee deserves appreciation because of his intense engagement with the cross section of the key actors of studied villages and his analytical acumen to focus on the nature of stratification, their implications on socio-political domains as well as the emerging realities of a frontier state.

As the supervisor, I am privileged to write a foreword for this book which is very comprehensive from the perspective of contemporary ethnography and hope it will pave the way for future research not only on the Sherdukpens but also on the other tribes located in similar context. As the Director of IGRMS, Bhopal, I am highly indebted to all members of our Academic Advisory Committee who unanimously recommended this book for publication as per the mandates of this prime national museum, which has always paved the way for a special focus on India's North East and its people.

The Academic Advisory Committee of IGRMS has decided to bring out a series of publications from the doctoral works under the title 'Recognition of Emerging Scholars in Anthropology and Related Disciplines' from 2017 onwards. This is the first volume in this series, written by an indigenous anthropologist on his own community located in Arunachal Pradesh.

Sarit Kumar Chaudhuri
Director, Indira Gandhi Rashtriya Manav Sangrahalaya,
Shamla Hills, Bhopal (M.P.), India

Acknowledgements

The completion of this thesis is the outcome of the endeavour of so many people at different phases of Ph.D. programme and fieldwork undertaken on the Sherdukpen community of Arunachal Pradesh.

Naturally, my sincere thanks and gratitude goes to my teacher Prof. Sarit. K. Chaudhuri, for encouraging and helping me with his valuable suggestions at all times. He has been friendly, resourceful and was always prompt in responding to whatever information I sought for. I remain grateful to him for all his suggestions and the hours long discussions.

My sincere thanks also to Prof. Tamo Mibang, Vice Chancellor of Rajiv Gandhi University, Dr. Sucheta S. Chaudhuri, Dr. H. Vokendro Singh, and Dr. Jumyir Basar for their cooperation. I am also thankful to Prof. A.K. Thakur, Department of History, NEHU for his valuable suggestions provided at different stages of my doctoral work.

My gratitude goes to Mr. Sonam Phunchu Khrime, Mr. Rinchin Wangdi Khrime, Mr. Sang Tsering Thongdok, Mr. Dorjee Khandu Sinchaji, Mr. Chumbi Megeji, Mr. Dorjee Khandu Megeji, Mr. Leiki Khandu Megeji and Mrs. Rinchin Wangmu Thongchi from Thongre village; Mr. Dorjee Khandu Khrime, Mrs. Pema Chomu Khrime, Mr. Sang Khandu Khrime, Mr. Nima Tsering Khrime, Mr. Dorjee Khandu Thongdok, Mrs. Yese Dema Thongdok, Mr. Rinchin Dorjee Mosobi, Mr. Rinchin Khandu Karma, Mrs. Tsering Dema Megeji, Mr. Sang Norbu Thongchi, Mr. Yeshi Dorjee Thongdok, Mrs. Nima Wangmu Thongon, Mrs. Pema Yangjom Khrime, Mr. Prem Thongdok, Mr. Wangchu Thongdok, Mrs. Pemchom Thongdok, Mrs. Pema Lozom Thongon Mrs. Chewang Dema Wangja, Mrs. Nima Wangmu Megeji, Mr. Dorjee Khandu Dingla and Mr. Rinchin Dorjee Thongdok from Rupa; Mrs. Pema Dema Megeji, Mrs. Namgey Wangmu Wangja, Mr. Kesang Tsering Megeji, Mr. Rinchin Dorjee Megeji, Mr. Rinchin Dorjee Thongchi, and Mr. Rinchin Norbu Thongchi from Jigaon – for their consideration and for taking time out from their hectic schedule and sitting with me for hours to share information. I am indebted to all of them for their immense help. Besides, my heartfelt thanks also goes to all the people of Rupa, Thongre and Jigaon villages who cooperated with me during my field survey and provided information in all possible manners. Mr. Dor Gombu Megeji, Mr. Pema Dorjee Megeji, Mrs. Tsering Chom Khrime, and Pengkhai deserve my hearfelt thanks as they assisted me throughout my field survey.

I am grateful to the officers of Anthropological Survey of India, NERC, Shillong, for helping me in providing the much-needed materials.

It is my humble acknowledgement to the authorities of Rajiv Gandhi University for allowing me to access the facilities available, including library, computers, internet, etc. Without the incorporation of all those resources, it would not have been possible for me to articulate this work. Further, several faculty members and the non-teaching staff of the university assisted me during the period of my research work, both academic and official, I express my sincere gratitude to them, for their kind acts.

I am grateful to the University Grant Commission for the fellowship grant which helped me financially to accomplish various Ph.D. related works both in the field and at the department.

I am thankful to all my friends – Pachang Miji, Tarun Mene, Mari Lollen, Wangrao Taidong of AITS, RGU, and Chow Nakunand Singkai of Geography Department – for their constant support and encouragement. I am also thankful to all my friends, who were always there to support me morally during the trying periods in completing my report. I am thankful to David Waikhomba Singh for extending help in getting the final draft of the thesis ready.

I am thankful to my parents who encouraged me to pursue my higher studies and who constantly provided me with the strength and comfort of their presence and assistance, without them I would never have been able to reach this far.

Mr. Rana Deb and Mr. N. Adhikari also deserve praise for typing of the handwritten script of my thesis.

Finally, I am extremely grateful to the members of Academic Advisory Committee of IGRMS who accepted my work for publication under a special series. Thanks to Mr. Sudhir Shrivastava who remained in touch with me to ensure that all necessary editing is done so that the book could be released at right time. I must acknowledge the valuable editorial assistance received from Rawat Publications for finalization of the manuscript.

Rinchin Megejee

List of Tables, Charts, Illustrations and Figures

List of Charts

List of Illustrations

List of Figures

Map of India showing position of Arunachal Pradesh

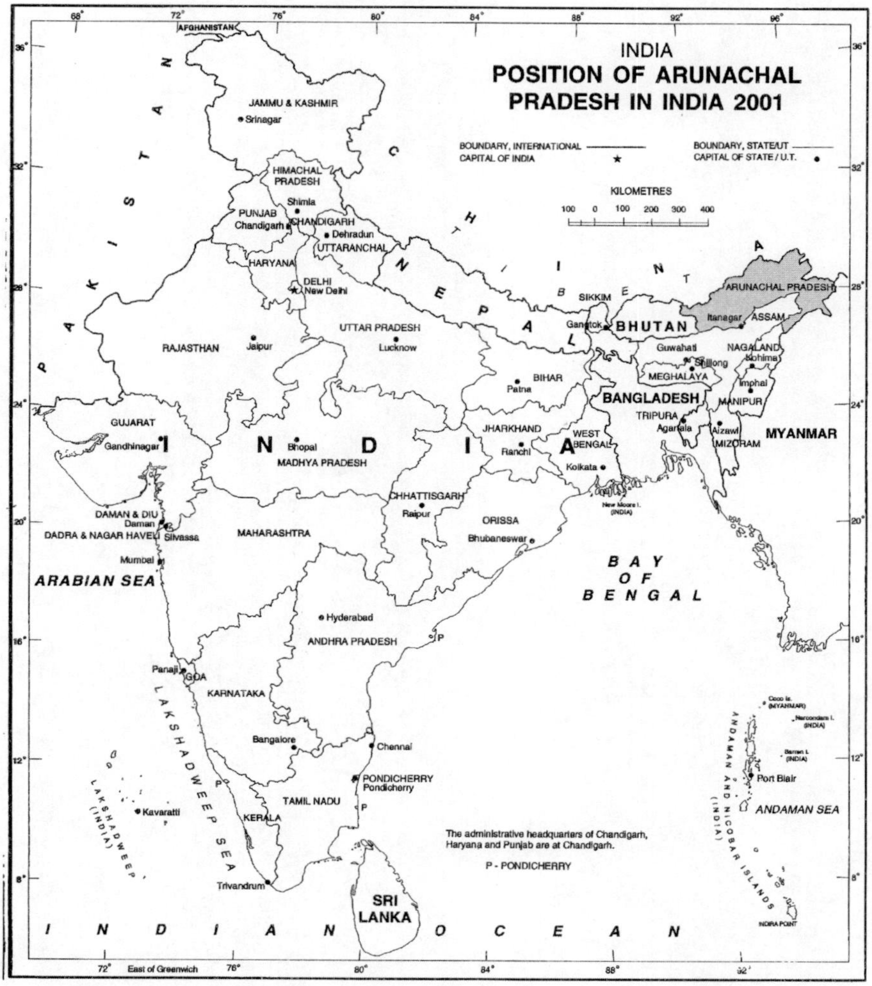

1

Introduction

Arunachal Pradesh is a land of multi-ethnic groups. It lies in the easternmost part of India and is also known as 'the land of rising sun'. Arunachal Pradesh lies between 26°–29° N latitude and 91°–97° E longitude. It spreads over an area of 83,743 square kilometres and has a long international boundary with Bhutan to the west, Tibet and China in the north and the north-east and Myanmar in the east. Extending its length to 1,628 km, the high Himalayan ranges with perpetual snow exist along the Tibetan border in the north outlining the border between India and Tibet through the McMahon line. These ranges are the source of the watersheds of the river system which penetrates into several river courses through the hills and valleys of the territory of Arunachal Pradesh (*Encyclopaedia of North-East India*, Vol-I: p. 2).

The state is divided into five river valleys: The Kameng, the Subansiri, the Siang, the Lohit and the Tirap. Besides these, it has many hilly slopes, deep forests and dales. The state is home to 26 major tribes and more than 100 sub-tribes. The state is predominantly tribal with 64.22 per cent of tribal population out of the total population according to 2001 census. The people of the state have a rich cultural heritage, their dance forms, songs, arts and crafts of magnificent beauty have enriched the culture of the state. The people mainly practise Donyi-Poloism and Buddhism with Christianity gaining grounds in the region.

With so much diverse culture and tribes within the state little has been known about them, as there is lack of research works undertaken through all the tribes. The number of research works undertaken, on Arunachal tribes, are very few leaving out some of the major tribes. For instance, no major works have been done on the Sherdukpen tribe leaving the ethnographic work entitled *The Sherdukpens* by R.R.P. Sharma (1960) and Verrier Elwin's (1958) *Myths of the North East Frontier of India* where Elwin has collected a good number of folktales regarding this tribe. Whatever writings that have come up after these regarding the Sherdukpens are not of much relevance as they usually follow on the previous writings, so, hardly any new information is incorporated in the later writings. As an opportunity to undertake a research and to write through my Ph.D. dissertation, I took this chance of concentrating on a small Buddhist tribe of Arunachal Pradesh, i.e. the Sherdukpen.

Statement of the Problem

Stratification can be seen in every society, even in the so called simple societies which have some differences in advantages based on ability or gender; adults have higher status than children, the skilled more than unskilled, and men more than women. Social stratification is a universal phenomenon, an unavoidable feature of all human societies, though found in different forms and degree (Sharma, 2010: p. 14). Thus, stratification in a society shows an unequal pattern of distribution of status, power, etc. among the individuals or group of individuals. According to Gupta (1991: p. 8), "Social stratification is the ordering of social differences with the help of a set of criteria or just a single criterion which ties the differentiated strata into a system". For Barber (1956), "it is the person in a society who rates one as high and low and treats another as better and worse, they value each other on various scales." According to the Sills *International Encyclopaedia of the Social Science* (1972: p. 138), "Social stratification in its most general sense, is a sociological concept that refers to the fact that both individuals and groups of individuals are conceived of as constituting higher and lower differentiated strata, or class, in terms of characteristics". For Merril (1962: p. 259), "Social stratification is the product of social interaction".

The concept of inequality is centred on stratification. Social inequality may be in social structure or among the members of the society and its entrance or exit depends on the model of stratification (Sharma, 1985). "Equality and inequality are relative phenomena, and undergo perceptible change over a period of time due to both structural and cultural factors of social change. There is always a striving for equality, and in this process, at times, new forms of inequality may also emerge, along with disappearance/weakening of the persisting inequalities" (Sharma, 2010: p. 34). The notion of stratification is intrinsically linked with the concept of "caste system" without which we can't understand the Indian socio-political realities (Srinivas, 1977; Bose, 1975). Many valuable studies have been done from anthropological, sociological or from other disciplinary perspectives on social stratification like that of Barber

(1956), Sharma (1997), Chauhan (1980), Berreman (1979), Beteille (1971), Ghurye (1957), Blunt (1969), Hutton (1951), Dirk (2001), etc. Though, such studies are on social stratification but pivoted around the caste system which is precisely an endogamous hereditary group showing a hierarchical system, not dependent on wealth but associated with distinct ritual status and is ascribed, whereas, a class is a division of society on the basis of wealth status and can be achieved.

On the contrary, traditionally, the notion of stratification is hardly used for understanding Indian tribes who are, by and large, portrayed as egalitarian in character. Quoting Shalin (1958) and Leach (1964) even Beteille (1972: p. 7) mentioned that the tribal or primitive societies differ greatly in the complexities of their organisations. The simpler ones are not marked by rigid social stratification although here even age and sex are important criteria of inequality. He added (ibid.) that Leach has shown how among the Kachins of Highland Burma, the rules of kinship and marriage serve to place individuals in a hierarchical order.

However, last three decades of research on the tribal situations in India have provided sufficient grounds to rethink on such myths, as one can see, the notion of stratifications in various forms in tribal society also. For instance, the study by Misra (1998) in which he talks regarding the emerging pattern of stratification among the Khamptis of Arunachal Pradesh. He tries to find out the role of the status; the interrelation of the status; property and power; its transformation and consequences. J.N. Chowdhury (1976) provides some evidences regarding caste like features in some Arunachal tribes. Thakur (1998) talks on the evolution of stratification among the Monpa, Nyishi and Sherdukpen of Arunachal Pradesh. He tried to show how the influential sections of the society made successful attempts to control both resources and productions. Along with this he also explains how the contact with the neighbouring society and British rule acted as a booster in the context of stratification. Deliege (1980) deals with the transformation of tribal section into caste among the Bhils. According to Ghosh and Soni (1990) the stratification and social changes among the tribes of central India resulted due to contact with non-tribal settlers. Dey (2004) focuses on the class structure of Sherdukpen community of Arunachal Pradesh and the impact of education on it. Understanding such stratification and its implication on the tribes is extremely essential in order to understand the tribes of India who are passing through a phase of transition.

However, in the context of North-East India in general and Arunachal Pradesh in specific, such studies are not so much traceable though the questions or the issues of stratification are very much imbued with the existing tribal social structure which need special attention from a holistic perspective in order to understand the emerging contemporary realities. In the context of Arunachal Pradesh, which is the core area of present study, the most glaring and referred work which distinctly surfaced on the very existence of social stratification is Haimendorf's work on the Apatani tribe (1962) which he restudied later (1979). Stratification can be seen in Apatani tribe, as Haimendorf (1962: p. 29) cited that "there can be two classes differing in status. An upper class whose members own the larger part of the land and wield political power in clan and village, and a lower class which consists of free men owning their own land as well as of domestic slaves".

Reference may be cited from Arunachal tribes where the society is shown to be stratified. Though few studies have been done in relation to this, reflections on stratification are traceable within numerous tribes from those works. Dutta (1990, 2005) in his ethnographic study on the Wanchos and Noctes also gave a brief account on the type of stratification which the Wancho and Nocte chieftainships reflect. Roy (1960) in his book *Aspects of Padam-Minyong Culture* has shown that the Minyong society is divided into moieties; but he does not tell about the status or inequality in the society. Stratification can be seen among the Khamptis also. Sarkar (1987) gave a brief idea on the stratification among the Khampti. In Borkhampti the differentiation of clans of the Khamptis is based on the specialisation of occupation, which is very similar to the Hindu caste system such as: (i) the noble (ii) ordinary farming class and (iii) the lower class (fisher man, pig keeper, butcher, etc.) (ibid.: p. 83). He tells, "though in the course of settlement in the recent settled village i.e. Momong, the earlier form of stratification does not exist but the feeling of higher and lower status persists, specially during marriage where the Royal clan generally do not marry with the clans who are not considered as the clans of the officials..." Mention can be found in Elwin's (1957) book regarding the social division among the Arunachal tribes. Elwin (1957: p. 9) cited, "There are social, but not caste, distinction, in many tribes… and marriage between them is not usually permitted. But all eat together and take part in the tribal councils, festivals and dances."

Stratification can be seen among the Sherdukpen tribes also, which constitutes the universe of the present study, where the society is divided into three classes—*Thong*, *Chao* and *Yanlog*. The *Thong* is considered to be the topmost in the hierarchy, *Chao* in the middle and *Yanlog* at the lowest. The *Thongs* are considered to be the king clans or aristocrat clans, *Chaos* the commoner and *Yanlog* the blacksmith who came from Bhutan and settled in

Sherdukpen area. However, the *Yanlog* have been abolished by the council (*Blu*) by letting them get absorbed in the main class of the society. Thus in the present context only two classes, i.e. *Thong* and *Chao* exist. The existing classes of Sherdukpen show shadows of caste characteristics in some ways. The class is ascribed and not achieved by a person. As economy is the main criteria for the class distinction but here the economic condition of the person does not define his/her class or to which class he or she should belong, rather one's birth is the criteria for the class classification.

Although the Sherdukpen society is changing and losing many of its traditional characteristics and social rigidity but in the collective psyche that sense of division still persists which regulates its social relations. For instance, if we look at the contemporary political leaders who emerged in the state electoral political system, it is found that they belong to the upper stratum only. However, no significant research work has been done so far to locate such a unique dimension of tribal life contesting the so called notion of "egalitarianism" and more importantly to understand the emerging realities of a frontier tribal state.

Some of the Earlier Works

In the context of stratification and its transformation in India, many studies are available. Dasgupta, Hennessey and Mukhopadhyay (2000) examined the extent to which class and caste continue to be closely related. Deliege (1980), Ghosh and Soni (1990) show how a tribe when it comes in contact with other society acquires their characters and creates differentiation within the tribes itself for the resulting stratification.

Chakraborty (1996) examines how the notion of caste persists in society even after the society has passed through many intermediate phases. Chattopadhyay (1966) also demonstrates how the society tries to rearrange itself into classes based on economic relation but falls back due to strong kinship ties. Mookherjee and Dasgupta (1970), Mookherjee (1967) in their papers attempt to show how the societies try to improve their status by adopting the characters of the caste higher than theirs.

Sharma (1970) and Srivastava (1970) compare the stratification system in terms of traditional caste hierarchy and the pattern of interaction among different castes, whereas, Kassebaum (1974) tries to show how far caste system in India poses a barrier to intergenerational occupational mobility and the social characteristics involved. Mukhopadhyay (1997) tries to keep forward the way in which the production relations in agriculture are unmeshed with caste and kinship structures.

Chakravorty (1989) tries to find out the evolution of caste stratification and its conversion into occupational basis. Behura (1993) on the other hand examines Dumont's concept of caste hierarchy based on twin concepts of ritual purity and pollution. Danda (1986) examines how along with other factors, differential control over information or knowledge indicates differential levels of distribution of prerogatives and adds new dimension in understanding the system of stratification.

Debnath (1995) made an attempt to reveal the continuity and change, in the caste system, from pre- to post-independence era. Kumar (2002), Jain (1967) and Srinivas (1962) show how politics has inculcated in caste and how individuals try to achieve higher social status.

Misra (1997) examines the contribution of some notable scholars on the debate where the tribe ends and caste begins. Mathur (1998) and Ali (1974) examine the stratification among the Muslim society, though the egalitarian social order of Islam stands in sharp contrast with the ideology of caste. On the other hand, Borthakur (1997) shows how the society of Assam is stratified but the division is different from the Hindu model of stratification.

Change is a social reality and everything keeps on transforming. Social change becomes necessary to enable people to march with the times and register progress (Mibang, 1994: p. 87). The change may be due to various reasons. Studies on this line have also attracted the attention of many researchers. Dubey (1972: p. 1) cited, "The main basis of increasing rate of mobility are equal opportunity to the aspirants, open competition and the sense of individual achievement". In the content of achievement, Srinivas (1977: p. 95) cited, "It is the Indian elite who have taken upon themselves the great task of modernising their society". Sachidananda (1988) tells how the impact of modern technology affects the social life.

Mahapatra (1977) makes an extension of the work of T.C. Das who worked on social change and examines the changes brought about due to culture contact and development. Deogaonkar (2005) provides evidence of social change which took place among Maria, Gond and Kolams due to the introduction of market economy and implementation of welfare schemes. Gowloog (2001) shows the change among the Lepchas of Sikkim with passage of time. Mibang (1994) examines various agents which lead to changes in the life of the Minyong after independence.

In the edited book *Transition, Change and Transformation* by Sarkar (2003) good number of papers can be traced on the issue of social change. Papers such as of Sathyanarayanan, Hazra, Mohidden and Ramanna, Bera, Athparia, Chaudhuri and Sahay have given a good account on the social change of Toda,

Gujjar, Chenchus, Riang, Noctes, Pao and Man tribes of India. The change may be due to the impact of social change but the degree of impact is different in their respective tribes which they have studied. In each study one can see that even if there has been an impact it has not totally altered the society. In each case, age-old practises are still being followed with the new ones. Sarkar (2003: p. 3) mentioned, "In the contemporary Indian situation such aspiration does not move beyond certain stage which would cause complete transformation, instead the process of transition tends to become static at some level which is suitable for continuance of tribal identity". Das (2005), Shah (2005), Sinha (1992), Patel (1997), Srinivas (1997), Debnath (1998) and Mondal (2006) demonstrate how the modern political system and educational system have changed the traditional social set up of Korwas, Kolis, indigenous groups of North Bengal and so on. Their study underscored the impact of modernisation. But change can also be due to compulsion. Singh (1993) and Prasad (1989) have shown how compulsion brought changes in the social set up.

In the context of Arunachal tribes very few studies can be traced regarding stratification, but, mention on stratification can be found in some books on Arunachal tribes, for instance, Roy (1960) on Minyong, Sarkar (1987) on Khampti and Elwin (1957) on tribes of Arunachal in general. Mishra (1998) made an attempt to study the stratification among the Khampti and the impact of modern political system on it. Dey (2004) worked on the class structure and the impact of education on the Sherdukpen tribe. Koley (1999) worked on tribal village council of the Sherdukpen and the effect of Panchayati Raj system over it. Sharma (1960) provided an ethnographic study on the Sherdukpen. Chakravarty (1973) wrote very brief ethnographic note on Sherdukpens while Sarkar (1990), Deuri (1977) provided a brief account on their religious life. Jatso's (2003) account on the history of migration of the Sherdukpen and Megejee (2006) examines the marriage system among the Sherdukpen society in general. He did not stress on the differences according to the so called class structure which exist in the society.

So far as the theoretical aspects are concerned, to understand the complex aspects of stratification we have two fundamental approaches given by Marx and Weber. The former one is called as reductionism where economy remains at the centre stage and the later one is called pluralist where the interplay between status and power holds the key to understand inequality (Beteille, 1972: pp. 4–9).

Objectives of the Study

In this study I have tried to understand the historicity and nature of stratification in the Sherdukpen's society. Even an attempt was made to see the implication of material as well as economic life on stratification within the society and on various traditional socio-political institutions, religious systems and on social structure and value systems and also tried to see the implications of stratification today when the Sherdukpen society is passing through a crucial phase of transition.

Area of Study

Sherdukpens settled in the West Kameng district of Arunachal Pradesh in three circles, i.e. Rupa, Kalaktang and Bhalukpong. The names of the villages of Sherdukpen's are Rupa, Thongre, Brokpublong, Chillipam, Jigaon, Shergaon, Musaksing, Mukhuting, Minkhyur, Dikshipam, Birpur (Gyung), Lumbaktang, and Membachur, but the main villages are Rupa, Jigaon and Shergaon. Leaving these three villages, all the villages of Sherdukpen are thinly populated with a population of less than 300 persons per village. All these villages fall under the Rupa and Kalaktang circles. Doimara (Ruchong) which used to be a winter camp in past comes under Bhalukpong circle. The people used to camp in this place for trading with the plains of Assam and also to avoid chilly winter seasons (*Encyclopaedia of North-East India*, Vol-I 2001: p. 133; Mackenzie, 1979: p. 19; Sen, 1986: p. 27). The total population of the Sherdukpen is about 3310 according to 2001 census which is spread over in different villages. The present study is concentrated on three villages—Rupa, Thongre and Jigaon. Rupa is the circle headquarter, the main village of the Sherdukpen people. Even till date the judiciary matter is controlled by the Rupa council. Thongre is a village which is to the south of Rupa is about 5 km inside, by the motor road, by the bank of river called *Dinik-Kho*. Jigaon village is located on the highway to Shergaon by the bank of the river called *Doblo-Kho*.

The Sherdukpen society as cited earlier is divided into two classes—*Thong* on the higher strata and *Chao* on the lower. However, besides these, there is another class which is considered to be on the lowest strata of the society is *Yanlog*. They are so called by the people of the society, as the smiths who came from Bhutan and were gradually accepted in Sherdukpen society. Reference on this relation can be found in *Encyclopaedia of North-East India*, (Vol-I, 2001: p. 135; Sharma, 1960: pp. 49–50). But whether the division of the society is a class in reality, as class is believed to be an achieved one but it is not the case with Sherdukpen.

What is class? Let's discuss this issue from the perspectives of renowned proponents, i.e. Marx and Weber. According to Marx, class within the society is based on the mode of production (Sharma, 2010: p. 69). Hence he refers to only two classes (a) owners of the means of production (bourgeoisie), and (b) workers (proletariat) (Ibid.: p. 70). To put his concept of class in greater context, Marx describes history in terms of three periods, namely, ancient, feudalism and capitalism, characterised by a predominant mode of production, consisting of a ruling class and an oppressed class (ibid.: p. 71).

For Weber class is an economic category, a product of market situation (ibid.: p. 79). To Weber the class component arises due to market situation where the group of people have in common a specific causal component of their life chance (Ibid.: p. 81). Thus, the term class refers to any group of people that is found in the same class situation (ibid.: p. 82). Thus "class" is created by economic interest involving "market" (ibid.: p. 81).

These ideas of class put by Marx and Weber do not fit the Sherdukpen society. In the Sherdukpen society the mode of production is not controlled by a particular section or group of people as viewed by Marx in his division of class. In relation to Weber too it is difficult to examine the Sherdukpen society, where he sees the division in relation to the market economy only.

In relation to class, MacIver and Page (1998: p. 348) define it as "...any categories or type within which individuals or units fall." They saw 'status' as the criterion for social class and said, "It is the sense of status, sustained by economic, political, or ecclesiastical power, and by the distinctive modes of life and cultural expressions corresponding to them, that draws class apart from class, gives cohesion to each class, and stratifies a whole society". Here the definition of social class is not formulated in economic terms, but they believed that it is an alternative approach to class put by Marx and Weber. Hence they categorised "social class" determined by status criterion and economic class determined by economic criterion.

In context of present study on Sherdukpen, I am going with MacIver and Page's concept on "class" which fits with the society. As the Sherdukpen division is not based on the market economy rather it is based on status. Though the term "class" will be used to refer to the division of the Sherdukpen society but it will be determined by "status" as in class concept of MacIver and Page.

Methodology

The whole work is based on extensive fieldwork covering three Sherdukpen villages, as mentioned in the area of study, by using conventional anthropological techniques of data collection such as interview, observation, case study, genealogy along with audio visual technique.

In interview method both structured and unstructured techniques have been applied. Interviews had been done from the different strata in which the society is divided keeping gender dimension in purview. Its validity was confirmed by doing cross verifications among the different groups wherever necessary. An attempt was made to collect a lot of folklore materials of different genres in relation to various strata and for understanding their own perception of migration.

It may be mentioned here that with the publication of books by James Clifford and George Marcus (1986), Marcus and Fischer (1986) and Clifford (1988), some important questions are raised about established practises of fieldwork, ethnographic preparations and interpretations. This critique of Anthropology is a part of ongoing movement in social sciences known as postmodernism. The researcher tried to take care of the emerging debates, so that the question of polyphony, contesting ideas and the intricacies of anthological knowledge as well as fieldwork tradition (Das, 1998; Thapan, 1998; Chaudhuri, 1998; Haider, 1998; Madan, 1998; Berreman, 2004; and Kloos, 2004) can be dealt with while collecting and analysing data and constructing ethnographic text on the Sherdukpen.

Moreover, the researcher, being a Sherdukpen by birth, is also aware about the current debates related to "emic" and "etic" perspectives in anthropology (Obeyesekere, 2004; Srinivas, 2004; Mascarenhaskeyes, 2004) which Narayan (1998) brings out excellently by arguing how "Native" is the native's point of view. Moreover, researcher believes what Lambek (2002: p. 3) said, "The best anthropology is also self critical; here our concern with overcoming the various and multiple forms of ethnocentricism and intellectual narrowness remains a characteristic feature of any contribution that wishes seriously to be taken as anthropological".

2

Land and People

Sherdukpen is one of the major tribes of Arunachal Pradesh inhabiting the western part of the state. The term Sherdukpen is defined as "The King of East Bhutan" by Grewal (1997) in his book *Tribes of Arunachal Pradesh: Identity, Culture and Language*. It may be right as *Shar* means East, *Duk* refers to Bhutan and *Pan* means King. However, during the course of fieldwork it was said by the mass that the term Shedukpen in actual is Shertukpen.[1] The term Shertukpen means the people of Sher i.e. Shergaon and Tukpen i.e. Rupa. The Monpas and Sherdukpens, together find mention in the British records as Bhutias (Chatterjee 1991). In Mackenzie's report these people were referred as *Chardwar Bhutias* under Extra-Bhutan Bhutias. He mentioned (1979: p. 18) that "Eastward of Kuriapara lies the extensive division of Char Dwar or the four passes, on the borders of which are the Rooprai Ganw and Sher Ganw Bhutias". Bose (1997: p. 57) mentioned the people of Rupa and Shergaon as Bhutia Roop Roe Gya (rooprai gaon) and Surgyah. It is also difficult to make a justification as this word does not belong to the so called Sherdukpen or Shertukpen tribe itself. It is a Tibetan word. The Sherdukpen used *Me* to denote themselves in the society. The term Shertukpen in present context by which they represent themselves to the outsider is not used within the society. However, in the present study the term Sherdukpen will be used as it was approved in the proposed synopsis.

Population

The total population according to 2001 census is 3,310 (see Table 2.1 for detail information). But this total population cannot be taken for granted as the division in census counting is done on ST and non-ST basis of the state. It is to be noted here that it may include other ST population of the state. However we

Map of Arunachal Pradesh

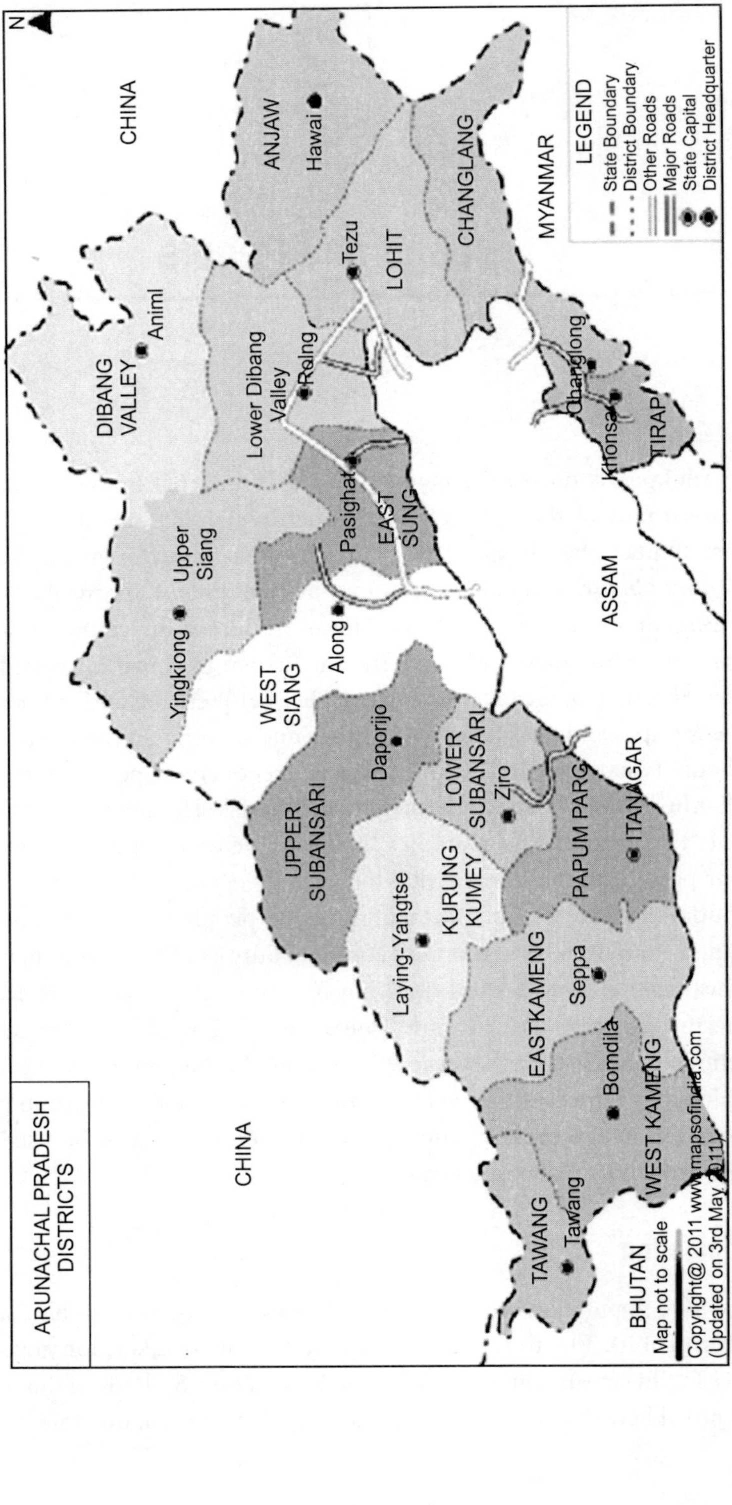

can say that there may be approximately 4000–5000 of Sherdukpen population throughout the state.

Table 2.1 Total population of the Sherdukpen villages

Villages	*Male*	*Female*	*Total Population*
Rupa	637	589	1220
Shergaon	334	327	661
Brokpublong	19	21	40
Thongre	124	126	250
Chillipam	71	58	129
Lumbaktang	54	51	105
Jigaon	182	163	345
Musaksing	47	43	90
Membachur	53	76	129
Mukhuting	36	38	74
Jungpam	54	44	98
Dikshipam	80	89	169
TOTAL	1691	1619	3310

Source: Census of India 2001

Location

The Sherdukpen's are distributed in three circles of West Kameng district i.e. Kalaktang circle, Rupa circle and Bhalukpong circle. But mostly all villages fall under Rupa circle. In Bhalukpong only the Doimara (Ruchong) falls which used to be the winter camp or a camping place used in past while trading with the plains. Shergaon falls under Kalaktang circle. The rest of the hamlets (*pams*) which are now villages such as Brokpublong, Thongre, Chillipam, Lumbaktang, Jigaon, Musaksing, Membachur, Jungpam, Dikshipam along with Rupa which itself falls under Rupa circle.

The Sherdukpen valley is traversed by many streams of which some are non perennial. During monsoon season the current of the water used to be strong and swift. The drainage is from west to east. The main river is *Ziding Kho* which flows from Mandala-phudung (monpa area) and descends to Kameng river. Two other rivers, *Dinik kho* flows from Thongre and *Doblo Kho* which flows from Shergaon and meet *Ziding Kho* at Rupa.

The altitude of the Sherdukpen areas ranges from 5000 to 6500 feet above the sea level (Sharma, 1960: p. 3), because of this variation the villages are scattered from the valley to the hills.

Topographically the area is at transition from the sub-tropical zone to the temperate zone (*Encyclopedia of North-East India*, Vol-I: p. 131). The sub-tropical evergreen forest or mixed forest forms an intermediate stage

West Kameng District Map

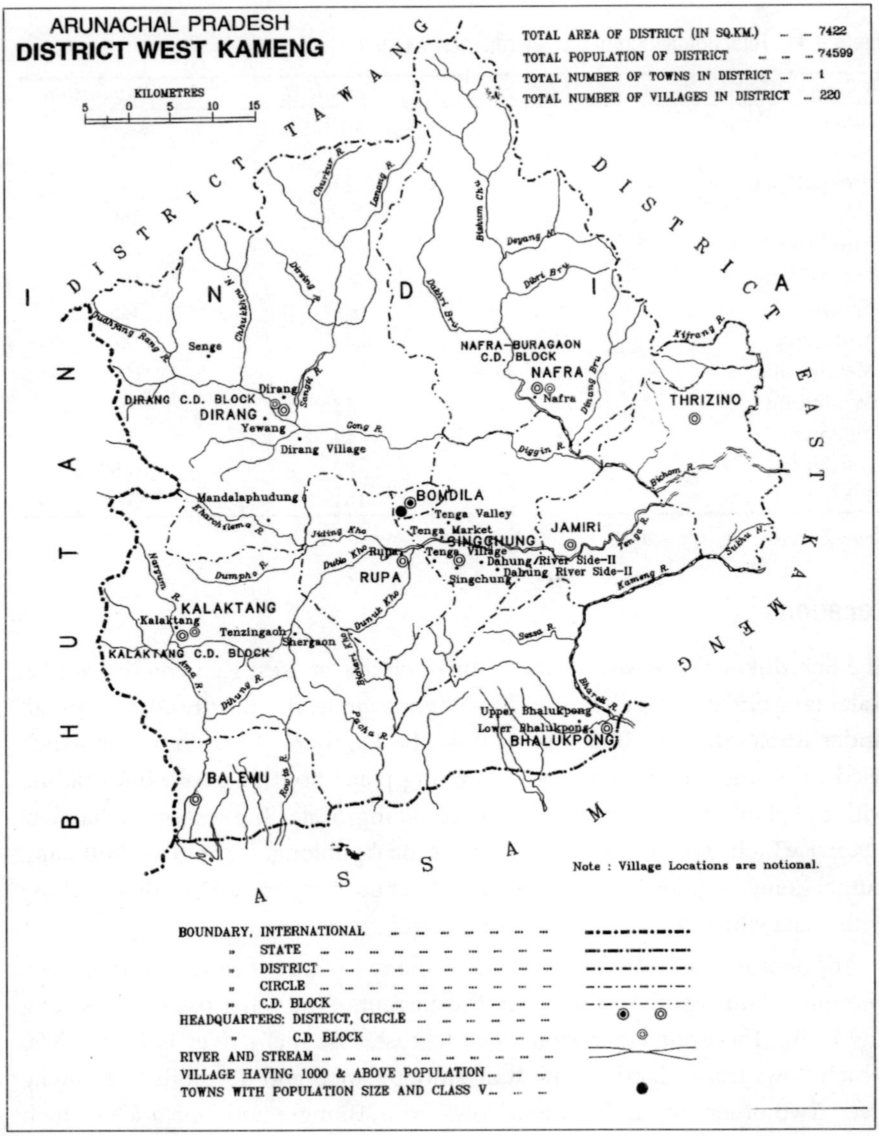

Rupa circle map

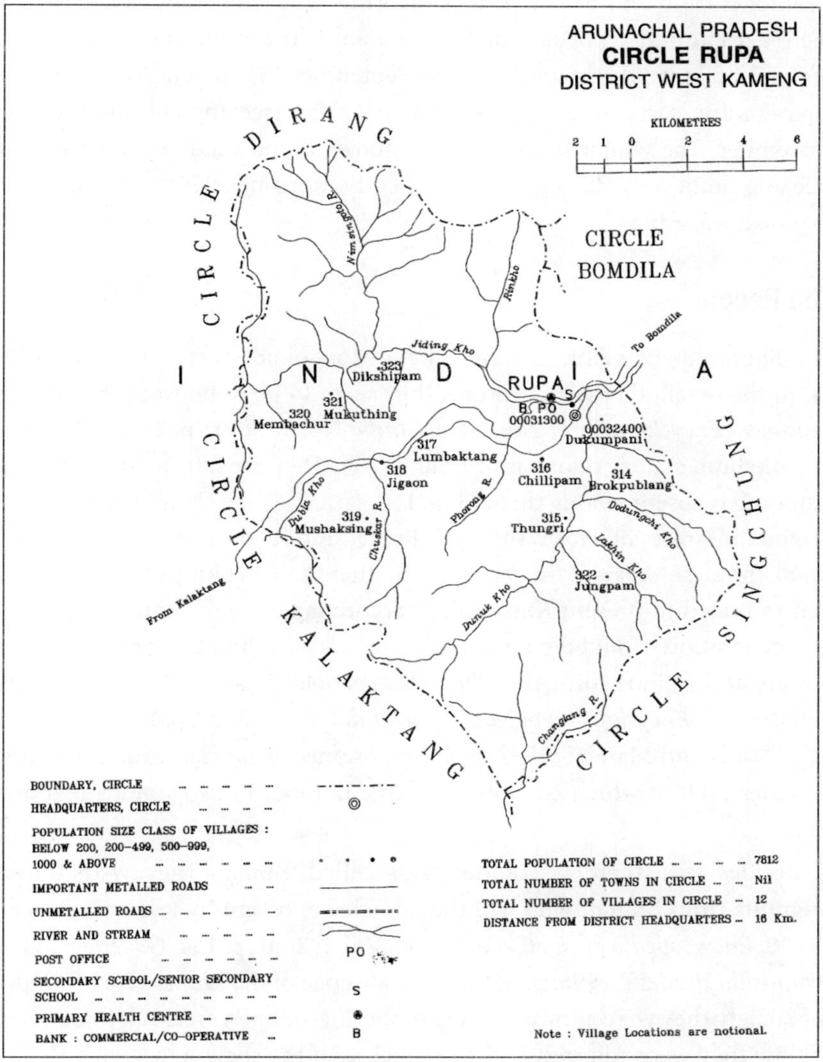

combining both tropical and temperate species. These forests are dominated by species of *Ficus*, *Castanopsis*, *Callicarpa*, *Sisni*, *Schima*, and *Englhardtia*. *Pinus wallichiana* mixed with *Rhododendron arboretum*, *Lyonia*, *Berberis*, *Quercus* and member of *Rosaceae* along the Rupa valley are predominant (*Gazetteer of India: Arunachal Pradesh*, 1996: p. 10)

In terms of fauna the area is rich with animals like tiger, wild goat, barking deer, spotted dear, boar, fox, monkey, wild cat and porcupine. Besides these, there are plenty of birds like wild fowl, eagle, pigeon, dove, owl, wood pecker, bulbul, fork-tail and sparrow (Census of India, 1981: p. 5).

It is not too hot during the summer which begins around early April. The weather is calm and bright. This is the time when the people are engaged in their agricultural work as much as possible. The monsoon approaches by the end of June which continues till September. By the end of October, the temperature starts to fall, and it may reach the freezing cold by the end of November. The winter passes without snowfall and the temperature reaches freezing point only during nights and early mornings which probably is due to global warming.

The People

The Sherdukpens belong to the Tibeto-Mongoloid stock (Sharma, 1960: p. 4). In the detail diagnostic features they seem to be in between the Akas and Monpas (*Encyclopedia of North-East India* Vol-I, 2001: p. 132). They are of low medium stature (Goswami, 1990: p. 11). They are fair in complexion and tattooing is absent among them (Sen, 1986: p. 27). They claim themselves to be original migrates of Tibet. They are divided into two main classes *Thong* and *Chao*, the aristocrat and the serf. It is said that the Tibet king's son *Asu*[2] *Japtang* had migrated to present Rupa village accompanied with potters and retinue. The generation of *Japtang* form the *Thong* class. While the generation of the potters and retinue form the *Chao* class people (Sharma, 1960: p. 49; Elwin 1958: p. 133; *Encyclopedia of North-East India* Vol-1, 2001: p. 134; Dey, 2004: p. 49). Danda and Mandal (1997: p. 35) mentioned these classes as endogamous moieties each of which consists of a large number of exogamous patriarchal clans.

Besides this, there is another class called *Yanlog*. They were the later migrants from Bhutan who had the knowledge of smithy (Sharma, 1960: pp. 49–50; *Encyclopedia of North-East India*, Vol-1, 2001: p. 134, *Gazetteer of India: Arunachal Pradesh*, 1996: p. 84). Due to absence of the knowledge of smithy in the society they were allowed to stay in the Sherdukpen area. But in due course of time they were adjusted in the main class of the society by giving them the clan title of that class. So at present no one represents the *Yanlog* class.

The neighbouring tribe of Sherdukpen are Aka, Miji, Bugun and Monpas. Amongst these the Akas and Mijis constantly raid the Sherdukpen areas. To keep them away from such constant raids they were paid annual tax. "To Miji kings one bullock, one load each of salt and jabrang spice, two goats and a cowrie waist band were paid. To Aka kings three bullocks, ten woven bags, one large and six small pieces of cloth, ten load of salt, twelve load of jabarang seed, twenty three fowls and two goats were paid" (Sharma, 1960: p. 6; *Gazetteer of India: Arunachal Pradesh*, 1996: p. 31).

Language

The language of Sherdukpens belongs to the Tibeto-Burman branch of Sino-Tibeto family (Grewal, 1997). It is basically a dialect as it has no script of its own. The people being predominantly Buddhist use Tibetan script on prayer flags, shrine (*mane*), gates (*kakling*), monastery (*lagong*). The elderly people have knowledge of Assamese language due to the neighbourly contact and trade relationships with the people of the plains of Assam. Some aged people have the knowledge of reading and writing in Assamese medium also, as they had their education in Assamese language. With the advent of modern education system the society now possess the knowledge of Hindi and English.

Land

Traditionally land was an important economic indicator of the people as land was the main source of livelihood. The person who possessed more land in comparison to others is considered to have higher economic status. The land is divided into three main forms: 1. Individual land (*Gu so*) 2. Clan land (*Rung so*) 3. Council land/village land/community land (*Blu so*). Beside these divisions of land there are some portions of river termed as *khroh* (portion in the river where it flows in two channels) and cliff for honey collection is termed as *chok* which is owned by the clan.

House

The Sherdukpen house is erected on a massive stone foundation the heights of which depend upon the topography of the area. Above this foundation the house is a double storey. The house is made up of wood, bamboo and cane strips. The first storey above the raised platform is used for domestic purposes. The first storey wall and floor used to be of wooden planks and the upper storey wall and its floor is constructed by matted bamboo. The roof is built with light wooden planks. Both the stories used to be of single room. However, an extra small room behind the first storey is constructed with wooden planks which is used as a prayer room (Sharma, 1988; *Encyclopaedia of North-East India* Vol-1, 2001).

Society

The Sherdukpen society is patriarchal in nature. The father is the head of the family. Descent is patrilineal (Koley, 1999: p. 13; *Gazetteer of India: Arunachal*

Pradesh, 1996: p. 84). In the domestic affairs of the family, the father wields a dominating influence. A woman plays an important role in the family by taking care of the house and the children besides the agricultural work though she is debarred from playing any role in the traditional political system of the society. Nuclear family is predominant.

Regarding the property, the immovable property of a Sherdukpen family consists of the house and the cultivable land, and the movable property includes livestock, clothes, ornaments, domestic utensils, agricultural implements and so on. The disposal of the property depends upon the head of the family. Usually the house is inherited by the youngest son as he is the last member in the house, besides these generally the eldest and the youngest sons of the family get the major share of the property in comparison to the middle son.

Dress

Traditionally the dress of the male members include a cloth which is wrapped diagonally (*sape*), a shash (*mukhak*) of red colour, sword with silver scabber engraved with design (*adok chongthok*) or knives with silver scabbard engraved with design (*achan chongthok*), a coat (*alphudung*), and a hat (*gurdom*) made of yak hair. The female dress includes frocks (*sinku*), shash (*mukhak*) of red colour, coat (*alung-dedik*) and a shawl (*snap*) (Sharma, 1960; *Gazetteer of India: Arunachal Pradesh*, 1996).

But in present day life, in general men wear shirts, trousers, jeans, pants, coats, jackets and sweaters, etc. The adult female generally wears *gale*[3], blouses, salwar-kameez/kurta-pyjama and sweaters. Young girls can be seen wearing jeans, pants, T-shirts and fashionable clothes available in the market, besides wearing chappals, sandals and shoes is a common sight among both males and females (Census of India 1981: series–25).

Marriage

The Sherdukpen people are exogamous clan and class endogamous. But is not a taboo to marry outside the class. Monogamy is the rule, polyandry and polygyny is not acceptable in the society. The cross cousin marriage is given preference. Other forms of marriages also take place like marriage by negotiation, marriage by capture, elopement, etc. widow marriage is not restricted. Extra-marital affairs are looked down upon and if caught may reach to the extent of divorce.

Economic Life

Agriculture is the main economic occupation of the Sherdukpens. The Sherdukpens practice both settled and jhum cultivation. But now, they generally go for settled cultivation. However, cultivation is not done throughout the year because of cold weather and winter wind. So during the cultivating season everyone puts in their hard labour to obtain maximum production and profit. For better crop production as well as to compete in the present market; hybrid seeds, fertilisers, insecticides and pesticides are also being used in large scale in the cultivation sector.

The crops which Sherdukpens cultivate are cabbage (*kobi*) potato (*gyu*), raddish (*mulu*), brinjal (*mantho*), tomato (*bilati*), maize (*fentang*), millet (*gacham*), chilly (*mong*), pumpkin (*bungbloh*), bottle gourd (*khlom*), mustard leaves (*pejo-dono* and *tho-doho*) beans (*thamplah*) cucumber (*mubung*), garlic (*mongsing*), etc.

Besides agriculture during the off seasons in winter the people go out for hunting and fishing. In the past during the winter season, the tribes migrated to the plains of Assam for trading purposes and to prevent themselves from the severe winter cold.

With the modern education and market system, the people have engaged themselves in works accordingly. Many people are engaged and prefer to work in government departments and some are earning their livelihoods by working as contractors. Due to the availability of market and knowledge of the importance or role of money in their lives the people are working hard. In the past the people sustained themselves on subsistence agriculture. With the aspiration for a better standard of living people are putting greater efforts in earning more so that they can afford all the material comforts and be able to send their children for better education.

Political Life

The village council of the Sherdukpen is called *Blu*. The *blu* consists of village head (*thik-akhao*), members (*jungme/junmebarso*) and workers/staff (*kachin*). The entire official work is done in honorary capacity and nobody receives any salary. The council (*Blu*) is responsible for the maintenance of law and order in the village which is checked by the workers (*kachin*). The village head (*thik-akhao*) is elected and presides over the council (*Blu*). The workers (*kachin*) are not selected but it is the responsibility which people own on a turn wise system.

Religion

The Sherdukpens like their neighbouring tribe, the Monpas belong to Mahayana sect of Buddhism. They regard Lord Buddha as the supreme god. Every household has a *Chesum*[4] where every morning they offer water and burn incense. Accordingly in a month or year the *lamas* are called to propitiate the deities to keep the house and family members in a good or healthy environment. One can see the religious structure all over the Sherdukpen villages like monastery (*lagong*), shrines (*mane*), Stupa (*chorten*), long flag (*Dadar*), short flag (lungtah) and small pieces of clothes or strip of papers (*phan*) tied on the roof of the house from the front to the rear (Sharma, 1960; *Gazetteer of India: Arunachal Pradesh*, 1996; Sarkar, 1980).

Besides Buddhism the Sherdukpens still continue to practice their traditional Bon religion which is propitiated by the local priest called *jiji*.

Some of the important festivals celebrated by the Sherdukpen are *Losar, Chokor, Wang* and *Khiksaba. Losar,* is the Buddhist new year following the lunar calendar. *Chokor,* is a procession carrying the religious text for the betterment of the society and the village. Wang is a blessing ceremony done by the head priest for the people on religious occasion. *Khiksaba,* is a bon religion festival where the *khik jiji* (local priest) propitiates the mountain god.

Trade

The Sherdukpens did not live in isolation and were in constant contact with their neighbouring tribes to obtain resources as well as to supply. Their annual migration to the plains of Assam by camping at Doimara was not the only reason for escaping from the severe winter cold but also for commencement of commercial purposes. The society is dependent on the plains for the resources which were not available within the society. While leaving for the plains the people took jabrang, dried chilly, powdered chilly, dried radish and dao and in exchange from there brought endi clothes, salt, paddy and utensils.

From the Akas, the Sherdukpens obtained Mithuns (*Bos frontalis*) which they used for cross breeding with their cows or else they sold these Mithuns to the Monpas and the Bhutanese. With the Buguns they exchanged clothes, salt and betel-nut. From the Monpas they obtained butter, coats, shoes, carpets, masks and caps made of yak hair in exchange for cows, endi cloth, maize and maize flour (Sharma, 1960: p. 10).

Endnotes

1. But it can be kept as a note for future reference that the people like to refer themselves as Shertukpen not as Sherdukpen as has been written in all the books.
2. Asu is a term referred to grandfather. In this case Japtang is being designated as grand father.
3. Gale is a wrapper. It is not a Sherdukpen term as the concept of gale was not there. It is procured from the nearby market.
4. A place or a corner where the picture or idol with religious stuffs are kept.

3

Migration Narratives and Nature of Stratification

Every culture and every society has a history of its own. It is beyond doubt that the place we live in and the way we live now may not be the way we used to live in the past. To know how a society functions, it is a pre-requisite to understand its past, because whatever has happened in the past or what and which situations the society might have gone through is responsible for moulding the society in its present state. So in this context the history cannot be neglected, as it is a universal fact that no society is static rather each one is dynamic. Historical memory is seen as primarily linked to the concerns of the "here and now" and leads to the question of self-definition and identity (Gaenszle 2003/2004: p. 8). The past only matters as long as it is made use of otherwise it is forgotten (ibid.). Imaginings of the past thus have to be examined as part of a social arena in which meanings are continuously under construction and at the same time may always be contested (ibid.).

It may be such that by this history we could make conclusions and trace the origin and the nature of division that emerged within the society. For instance, the Indian Hindu society is structured on caste system which is concerned with the idea of pollution and purity, where the Brahmin is at the top most strata followed by Kshatriya then Vaishya and Shudra at the bottom. But this division is not in the form as we perceive today. K.L. Sharma (2007: p. 160) in his book wrote:

> The origin of caste system dates back to the age of the RigVeda. There is a reference to the word varna (colour) in the RigVeda. The Arya is referred to as fair and Dasa as dark. However, there is no reference to Brahmin or Kshatriya. The people of the two varnas differed not only in their skin colour but also in their worship and speech. Thus, the differences were both racial

and cultural. Brahmanas, Rajanyas (Kshatriyas) and Vaishyas constituted the Arya varna, whereas the non-Aryans made up the Dasa varna.

> The Purusha-sukta, a part of the RigVeda, states the Brahmanas, Rajanyas and Shudras sprang up from the mouth, arms, thigh and feet of the Purusa (God). Later on these became castes. However, there is no reference to the classes becoming hereditary classes were merely functional. The priest and the worrior occupied positions above the Vaishyas and the Shudras, but they were neither hereditary position nor exclusive ones. There was interchange of duties and inter-class marriage prevailed. The ban on eating food cooked by Shudras did not exist. There was no trace of untouchability.

Later on, with the occupational attainment the classes were divided into various castes. The Brahmins became a distinct class and were highly respected because they performed religious duties. The Aryans who stood to fight and protect the conquered territories formed another group known as Kshatriyas. The remaining Aryans became a separate class and were named as Vaishyas. The non-Aryans became the fourth class and were known as Shudras. Later on further sub-divisions occurred and restrictions were imposed (Sharma, 2007: pp. 160–161). We can conclude here that in earlier days the concept of social stratification was different from the present situation. Hence it can be said that the society in the remote past may not have been stratified socially as later. Maybe, the concept of egalitarianism does fit the society of that time. But even in the so called egalitarian society the people within the society are not same. There will be differences among the individuals in age, gender, skill and intelligence.

It is interesting to note here that the tribal societies which are considered to be egalitarian in nature do not befit all the tribes. Stratification has been found in the tribal societies too. This social stratification has been found in the Sherdukpen society of Arunachal Pradesh which is Buddhist by religion. To know the roots of the stratification and its nature, the history of the society must be brought into consideration. The history of tribal society is mainly based on oral traditions. However, we cannot rely on oral traditions as in the process of passing of oral history from one generation to another, it gets diluted and distorted to certain extent. So the exact prevailing condition of that period cannot be ascertained. But somehow these oral stories can give a glimpse of the history of the society.

Thus, the history of migration of Sherdukpens also holds multiple views.

Folktale No.1[1]

Sherdukpens consider themselves to be the descendant of the king of Tibet *Sangtsen/Sangchen Gombo*. The tales of Tibet trace the origin of the king of

Tibet in India. It is said that a deformed kid was born in a kingdom in India. When he was a child, his feet were webbed like swan, his eyebrows were green. The father, ashamed of the child's deformity, put him in a basket and floated him in the river Ganga. Some fishermen found him and brought him up. When he grew, he saw he had swan like feet and green eyebrows. Embarrassed, he ran away to Tibet. When he reached Tibet he met some villagers. There they asked him, where he came from. Unable to understand and to speak their language, he just pointed towards the mountains beyond which he had come climbing. The villagers took it the other way and thought that he had descended from heaven. They took him to the village and made him their king. After 33 generations king *Sangchen Gombo* became the famous king of Tibet. *Sangchen Gombo* had five wives; one from the Tang dynasty of China, her name was *Wangchen*, another one from Nepal of Mala dynasty named *Bhriguti Devi* and three local princesses. He was influenced by his Buddhist Chinese wife and Nepali princess so he brought Buddhism in Tibet. One of the descendants of the king of Tibet called *Lasa Changma* was exiled to Bhutan. He established there a new kingdom but didn't like it much. So in search of better place he proceeded south-east and reached Nafra. *Lasa Changma's* descendant, son or grandson named *Gyapton/Japtang*, locally called *Asu Japtang* (*Asu* means grandfather) became king of Nafra area. Later on he had a fight with the natives of Nafra, the Mijis. He then moved out of Nafra and established a kingdom at Rupa. At Rupa, *Asu Japtang* killed the local king named *Tsewang Ganggan Thong*. He built a fort at Rupa called *Tukpen Lomekhar* (*tuk* = clash, *pen* = thrown; *lo* = south, *me* = rear; rear side of the south; *khar* = stone house). As he was very strong, he was known as *Sarbapu* (*sar* = east, *bapu* = king) by the people of Tawang and Bhutan. We can conclude from above that *Japtang* was born and brought up at Nafra.

But the same person[2] in another interview with me gave a different picture which is as follows:

> *Japtang* migrated alone from Tibet. *Japtang* was born at Lhasa, King *Sangchen Gombo's* son. The elder son of the king was *Khiburathe*, *Japtang's* elder brother. He was actually the son of King's minister. The minister seduced the queen on her journey from Assam to Tibet. *Japtang* was the real son of the king. He had a mark of moon crest on his forehead. When both of them grew into adults, *Japtang* killed *Khiburathe* and ran away from there and reached Ligam. From Ligam he kept migrating and reached Rahung, stayed at Binthonglo from Binthonglo again he migrated and stayed at Chakhe. Then he migrated to Phlong. In Phlong *Tsewang Ganggan* was the king. At first the *Megejis* also migrated from Lhasa and stayed there supporting

Tsewang Ganggan. Actually Megejis were the civilians of the king *Tsewang Ganggan*. Japtang, by killing *Tsewang Ganggan* took over the power and ruled Rupa. He was killed with the help of *Tsewang Ganggan Thong's* subject the *Megeji*. While migrating, *Sinchaji* and *Dingla* accompanied *Japtang* as guard. *Megejis* are the native settlers of Rupa, others have migrated from Butkhoina, the present Jerigaon.

Folktale No.2[3]

It is said that *Asu Japtang's* father was the king of Lhasa and that his mother was the daughter of king of Assam. The Lhasa king had sent his *Chao*[4] to fetch the Assam king's daughter. On the way the princess was seduced by the Chao and she conceived. The *Chao*'s name was *Khepu Berichan*. The *Chao* was very clever, so he told the princess not to face the king but to bend her head while speaking to him. The king however doubted while putting the ring in her finger as he saw her face. Despite his doubts he married her and the queen delivered a boy who originally was the *Chao's* son. His name was *Khiburathe* (*Khi* = dog, *rathe* = shape). Later he bore a second son whose name was *Japtang*. But in all gathering and function the elder son took part being the next probable successor. When *Japtang* grew up he came to know about the fact and realised that his elder brother was not the king's son in reality.

Whenever the elder brother attended a public gathering he would hide his face as he had a dog like feature. When *Japtang* realised it, it hit his ego and by his power he let the wind blow and lifted the veil of *Khiburathe* in public gathering. When the public saw his unveiled face, *Khiburathe* ran away from there in shame. When the mother came to know about this she scolded *Japtang* for his unruly act towards his elder brother. So he ran away from Tibet and came to present Rupa.

He ran away alone and settled down at *Binthonglo*. Later he was accompanied by two people *Hudu* and *Chaki*. Regarding these two persons, it is not clear whether they came along with *Japtang* from Tibet as some say they came along with king from there while some say they joined him when he (*Japtang*) reached present Rupa. When *Japtang* was staying at *Binthonglo* he went hunting one day and reached Chinggi at Kalaktang. There he took shelter in a house of a woman who lived with her only daughter. There was no one except the lady and her daughter. That village was terrified by a demon snake that used to eat human beings. The snake was called *Midelabdar de* (*de* = demon). The day *Japtang* reached the village he was provided food and shelter. At night *Japtang* overheard that one of them had to go as food for that demon (snake). So *Japtang* insisted on going himself in and when he got there he killed the demon snake. So in Kalaktang there is a shrine (*mane*) whose length is equivalent to the length of that snake. After killing the snake *Japtang* asked for the hand of the daughter in marriage which was accepted by the mother. They bore a son who was named with the title of *Thongdok* and who later settled at *Khleng*. So the generation from that *Thongdok* is called *Khleng Thong*.

Japtang leaving the wife and son again went for hunting and shot a pig somewhere in Kalaktang. That slightly injured pig escaped. *Japtang* followed the blood drops and at last reached Assam and saw the pig hiding below the rice store as a result of which an argument arose. *Asu Japtang* claimed that the pig had been shot by him so it belonged to him. But the local person argued on how one could shoot the pig in the forests as it was not wild but a domesticated animal. As the argument stretched, they finally resolved by offering each other eatable items. The people of the plains offered *Japtang* some rice to eat and in return *Japtang* gave them chilly powder. Both relished each other's items so much so that it was decided from that day onwards one would provide paddy and the other would provide chilly and other products. So in this way the trade relations with Assam started.

After that *Asu Japtang* returned to his area leaving his wife and son at Chinggi, where he was accepted as a king by the Akas and Mijis there he married a *stongma*[5] lady. The Akas and Mijis frequently came to pay their tax at his place. *Asu Japtang* had instructed his wife not to speak when these people were around. But unfortunately that day when the wife went upstairs to the store, to collect some rice beer, her cloth got stuck and she shouted and from her accent everyone made out that *Japtang* had married a *stongma* woman. They decided not to allow *Japtang* to stay there any longer and to kill him. As they were coming to kill him, *Asu Japtang* left his *stongma* wife and escaped with the help of *Hudu* or *Chaki* who misled the the Akas and Mijis by wearing the *Japtang* robe. *Japtang* wearing *Hudu* or *Chaki* dress went in the other direction. The Akas and Mijis followed the disguised person and killed him. *Japtang* after fleeing finally managed to reach Rupa.

Folktale No. 3[6]

While migrating, *Japtang* came from Tibet via Bhutan and stopped at Nafra. There he married two women, one of Rahung and another of Salari. During those days Nafra was ruled by chiefs. *Japtang* did not have good terms with the Nafra chiefs. He was chased away from Nafra. So he came and settled at Salari. The place where he settled is called *Japtang Dungcha* (*Dung* = house, *cha* = land) the ruins of which exists even now. There he stayed for some time. When the people of Jerigaon came to know about his presence they came in search of him. So during the day time *Japtang* would go and hide in a nearby cave on the other side of a stream and would come back at night. When the people came to know about his escape they found him and chased him away, from Salari. So from Salari he went to Rahung and stayed there. According to the informant it is from Rahung that two versions arise. Our (Sherdukpen) version is that from Rahung he came to Rupa. But from the Tawang monastery records it is found that from Rahung he went to Mandala Phudung from where he went to Domkho. There he met a religious leader called Lama *Tanpo Drema* who was preaching out there. Along with him there was a person called *Trangpodar*.[7] So the *Japtang* got introduced with them and then three of them started preaching together. So it is believed that the propagation of Buddhism in the region started from Domkho, and it is also believed that *Japtang* brought the fellowship of Buddhism in Sherdukpens.

There is a shrine (*mane*) out there which is about 150 metres in length". The informant said that "on enquiring on who had constructed this double storeyed shrine one of the monks had said that long time ago lama *Tanpo Drema*, *Trangpodar* and *Japtang* were spreading Buddhism out there, wherefrom they started for Assam. But on leaving for Assam they were accompanied by many people. So to keep the record of the number of followers it is said that each person placed a stone which later converted into a huge shrine. When *Japtang* and the group reached Assam, the relation between the Sherdukpen and Kachari started on religious terms. While coming back *Japtang* had an affair with one of the princesses from there. This led to the beginning of trade relations. From Domkho, *Japtan*g and the Lama came to Rupa through Gacham.[8] So after coming from Gacham side to Rupa the story of *Megeji* and *Megeji* king started. There was a king here named *Tsewang Ganggan Thong* who was killed by *Japtang* and he established his rule. But there is no substantial proof that *Thongdok*, *Thongchi*, *Thongon* and *Khrime* are the sons of *Japtang*. When he came from Tibet he was not married. He married two women at Nafra and when he ran away from Nafra he left alone leaving the wives behind. Again he got married with an Assamese lady. Even from there he came alone leaving the wife out there so of what is said of *Japtang* had three sons is a bit controversial.

But if one visits Dibbin at Nafra circle, one can see the characteristics of the people who resemble the *Thongdok* of the sherdukpen community, their body built and way of talking, bit dominating, likewise. It is said in Nafra that in earlier days Dibbin was the centre of power and the warrior clans stayed there. When *Japtang* came to Nafra (being a prince he had the administrative strategy) he collected people along with him. Maybe he collected some warriors from Dibbin that's why he could stay for a longer period at Nafra. If he had not done so he would not have been able to stay even for a day at Nafra, as they already had their own administrative system. So obviously he took some warriors along with him from Dibbin. And if these warriors came with him upto Rupa then *Thongdok* can be traced out from there. As in Kingdom by virtue the king used to offer position and give a title as Borbarua the commander, Kalita the inspector. Now these are mere titles. At that time these were the positions or ranks held by an individual. From the rank of a soldier you were upgraded to inspector and so on. Maybe this way *Thongdok* has a meaning and the *Thongdok* position was given which is used as a surname in the present generation.

For *Thongon*, one can still see that even now in Lower Jung they are official mediators. If there is any dispute at Nafra the mediator will be from Lower Jung. They were experts in conversation. They were expert in handling the situations, and to dispose the cases of worst matter. *Thongon,* did the same in Rupa. Because of their oratory skills and ability to resolve situation, they were sent to dispose the matters. So when *Japtang* came, he had the warriors and wanted an interlocutor. When he stayed at Nafra and wanted to dominate he wanted such a person who could convince people and so he found one from the Lower Jung among the mediators for the nearby villages. These mediators were diplomatic people. So, *Thongon* belongs to Lower Dzong. Even now one can find a staying place of *Japtang* at Lower Jung. So when these people came with *Japtang* upto Rupa they were given the title *Thongon*.

For *Mijiji*, one can see that they are found in hilly areas of Mukhuting, Membachur. If one sees the topography they are very close to Mandala-Phudung and Morsing. They have marital relationship with Mandala Phudung and Morsing. They have relatives at both places also, so it might have happened that they came from Mandala-Phudung and Morsing and settled at Mukhuting, Membachur. Later they were accepted and given the title like the Musaksing people who are runaway people of Bhutan and settled out here.

Megejis were already here. *Dinglas* as you can see in the *Khiksaba* festival, wear a cap. That cap is possessed by the *Dinglas* only. And this came with us from *Jerigaon*. In Jerigaon you will see that the head priest wear that kind of cap, even in Rahung. When *Japtang* came he saw that he already had the warrior and a diplomatic interlocutor. Now what he needed was a priest. So he took along the priest from there who came with him upto Rupa who is said to be a *Dingla*. When the Rangradus clan of Jerigaon come to Rupa they write *Dingla*. *Dingla* and *Rangradus* are brothers. By profession they are priests.

In this way, if we see then *Thongdoks* are the warrior clan who came along with *Japtang* from Dibbin, *Thongons* came from Lower Dzong and are the mediators. *Dingla* who are the priests came from Rahung and Jerigaon. In case of *Khrime Japtang* had an immediate cousin *Khrime Leiki Wanchu* but it is bit difficult to trace their origin. However it is said *Khrimes* were the descendant of that immediate cousin Khrime Leiki Wangchu. So it is undisputed that they are of the lineage of *Khrime Leiki Wangchu*. *Megejis* were already there at Rupa. *Thongchi* came from Domkho. So there is no proof that they are immediate son of *Japtang*. For *Khleng Thong* it is said that *Japtang* had *duflo* (bastard) who was adopted by the Rupa people and settled there.

So it may be an undisputed story regarding the *Khleng Thong* and if we look through this perspective the *Thongdok*, *Thongon*, *Thongchi* and *Dingla* came from outside along with *Japtang* as a retinue and later *Yanlog* came to society. *Khrime*s were the descendants of the cousin who came and stayed with *Japtang*.

Regarding the *Yanlog* class in due course of time by participating in various activities and giving their service to the society were merged into the *Chaos* class. So today, the *Yanlog* class no longer exists in the society.

Folktale No. 4[9]

In this story by Urgen Jatso, the descendant was traced from the Tibet king *Sangchen Gombo*. Here it is mentioned that among the later generations of the of *Sangchen Gombo*, a king name *Krisong Deochan* bore three sons named *Mune Chenpo*, *Murup Chenpo* and *Muti Chenpo*. *Muti Chenpo*, the last son of *Krisong Deochan* had three sons named *Lhase Changma*, *Lang Darma* and *Khrirepa Chen*. Then *Lhase Changma* had two sons namely *Khrimelsing Wangchuk* and *Chebu Thonglokchen*. *Khrimelsing Wangchu* was taken to Lhao where he became the king and settled at Lhao Khampa. Thus the *Khampa* Lineage came into existence. *Chebu Thonglokchen* had three sons named *Thrijenpal*, *Gongerjel* and *Pelkedar*. *Gongerjel* had four wives namely *Peldrenke*, *Dorjompa*, *Athungki* and *Yang Pema*. From *Peldrenke*, he had two sons namely *Thonglok pel* and *Chengongjel*. Other three wives were driven out by *Peldrenke*. But the king retained them as maid servants. They also became pregnant and in due course of time conceived sons. *Dorjompa* hid her son inside a big pot away from the harmful hands of *Peldrenke*. *Athungki* hid her son in a basket. *Yang Pema* hid her son in bunker who was later known as *Gebdechen* or *Gyapten* or *Gyaptong*.[10] With the assistance of a minister the three women showed their children to the king. The king became happy and assigned all the three a clan each—son of *Dorjompa* with

Yede clan, son of *Athungki* with *Tungde* clan and son of *Yang Pema* with *Wangma* clan.

Gebdechen moved further north-east and settled near present Nafra and Salari and selected four body guards for his safety at Khoina namely *Chage, Huju, Mije* and *Yayee.* At Khoina, a rich wise man named *Lhabe* had two sons. One day they were caught stealing fish from the channel prepared by *Gebdechen* and were beaten severely and thrown into the river. *Lhabe* thought *Gyapten* and his body guards were murderers but had no proof. He therefore announced that whosoever found out the truth would be rewarded with a precious stone (*nayu*) and Mithun (*Bos frontalis*). The wife of *Gebdechen* became greedy and told the facts to *Lhabe*. This created a lot of problems for *Gebdechen*. However, he along with his sons went to Jerigaon, took shelter in a cave at a small hill called Buthalong. *Gebdechen* used to play on his flute to show his presence but *Lhabe* could not locate him. Ultimately, the follower of *Lhabe* performed *Yakcham* to lure the wife of *Gebdechen* from hiding. She was caught and murdered. *Gebdechen* and his sons then moved on to Khoitam Salari and constructed *wangmakhar* (*Wangma* = clan, *Khar* = stone house) now known as *Japtong Dungcha*. *Gebdechen* had two sons *Gunglajel* and *Peladar*. *Peladar* along with his load carrier went to *Lhase Changma*. *Gebdechen* had already kept a girl of low birth secretly as domestic servant. The people came to know about this and reported the whereabouts of *Gebdechen* to *Lhabe*. He was driven away. He later settled at Rahung Namphing Jung. *Lhabe*'s men drove him from there to Chok. *Apa Gyapten* now dressed like Monpa started tilling land like farmer when *Lhabe*'s men reached there. He assured *Lhabe*'s men that he would bring *Apa Gyapten* and demanded an Ox. Then he changed his dress and fled away with his supporters. *Lhabe*'s men caught a man with rich gold ornaments. In the meantime *Apa Gyaptang* showed his real identity and fled away and settled at a cowshed. He came across an old lady and gave her a precious stone (*nayu*) to keep him secretly by wiping his footsteps. On arrival of *Lhabe*'s men she denied the arrival of even a dog. *Apa Gyapten* and his son remained there for three days. The old lady advised them to visit Domkho-Morshing area to meet *Trangpo Darge* and Lama *Tranpe Dreme*. He related his journey from Buthalong and intended to join them due to *lopa*[11] majority. The *lama* told about the past and hoped for a better future. *Gebdechen* or *Apa Gyapten* was gifted with the power to kill the demons. Lama *Tanpe Dreme* asked him to kill the demons through his power.

An agreement was made wherein *Gebdechen* was to be the bodyguard, *Trangpo Darge* the householder and Lama *Trenpe Dreme* the priest. From here they went east to a place called Liding Palingsengpa (sanctuary of devils). They reached Khalaktang where they met a girl named *Yunten Rema*, who was the manifestation of Goddess Tara. She prepared food for them. They were informed that in the land of Tsing Dangkhar, there was a devil called *Midhe Labdhar*, who ate human flesh and drank human blood and that as a tax it was the duty of the human beings to go to him. The next day would be the girl's turn. *Apa Gyapten* and his companions went after the devil, which fled to higher altitudes known as Rajalok. In the course of the fight the monster went to Sinkong and downwards on the river path. The chase continued through Saksingma, Adola, Wangmatong, Brongsingma, Bapyongri, Kurtabilam, Rangchilu, Bachilu and ended at Bumthang cave. There *Apa Gyapten* captured the monster. There they hunted a dove and found paddy inside the intestine of the dove. The devil pleaded for mercy and said that the lands such as Salidugar (present Chariduar in Assam) and Kherabara was under his possession and that if *Meme Gyapten* left him he would give the land to *Meme Gyapten* and the others. However, they continued their journey with the devil in their captivity and halted at a place called Ngam-tsabhur (bright with sunshine). Here Lama *Trenpa Dreme* was warned by God that if the devil was not killed he might bring harm to them. *Apa Gyapten* then killed the devil and his head and limbs were left at Phiratse and offered to *Ama Jomo*. After that they went to Morshing-Domkho area and built the Taglung, and came across Domkho Melong Khar, Sher Bumtangkhar and Tukpan Lukpaikhar where they constructed the Lomeod Fort.

The three finally decided to settle down. An agreement was reached upon wherein upper and lower Rongnang (Jakarapara, Assam) was given to *Trangpo Darge* and *Apa Gyapten* was given the Sherdukpen area upto Chariduar in Assam. As *Gyapten* had got rid of all the demons in this region, he is therefore also known as *Shar Bapu Thongla Thongsten*. *Apa Gyapten* then settled at *Tukpan Lukpaikhar* and accepted his brother's proposal for separation.

By the story of Urgen Jatso a chart can be drawn on next page.

In the meantime *Apa Gyapten* sired a son out of wedlock whom the village folks considered as ill omen. Therefore, this son was made to leave *Tukpan Lukpaikhar*, but was allowed to settle at Khleng where he established his principality, and there after called *Khleng Thong*.

Gongerjel, who had given a clan name to his son as *Yede*, *Tungde* and *Wangma* were renamed again by their grandfather *Thonglokchen* as *Thongchen* (*Thongdok*), *Thomber* (*Thongon*) and *Thongchuk* (*Thongchi*). However, *Wangma Gunglajel* wanted to retain his identity, so his descendents are known as *Wangma*. And the *Khrimes* are descendants of *Khrimelsing Wangchu*.

Chart 3.1 Geneological Chart according to Urgen Jats.

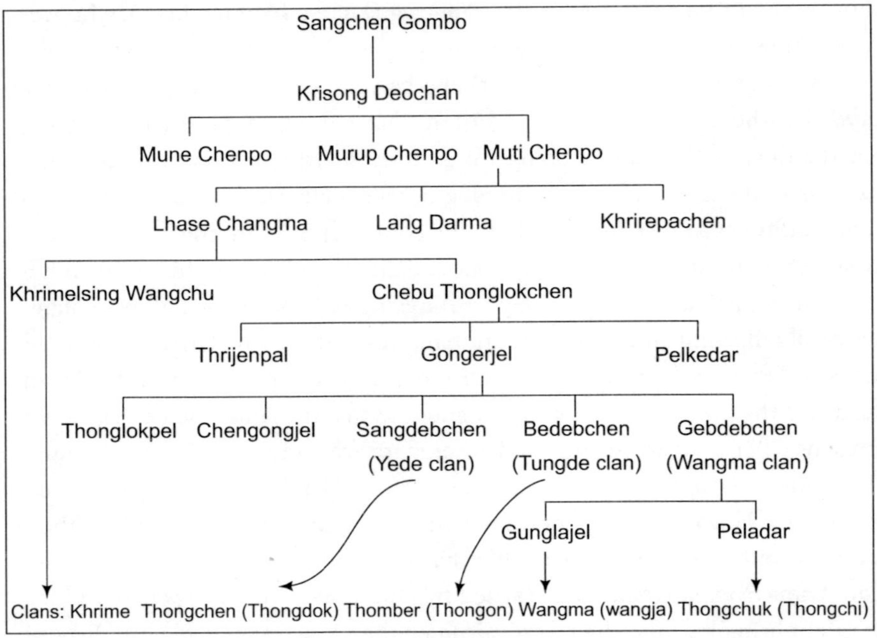

Folktale No. 5[12]

The king *Geporading Dorjee* lived in Debolojari with his queen from whom he had a son. But he heard that the Ahom King of Assam had a very beautiful daughter and his desire for her was kindled. He sent his minister with a strong force to Sibsagar to ask for her in marriage. But the Ahom king refused to send his daughter to an unknown, distant land, and it took the minister twelve years to persuade him to let the girl go.

At last they started on their journey home and came to the Brahmaputra and crossed the far side. There sin entered the Minister's mind and he seduced the princess. When they arrived at Debolojari, the king of Lhasa was delighted with his bride and married her with great ceremony. But very soon he noticed that his wife was pregnant and he asked his minister how this could be. The minister replied, "How can I tell? I lived twelve years in exile and brought her to you with great pain and difficulty. The child must be yours." But when the child was born, although he had the body of a human being, he had the face of a dog and the horns of goat. When the king saw the child he had him taken to the forest and was left to die there.

But as he loved his young wife he forgave her and in due course of time had two other sons from her. The elder was named *Jabdung Nawang Namja* and the younger *Gyaptang Bura*. When the boys grew up, the king gave his kingdom to the son of his elder wife. He gave Bhutan to the prince *Jabdung Nawang Namja* and the country around Rupa and Shergaon to *Gyaptang-Bura*, who was the first Sherdukpen king.

When *Gyaptang Bura* came to Rupa, the Ahom king heard of it at Sibsagar and invited his grandson to come and see him. He gave him all the land which lies between the Donsiri and Gabru rivers as they flow into the Brahmputra and told him to collect tax from people living there.

Gyaptang Bura was told by his father, the king of Lhasa that his people should not pay taxes to the Tibetans or carry loads for them. But he should be aware of the Hrussos, for they were demons at that time, and should give them cows and other tribute to satisfy them.

When *Gyaptang Bura* came from Lhasa to Rupa, he brought with him great trail of porters and servants. The king's descendants are now called Thongs and the descendants of the porters are called Chaos.

Yanlog

However, there was another class in Sherdukpen society the *Yanlog*. This class of people had migrated from nearby Bhutan in later period and came to settle along the Sherdukpen areas. *Yanlogs* were the newly migrated groups accepted in the Sherdukpen society but not main *Chaos*. However later on they were merged into the *Chaos* class. So the new comers were identified as *Yanlogs* who were not given all the rights specially the political rights. *Chaos* elders could participate in important political meetings always but *Yanlogs* were not allowed to attend the meetings.[13]

Yanlog was a statutory provision in which non-Sherdukpens could include themselves initially and later in the main clan of Sherdukpen by committing themselves in the work of community for fixed period followed by a ceremony.[14] It can be considered as a transitional phase where they were neither considered as an outsider nor a full fledged native. It is a doorway for a person to become a part or a member of the society.

Regarding them it is said that actually they were runaway people of Bhutan who came to Sherdukpen area and asked for shelter from *Asu Japtang*. About six families from Bhutan came and stayed while the Bhutan king came in search of them. Then the Rupa village paid six or nine mithuns (*Bos frontalis*) to the Bhutan king.[15] The payment was made with a plea stating "as we do not have smiths and have to go to Doimara every year to procure metallic tools. And as these people know the art of smithery we want to keep them with us". So a settlement place was given to them i.e. Musaksing and are called Musaksingpa.

Yanlogs practised black smithery and provided utensils and agricultural tools to the society. *Yanlogs* were the reserve people of the council. *Yanlogs* were people who did not belong to any *Chkok* (group) and had not been assimilated to any clan of the society. They were used for petty work or extra work of the society or as servants. For instance after going for winter camps and if a ritual has to be performed, it was difficult to engage the *Chkok* (group) in those kinds of works as it was a big group. So from *Yanlogs* a person was engaged to collect the drum, the idol, religious text, etc. for the ritual. The *Yanlogs* included, people from outside like Bhutanese, Nepali, Adivasi, etc. Later they were put under different *Chkok*[16] and at last incorporated into different clans.

There is a general acceptance regarding the '*Thong*' that the word *Thong* means king. But regarding the *Chaos* there is inconsistency as people have their own views on this as for some *Chaos* are subjects. Others interpret them to be the *Mantri* or body guard while some opine they were the servants who came along with *Asu Japtang*. One of the respondents belonging to *Khrime* clan said "The *Chaos* are not servants. Servants are normally taken from the *Yanlogs*. They are subjects. They are important citizens. The food habits among the *Thongs* and the *Chaos* are same unlike the *Yanlogs*. Both the *Thongs* and the *Chaos* do not take the meat of the domestic animals except for that of sheep and yak which are not reared by them. In contrast to this the *Yanlogs* consume the meat of domesticated animals. Inter marriage between *Thongs* and *Chaos* is somehow acceptable but marriage with the *Yanlog* was not allowed. Nobody married them, now of course liberalised".

Khleng Thong

Japtang taking his troop (*Sinchaji* was the warrior, *Megeji* and *Dingla* were the priests) reached *Chinggi* village of Kalaktang circle. In that village there was a big snake that used to eat the humans. When *Asu Japtang* reached there, there were only two survivors, an old lady and her daughter. The lady and the daughter decided to have whatever delicious food available as one of them was to die that night. By the moment they finished preparing their food, *Asu Japtang* and his troop reached there and they were hungry. *Asu Japtang* asked the lady of what she was doing. The lady replied, "As one of us is going to die tonight so whatever delicious food is left with us we were preparing and will die after having it. And if possible all of you must leave this place as there is a very big snake that comes and hunts us every night". On this *Asu Japtang* replied, "Do not worry, you do one thing, cook food for all my people and we shall kill that snake". The lady agreed and cooked food for all of them. After having meal at night the priests, *Megeji* and *Dingla*, performed some rituals and the warrior *Sinchaji* was ready for the snake to come. The lady said, "you will know when the snake comes as it usually comes whistling." As said the snake came whistling and *Asu Japtang* and the warrior killed the snake. After killing the snake *Asu Japtang* stayed in that village for couple of days and in the intervening period the daughter conceived. As *Asu Japtang* was always on move, he moved on. By the time he reached Rupa the lady at Chinggi delivered a baby boy. The boy grew up to excel in everything. But the other boys used to rag him saying that he was a bastard (*duflo*). One day when he had grown into a fine young man he pointed an arrow on his mothers head and asked her to tell him who his father was or else that he would kill her. Then his mother told him about his father and told him to go east ward. The son enquired on how he would recognise his father. The mother replied that his father had a moon crest sign on his forehead. The son set for his journey and reached Rupa. There he met his father and revealed his relation and pleaded for provision of some property there as at Chinggi no one liked him. As *Japtang* had already distributed his property among his other sons he sent him to *Khleng* (on the way to foothill road) which the son accepted. There he married a *Megeji* girl. That's why *Megeji* and *Khleng Thong* used to marry earlier.

Before the onset of winter camps at Doimara, the council first sent three people to take a look at the way. The *Khleng Thong* killed two people and let the one go back and said "until and unless you don't provide better land for me the situation will remain the same". This happened every time. Then the *Thoji Blu* (tukpen council) decided that it could not be tolerated anymore and so it would be better to kill *Khleng Thong*. So the *Thoji Blu* along with *Junyu Blu* (youth council) went there. There was a young boy, may be of Rahung, in that group. The troop stopped at Bompu and made preparations to kill *Khleng Thong*. They poisoned their arrowheads and by twilight set off to find *Khleng Thong* towards Khleng. The Rahung boy said, "I will also go to kill *Khleng Thong*." He was poisoning his arrows with the leftover poison. But the young group told him to stay there and take care of their goods. After they left he sat under a big tree. He saw something coming down from that tree. He took his bow and arrow which he had rubbed with poison and shot at that person. The group on reaching the Khleng saw that *Khleng Thong* was not there. They returned to Bompu and were having a discussion. The Rahung boy interrupted and said "A person was coming down the tree having huge thighs so I shot him with my arrow and he ran away." No one paid any attention to him but kept talking among themselves. Suddenly one old man asked everyone to keep quiet and to listen to what the Rahung boy kept saying. Every one stopped talking and turned to him and he said "A man having huge thighs came down from the big tree and I shot him with my arrow." After that they started enquiring about the time when he had shot him. On gathering the information the group started again for ambushing *Khleng Thong*. As *Khleng Thong* was strong he reached a place called *Choduchok* and was sitting on the banks of a stream. He pulled out the arrow and was cutting off the wounded flesh. By that time the group also reached there and killed him.

But at that time *Khleng Thong*'s *Megeji* wife was pregnant. So the brother of the *Megeji* wife said in the council (*Blu*) that if a girl was born then they would keep her as a servant for household chores. And if a boy was born they would keep him to look after the animals. In this way, the mother with the unborn child was saved. Later a boy was delivered and from this boy the *Khleng Thong* regenerated.

Stratification

As mentioned in all books Sherdukpens are divided into two main classes *Thong* and *Chao* (Elwin, 1958: p. 133; Sharma, 1960: p. 49; Dey, 2004: p. 49; *Gazetteer of India: Arunachal Pradesh*, 1996: p. 84; *Encyclopedia* of *North-East India* Vol-I, 2001: p. 134). The *Thongs* are the king class while *Chaos* were their servants. This division also came with the view that *Japtang* (Gyaptang) the forefather of *Thongs*, who was the son of the king of Tibet, on his migration, was accompanied by some potters and servants. And these potters and servants were considered as *Chaos* in the Sherdukpen societies. But in due course of time few families came from Bhutan, who were given settlement areas and were put in another class called the *Yanlogs*. But in the present society there are no more *Yanlogs* as they had been conferred with different surnames and incorporated within the *Chaos* long time back.

Basically, the Sherdukpen society is divided into two main classes *Thong* and *Chao*. The *Thongs* are divided into three clans *Thongdok*, *Thongo* (used to write *Thongon*) and *Khrime*. According to the tale, *Japtang* had three sons to whom he gave the names of three clans. It was done so by *Japtang* to keep the sanctity of the *Thongs* by inter-marrying within these three clans if they did not get any bride from outside society belonging to king's clan. As cited by N.T. Khrime "the rulers have to be of pure royal blood and could not mix up with the locals. The *Thongs* had to marry from the king's family itself. But in cases where one could not get such partner then to keep the class clean *Japtang* classified his three sons into three different clans—*Thongdok*, *Thongo* and *Khrime*. So these three sons became the progenitors of the three clans and till today there is an inter-marriage between the three".

These clans were further divided into sub-clans. *Thongdok* had three sons so he made—*Thongdok bukhao* (bukhao came from two words *abu*=brother and *akhao*=elder), *Thongdok chung* (*chung* is from *achung*=middle), then *Karma* (karma itself mean youngest in Tibetan language). But besides it, there are *Yangfan* and *Khleng Thong* (*Khleng Thong* is not a title but is the king of a place called Khleng and they write *Thongdok*) who also came under the *Thondoks*.[17]

Chart 3.2 Sub-clan of Thongdok

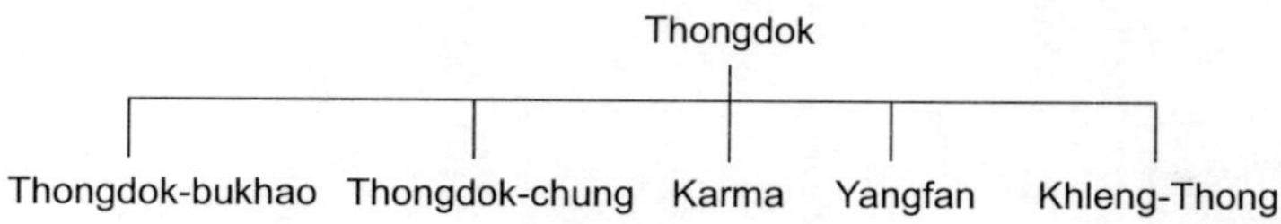

Then in *Thongo* (written *Thongon*), the *Thongo* had two sons—*Thongo* and *Thonchi*. *Khrime* had three sons eldest *Khrime*, *Mosobi* and youngest *Wangja* (see Chart 3.4).

The *Chao* class comprises of five clans *Sinchaji*, *Megeji*, *Dingla*, *Manoji* and *Mijiji*. *Megejis* are again divided into three—elder (*Akhao*), the middle (*Achung*) and the younger (*Achan*). The *Yanlogs* were the later migrants comprising of *Ibi*, *Dunkhar*, *Serthipa* and *Kengkhar*. But these surnames are not present as they have been merged into the main clans of the society (see Chart 3.4).

All the sub-divisions that are found in *Thongs* as well as in *Chaos* (in *Megeji*) do not represent or show any hierarchy within themselves. It is to be noted here that the sub-divided clans cannot intermarry. This was done so, for better management of the involvement during the *khiksaba* festival due to increase of population within the clan.

On the basis of hierarchy the *Thong* was considered at the topmost level, *Yanlog* at the lowest and *Chao* at middle. Both *Thongs* and *Chaos* considered *Yanlogs* as of low status and did not inter dine with them in the past. However, both *Thongs* and *Chaos* dine together. Beside these, all the classes were endogamous.

Here the class is hereditary. The class system is not an open one but closed not in strictest sense. People born in their respective classes are bound by it. It means a particular class is determined by birth not by selection. Hence, it is an ascribed rule as in caste system. Though, changes have been seen as the *Yanlogs* have been converted to *Chaos* by giving or letting them to enter into the clan of the *Chaos*. This decision was taken as the *Yanlogs* had been staying within the society since long time back and were using the resources of the society like land and forest. They were helping the society by providing their labour whenever and wherever necessary.

Chart 3.3 Social structure of Sherdukpen Society

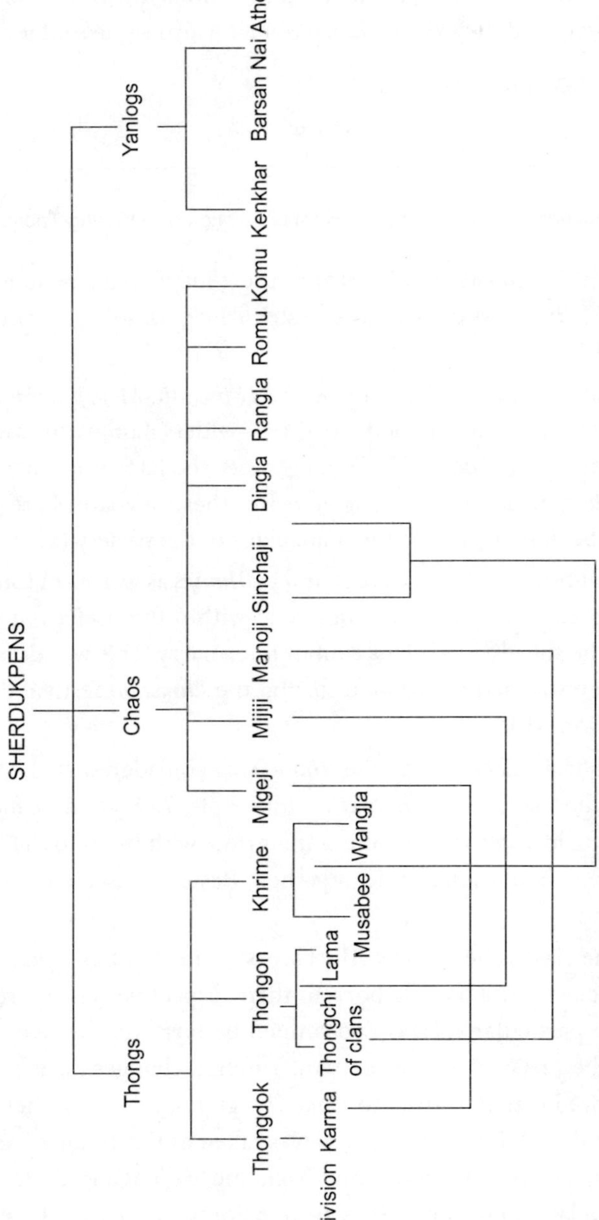

Source: R.R.P. Sharma, *The Sherdukpen* (Shillong: PC Dutta, 1960).

Chart 3.4 Social structure of Sherdukpen society

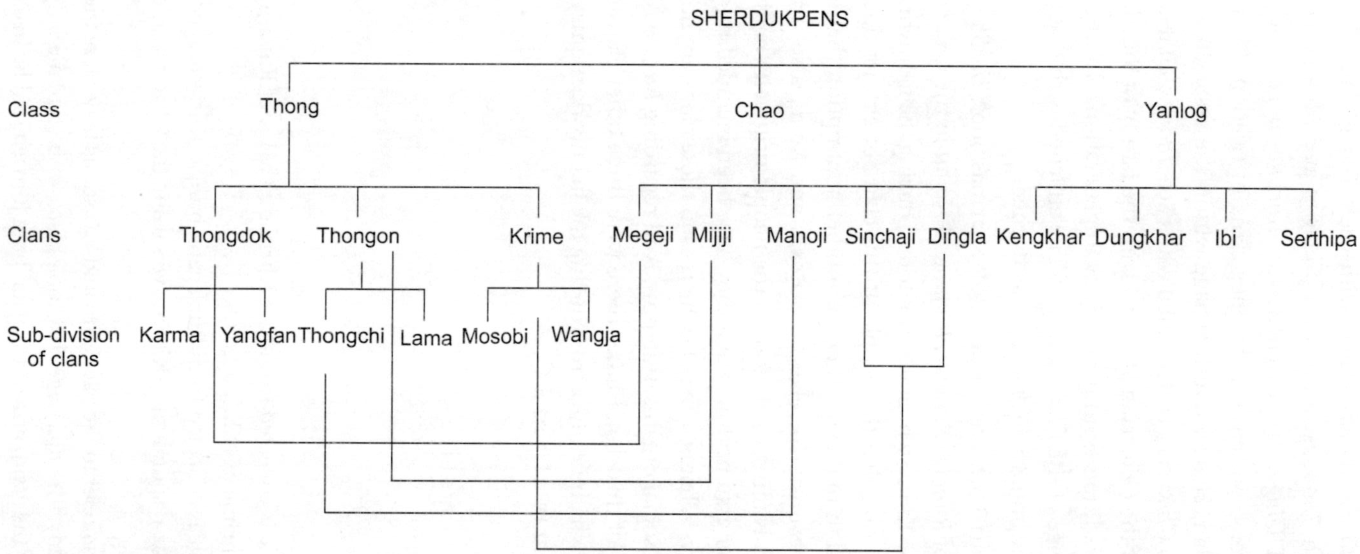

Source: Fieldwork

Each *Chao* clan is associated with each *Thong* clans. The *Megeji* clan is attached with *Thondok*, *Mijiji* with *Thongon* and *Manoji* with *Thongchi* and *Sinchaji* and *Dingla* are attached with *Khrime* in general (see Chart 3.4). They consider themselves as brother clans in relation. It can be considered as phratry clan. Hence, intermarriage within the associated clans is a taboo. Though each *Chao* clan is associated with each *Thong* clan it is to be noted that the family of the *Chao* clan attached with the family of the *Thong* clan follows the same tradition from generations to generations. In one way we can say that the lineage of the *Chao* family will be attached with that particular *Thong* lineage with whom that *Chao* clan is attached.

In the Chart 3.3, according to R.R.P. Sharma's book *The Sherdukpens* there is a reference of *Rangla* (*Rongla*), *Romu* and *Komu* in the *Chao* class and *Barsan Nai Athok* for *Yanlog* which was not found during the fieldwork. Regarding the *Ronglas*, it is said that the people of this clan got extinct due to non bearing of male child in that clan. There is another assumption that they migrated to Dirang and Namsu. In relation to *Romu* and *Komu* also it is said that they went back to Namsu, as they were the people originally hailing from Namsu while another assumption is that they have been included into the other clans of the society. Whatever may be the reason these clans are not counted in the Sherdukpen social organisation now. And regarding *Barsan Nai Athok* no one has any idea of this clan. Rather there were three other clans belonging to the *Yanlog* class which I came across during the fieldwork enquiry i.e. *Ibi*, *Serthipa* and *Dungkhar* (see Chart 3.4).

Endnotes

1. This tale is collected from N.T. Khrime ex MLA of Rupa, aged 68.
2. N.T. Khrime ex MLA, aged 68.
3. This tale is collected from Rupa gaon bura S. Khrime, aged 65.
4. Here the respondent S. Khrime was using the Chao term for the minister of the king.
5. *Stongma* refer to the backward and low status lady. Here they refer to Sulung tribe lady. The marriage that took place with stongma lady was told by the wife of the gaon bura as the gaon bura himself said he had not heard or had any idea that Japtang married a stongma lady.
6. This tale is collected from R. D. Thongchi, aged 37 of Jigaon.

7. *Trangpodar* is a clan name who settled down at Domkho.
8. Gacham is a place name nearby Rupa along its valley while coming from Morsing going through Mukhuting and Membachur.
9. This folktale is taken from Urgen Jatso book. Urgen Jatso is a monk from Kalaktang in whose name the book *History of Shertukpen Monpa* was published in the year 2003. It is said that he narrated the story while a teacher translated it in English.
10. *Gyaptang* is referred as *Japtang* in other story mentioned.
11. *Lopa* is denote to the Akas and Mijis.
12. This folktale is taken from Verrier Elwin's book *The Myth of the North-East India*, 1958.
13. N.T. Khrime, S.P. Khrime, P.D. Megeji and D.K. Dingla of Rupa.
14. R.N. Thongchi aged 29, teacher of Jigaon.
15. Informant Y.D. Thongdok, aged 74.
16. *Chkok* is a division of people in a group within the society. This is done especially for distribution of work in social functions.
17. It is to be noted that in writing of the title only *Thongdok*, *Yangfan* and *Karma* is used. The *Thondok bukhao*, *Thondok chung*, *Karma*, *Yangfan* and the *khleng thong* are the subdivision of *Thondok*.

4

Economic System and Material Life

The notion of stratification, to a great extent means relation between the economic system and material life within the society. For instance, the Hindu caste system is mainly based on occupation which is not achieved but is determined by the birth of the individual in a specific strata. The individual inherits that occupational frame automatically. But in the context of class, such occupational fixities are not found. This occupation reflects their status or rank within that society. It can be said that the work is given priority to determine the individual status. In this relation the religious work is placed at the topmost level and the individual who practises it is on the highest position in ranking within the caste based society. The people who do the cleaning or scavenging works are ranked in the lowest position within that society. Material life is also an important aspect to look into the issue of stratification. The ranking within the society also came with the notion of the possession of material life. The person possessing more wealth possesses more day-to-day comforts and materials of priced value. Hence, the economic system as well as the material life determines the issue of stratification system.

Economic Life

Traditionally, the *Thongs* are considered to be economically well established in comparison to the *Chaos*. One of the respondents[1] justifies by saying "because *Thongs* received tax or say that the tax went to them directly, they got better facilities and better land. When *Japtang* came to Rupa and killed the local king, he kept all the properties. That is the reason why the *Thongs* became rich. Besides, *Thongs* used to collect tax from Assam". But another respondent[2] justifies it by saying "*Thongs* never gave a thought to elevate the status of *Chaos*. If one tries to climb up in the social rank in the society he is pulled down, that's the mentality as I have seen. For instance, even during elections if we plan to contest and go for campaigns anywhere, they would say 'why are you contesting?' They do not support us. Because they have the mentality that if the *Chaos* move forward in political field then the *Chaos* will suppress them. That is why they do not allow us to get elevated. I think the *Chaos*' heads are empty, because whatever the *Thong* says the *Chaos* obediently follow. But if we are in difficulties and ask for the help they will not help. Even if a *Chao* works for a *Thong* and there is any economic gain or money is earned from the work everything will be kept by him (*Thong*), I will not get any share from it. Maybe because of this reason they became economically well established".

Traditionally, the Sherdukpens mainly indulged in agriculture for their livelihood besides hunting, fishing and trading. However, the traditional system of trading through the barter system with the neighbouring state Assam has stopped, as with the growth and expansion of market economy everything at present is available at the Rupa market. On some occasions they go for marketing in the nearby places like Tenga[3] and Bomdila[4]. New trend of trading has sprung up within the society. The contractors from outside come and provide every possible assistance for cultivation from the supply of seeds to fertilisers. Whatever assistance is provided, records are kept by them so that during the harvesting period when these contractors come to buy the harvested crop the money is adjusted accordingly. A change, not only in the agricultural practise can be seen but also in the occupational shifts. The shift in the occupation is due to the modern education system which provides an opportunity for every one to get absorbed in different governmental agencies (see table below).

Table 4.1 Number of people, class wise, involved in different economic activities of three villages

Class	*Main Occupation*							
	Male				*Female*			
	A	S	B	O	A	S	B	O
THONG	105	54	34	8	17	19	1	143
CHAO	52	34	4	4	12	1	-	66

A = Agriculture, S = Service, B = Business, O = Others
Source: Fieldwork 2010

It is found that the people beside agriculture are engaged in various economic activities also for their livelihood. However, large number of people are engaged in agriculture.

According to Table 4.2 it is found that the main economic occupation of the Sherdukpen when compared genderwise, in case of males is agriculture, while females are mostly engaged in house hold works. But here it does not mean that the females are not involved in agriculture. The females also engage themselves in agriculture as their secondary activity. In comparison the percentage of *Chaos* males engaged in agriculture is three per cent higher than the *Thongs*, while in case of females, it is two per cent. The percentage of females engaged in agriculture as their main occupation constitutes from the females who are unmarried and staying with parents.

It also includes those female members like the daughters-in-law living in joint families and doing the household work while the mothers-in-law help in the agricultural work. In case of the male population engaged in government services, the percentage is five per cent higher than *Thongs*. But in case of female population it is found that the females of the *Thong* clan are ahead by four per cent. In business entrepreneurship it is the *Thongs* who dominate the scenario, in case of both males and females. In other economic activities like daily wage earnings in case of male and the role of house wives for female the percentage do not show much variation apart from slight fluctuation.

Table 4.2 Percentage of people involved in different economic activities combining the three villages within own class

Class	*Main Occupation*							
	Male				*Female*			
	A	*S*	*B*	*O*	*A*	*S*	*B*	*O*
THONG	27.56	14.17	8.92	2.10	4.46	4.49	0.26	37.53
CHAO	30.06	19.65	2.31	2.31	6.94	0.58	0.00	38.15

A = Agriculture, S = Service, B = Business, O = Others
Source: Fieldwork 2010

Fig. 4.1 Chart showing percentage of people, class wise, engaged in different economic activities

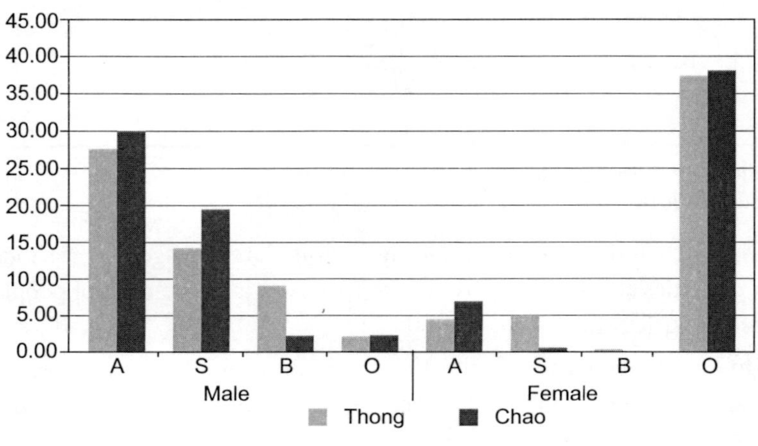

Table 4.3 Percentage of people involved in different economic activities combining the three villages within classes

Class	*Main Occupation*							
	Male				*Female*			
	A	*S*	*B*	*O*	*A*	*S*	*B*	*O*
THONG	18.95	9.75	6.14	1.44	3.07	3.43	0.18	25.81
CHAO	9.39	6.14	0.72	0.72	2.17	0.18	0.00	11.91

A = Agriculture, *S = Service,* *B = Business,* *O = Others*
Source: Fieldwork 2010

But when the economic activities of males and females in class are checked with the total population involved in it, it is found that the percentage of males engaged in agriculture for the *Chaos* is fifty per cent less than that of *Thongs* involved in it. Even in rest of the economic activities the percentage of *Thongs* is higher in every field in comparison to that of *Chaos* within the population.

Fig. 4.2 Chart showing percentage of people, class wise, engaged in different economic activities

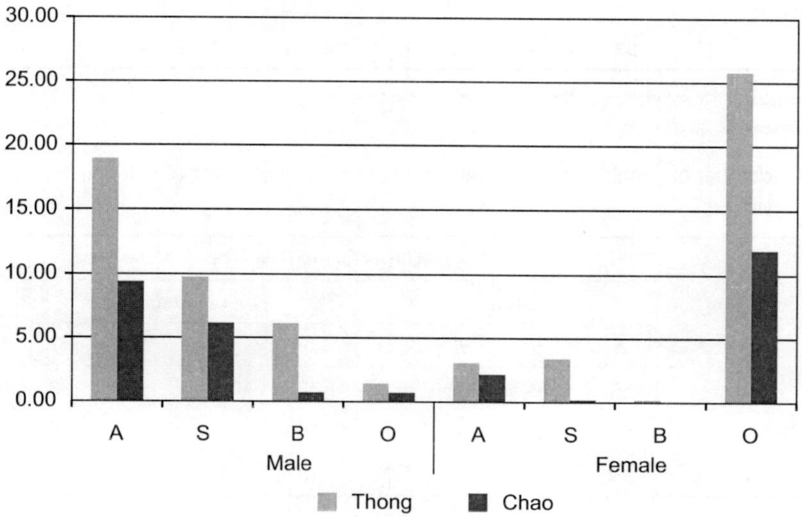

This fluctuation in the percentage within the two tables is due to the population involved in the economic activities. The population of *Thongs* is higher in comparison to the *Chaos*. So when the percentage is taken in relation to their respective class the *Chaos*' percentage is higher in comparison to the *Thongs*'. But when the percentage is taken with respect to the total population, the percentage of the *Thongs* is higher in comparison to the *Chaos*.

Table 4.4 Clan wise involvement of people in different economic activities of the three villages

Class	*Clan*	*Main Occupation*								*Subsidiary Occupation*							
		Male				*Female*				*Male*				*Female*			
		A	*S*	*B*	*O*	*A*	*S*	*B*	*O*	*A*	*S*	*B*	*O*	*A*	*S*	*B*	*O*
T	THONGDOK	38	16	10	3	4	2	-	53	6	1	2	-	44	-	-	-
H	KHRIME	13	9	9	3	5	2	1	21	6	-	-	-	20	-	-	3
O N	THONGON	12	10	3	1	3	5	-	12	1	-	-	-	8	-	-	-
G	THONGCHI	22	6	5	1	4	4	-	29	7	-	-	-	29	-	-	-
	WANGJA	5	7	3	-		4	-	10	2	-	-	1	7	-	-	-
	MOSOBI	9	3	4	-	1	2	-	10	3	-	-	1	8	-	-	-
	KARMA	5	3	-	-	-	-	-	7	-	-	-	1	5	-	-	-
	YANGFAN	1	-	-	-	-	-	-	1	-	-	-	-	1	-	-	-
Total		**105**	**54**	**34**	**8**	**17**	**19**	**1**	**143**	**25**	**1**	**2**	**3**	**122**	-	-	**3**
C	MEGEJI	24	17	2	1	8	1	-	35	5	-	1	-	27	-	-	-
H A	DINGLA	18	7	-	2	-	-	-	19	-	-	1	-	19	-	-	-
O	SINCHAJI	7	6	-	-	2	-	-	7	-	-	-	-	5	-	-	-
	MIJIJI	3	4	2	1	2	-	-	5	2	-	-	2	5	-	-	-
Total		**52**	**34**	**4**	**4**	**12**	**1**	-	**66**	**7**	-	**2**	**2**	**56**	-	-	-

A = Agriculture, *S = Service,* *B = Business,* *O = Others*
Source: Fieldwork 2010

Table 4.5 Number of people engaged in different economic occupation of different villages

Village	*Main Occupation*							
	Male				*Female*			
	A	*S*	*B*	*O*	*A*	*S*	*B*	*O*
RUPA	55	65	29	2	9	17	1	93
THONGRE	63	6	1	5	10	0	0	66
JIGAON	39	17	8	5	10	3	0	50

A = Agriculture, *S = Service,* *B = Business,* *O = Others*
Source: Fieldwork 2010

According to Table 4.5 the least number of people involved in other economic activities is of Rupa while for business it is of Thongre. The female in relation to business is negligible.

According to Table 4.6, it is found that the people of Rupa have a high concentration in other economic activities within the village. If we see the percentage of male, engaged in government service, it is higher than that of agriculture in Rupa. The percentage of females engaged in government services is also high in Rupa while it is nil for Thongre and a small percentage can be seen at Jigaon. In relation to business also small percentage of female is found in Rupa but it is nil for Thongre as well as for Jigaon village. It can be concluded that the population of Rupa is showing a great shift in economic occupations from the rest of the two villages. This is because Rupa has an

Table 4.6 Percentage of people, within respective village, engaged in different economic occupation of different villages

Village	*Main Occupation*							
	Male				*Female*			
	A	*S*	*B*	*O*	*A*	*S*	*B*	*O*
RUPA	20.30	23.99	10.70	0.74	3.32	6.27	0.37	34.32
THONGRE	41.71	3.97	0.66	3.31	6.62	0.00	0.00	43.71
JIGAON	29.55	12.88	6.06	3.79	7.58	2.27	0.00	37.88

A = Agriculture, S = Service, B = Business, O = Others
Source: Fieldwork 2010

Fig. 4.3 Chart showing percentage of people, village wise, engaged in different economic activities in the three villages

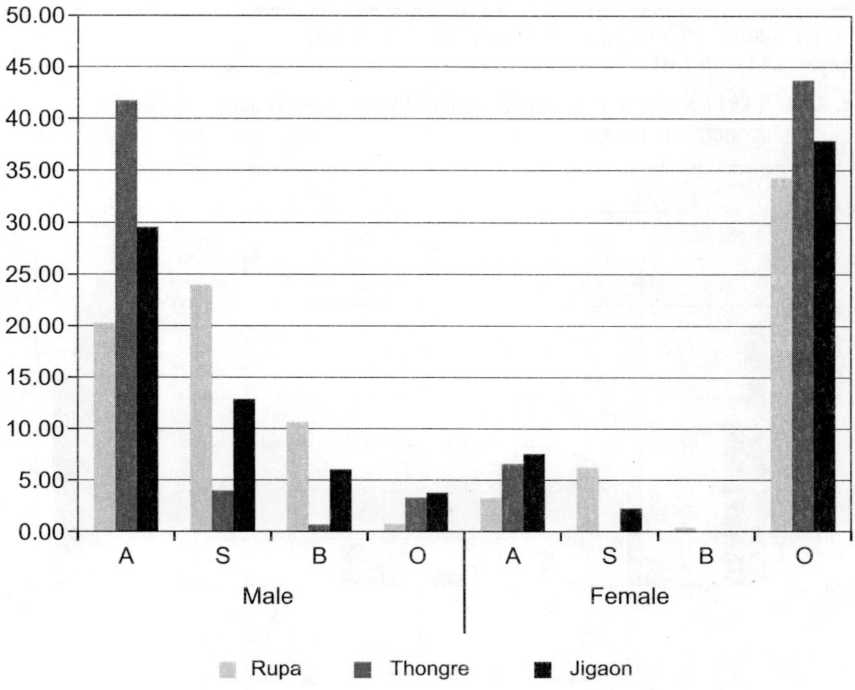

urban set up. Being the circle headquarter all the administrative set up is located here. The people of Thongre are still concentrating on the traditional economic activity i.e. agriculture, for their livelihood. Somehow, Jigaon is showing a transitional phase. In relation to business undertaking Jigaon is ahead of Thongre village in case of male population.

According to Table 4.7 it is found that the percentage of Rupa, as a whole, is high in every aspect of occupation. The percentage of male engaged in service is higher than the male engaged in agriculture in Rupa. This is due to the presence of administrative set up at Rupa. Females are also dominant in this sector in comparison to Thongre and Jigaon. In business sector also, the females show some concentration in Rupa while the females of Thongre and Jigaon have not come up in this sector.

Table 4.7 Percentage of people engaged in different economic occupation of different villages

Village	*Main Occupation*							
	Male				*Female*			
	A	*S*	*B*	*O*	*A*	*S*	*B*	*O*
RUPA	9.93	11.73	5.23	0.36	1.62	3.07	0.18	16.79
THONGRE	11.37	1.08	0.18	0.90	1.18	0.00	0.00	11.91
JIGAON	7.04	3.07	1.44	0.90	1.81	0.54	0.00	9.03

A = Agriculture, *S = Service,* *B = Business,* *O = Others*
Source: Fieldwork 2010

Fig. 4.4 Chart showing percentage of people, village wise, engaged in different economic activities

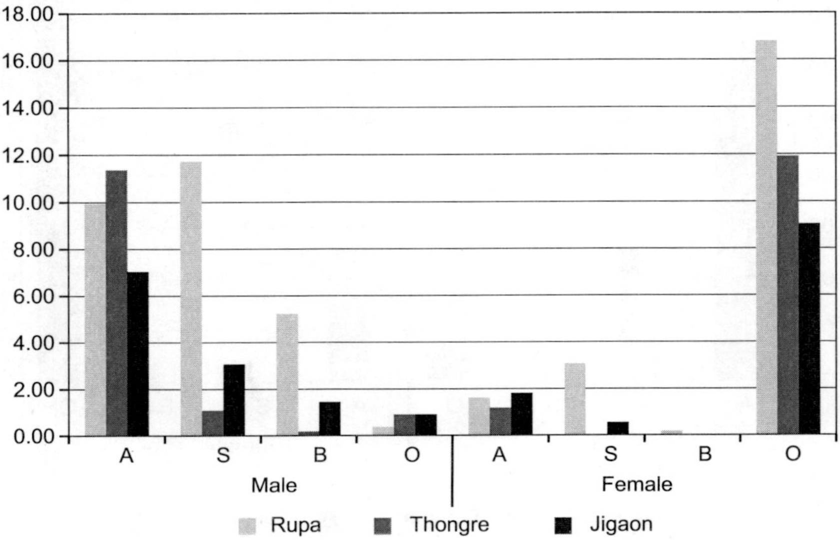

Table 4.8 Number of people, class and clan wise, involved in different economic activities of Rupa village

Class	*Clan*	*Main Occupation*								*Subsidiary Occupation*							
		Male				*Female*				*Male*				*Female*			
		A	*S*	*B*	*O*	*A*	*S*	*B*	*O*	*A*	*S*	*B*	*O*	*A*	*S*	*B*	*O*
THONG	THONGDOK	11	10	7	1	1	2	-	22	3	1	2	-	16	-	-	-
	KHRIME	8	7	8	1	2	2	1	11	4	-	-	-	10	-	-	3
	THONGON	4	10	3	-	1	5	-	6	1	-	-	-	2	-	-	-
	THONGCHI	2	1	1	-	1	1	-	3	1	-	-	-	2	-	-	-
	WANGJA	5	7	3	-		4	-	10	2	-	-	1	7	-	-	-
	MOSOBI	6	3	4	-	1	2	-	8	3	-	-	-	6	-	-	-
	KARMA	5	3	-	-	-	-	-	7	-	-	-	1	5	-	-	-
	YANGFAN	1	-	-	-	-	-	-	1	-	-	-	-	1	-	-	-
Total		**42**	**41**	**26**	**2**	**6**	**16**	**1**	**68**	**14**	**1**	**2**	**2**	**49**	-	-	**3**
CHAO	MEGEJI	5	14	2	-	1	1	-	14	2	-	1	-	7	-	-	-
	DINGLA	5	2		-	-	-	-	5	-	-	1	-	5	-	-	-
	SINCHAJI	2	4		-	-	-	-	3	-	-	-	-	2	-	-	-
	MIJIJI	1	4	1	-	2	-	-	3	1	-	-	-	3	-	-	-
Total		**13**	**24**	**3**	-	**3**	**1**	-	**25**	**3**	-	**2**	-	**17**	-	-	-

A = Agriculture, S = Service, B = Business, O = Others
Source: Fieldwork 2010

Table 4.9 Number of people, class wise, involved in different economic activities of Rupa village

Class	*Main Occupation*							
	Male				*Female*			
	A	*S*	*B*	*O*	*A*	*S*	*B*	*O*
THONG	42	41	26	2	6	16	1	68
CHAO	13	24	3	-	3	1	-	25

A = Agriculture, S = Service, B = Business, O = Others
Source: Fieldwork 2010

Table 4.10 Percentage of people, within own class involved in different economic activities of Rupa village

Class	*Main Occupation*							
	Male				*Female*			
	A	*S*	*B*	*O*	*A*	*S*	*B*	*O*
THONG	20.79	20.30	12.87	0.99	2.97	7.92	0.50	33.66
CHAO	18.84	34.78	4.35	0.00	4.35	1.45	0.00	36.23

A = Agriculture, S = Service, B = Business, O = Others
Source: Fieldwork 2010

According to Tables 4.9 & 4.10 the number and percentage of people, within the class, engaged in service is higher in both the classes in comparison to agriculture. The percentage of males, within the class, is much higher in comparison to the *Thongs* with a difference of fourteen percent. But in case of females the percentage of *Thongs* is higher in comparison to the *Chaos*. In case of business also the *Thongs* are ahead in comparison to the *Chaos* in both the genders. In case of other economic activities, in males, the percentage of *Chaos* is nil while there is a small percentage of *Thongs* engaged in it. In relation to this the female percentage of *Chaos* is higher in comparison with the *Thongs*. However, this same female population is also engaged in agricultural activities as secondary activity. The percentage of females in agriculture as their main occupation is from the females who are unmarried and living with their parents and are engaged in agriculture.

Fig. 4.5 Chart showing percentage of people, within own class, engaged in different economies of Rupa

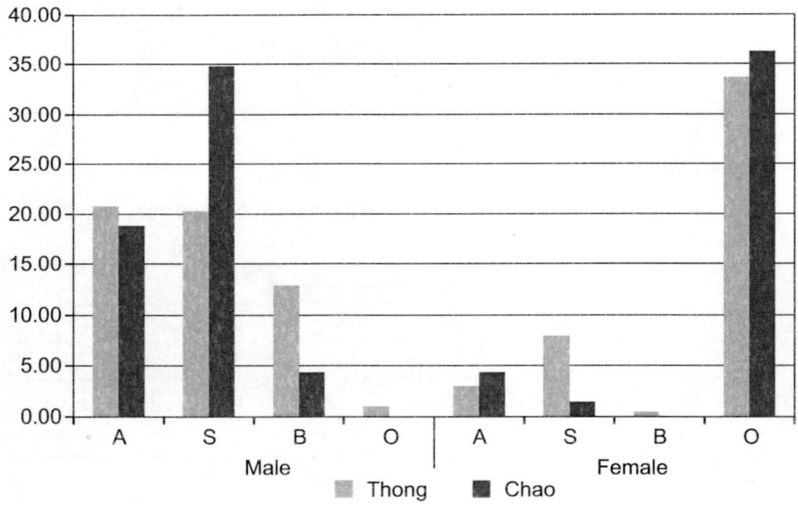

Table 4.11 Percentage of people, in class, involved in different economic activities of Rupa village

Class	*Main Occupation*							
	Male				*Female*			
	A	*S*	*B*	*O*	*A*	*S*	*B*	*O*
THONG	15.50	15.13	9.59	0.74	2.21	5.90	0.37	25.09
CHAO	4.80	8.86	1.11	0.00	1.11	0.37	0.00	9.23

A = Agriculture, S = Service, B = Business, O = Others
Source: Fieldwork 2010

Fig. 4.6 Chart showing percentage of people, in class, engaging in different economies of Rupa

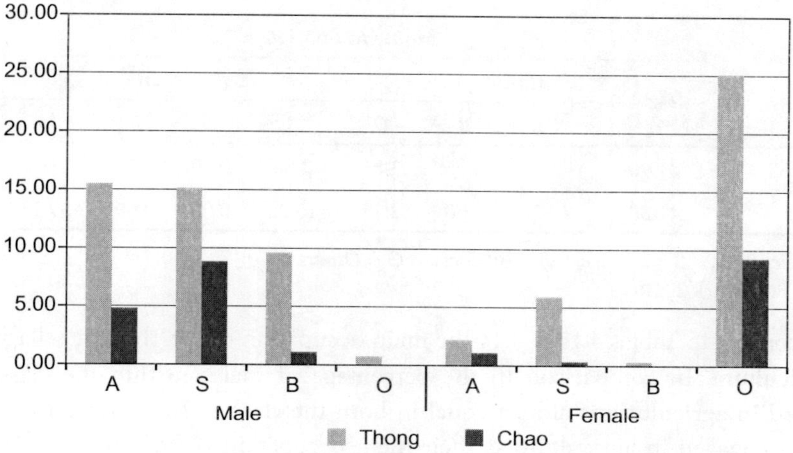

Table 4.12 Number of people, class and clan wise, involved in different economic activities of Thongre village

Class	*Clan*	*Main Occupation*								*Subsidiary Occupation*							
		Male				*Female*				*Male*				*Female*			
		A	*S*	*B*	*O*	*A*	*S*	*B*	*O*	*A*	*S*	*B*	*O*	*A*	*S*	*B*	*O*
T	THONGDOK	24	3	-	1	-	-	-	23	2	-	-	-	23	-	-	-
H	KHRIME	5	2	1	2	3	-	-	10	2	-	-	-	10	-	-	-
O	THONGCHI	10	-	-	1	-	-	-	11	-	-	-	-	11	-	-	-
N G	THONGON	5	-	-	-	-	-	-	4	-	-	-	-	4	-	-	-
Total		**44**	**5**	**1**	**4**	**3**	-	-	**48**	**4**	-	-	-	**48**	-	-	-
CHAO	MEGEJI	17	1	-	1	5	-	-	17	2	-	-	-	16	-	-	-
	SINCHAJI	2	-	-	-	2	-	-	1	-	-	-	-	1	-	-	-
Total		**19**	**1**	-	**1**	**7**	-	-	**18**	**2**	-	-	-	**17**	-	-	-

A = Agriculture, S = Service, B = Business, O = Others
Source: Fieldwork 2010

Table 4.13 Number of people, class wise, involved in different economic activities of Thongre village

Class	*Main Occupation*							
	Male				*Female*			
	A	*S*	*B*	*O*	*A*	*S*	*B*	*O*
THONG	44	5	1	4	3	-	-	48
CHAO	19	1	-	1	7	-	-	18

A = Agriculture, S = Service, B = Business, O = Others
Source: Fieldwork 2010

Table 4.14 Percentage of people, within own class, involved in different economic activities of Thongre village

Class	*Main Occupation*							
	Male				*Female*			
	A	*S*	*B*	*O*	*A*	*S*	*B*	*O*
THONG	41.90	4.76	0.95	3.81	2.86	0.00	0.00	45.71
CHAO	41.30	2.17	0.00	2.17	15.22	0.00	0.00	39.13

A = Agriculture, S = Service, B = Business, O = Others
Source: Fieldwork 2010

According to Tables 4.13 & 4.14 the main occupation of the Thongre village is agriculture. In comparison to the percentage of males, within the class, involved in agriculture is almost equal in both the classes. The percentage of females engaged in agriculture as their main occupation is from the females who are unmarried and staying with their parents. However, the percentage of females engaged in agriculture is higher in comparison to the females of *Thongs*. This is because of the higher number of females who have left their study and are engaged in agriculture. The percentage of females engaged in service and business is nil in both the classes. In case of males a small percentage of *Thongs* are involved in business while the *Chaos* are not represented in it.

Fig. 4.7 Chart showing percentage of people, within own class, engaged in different economic activities of Thongre

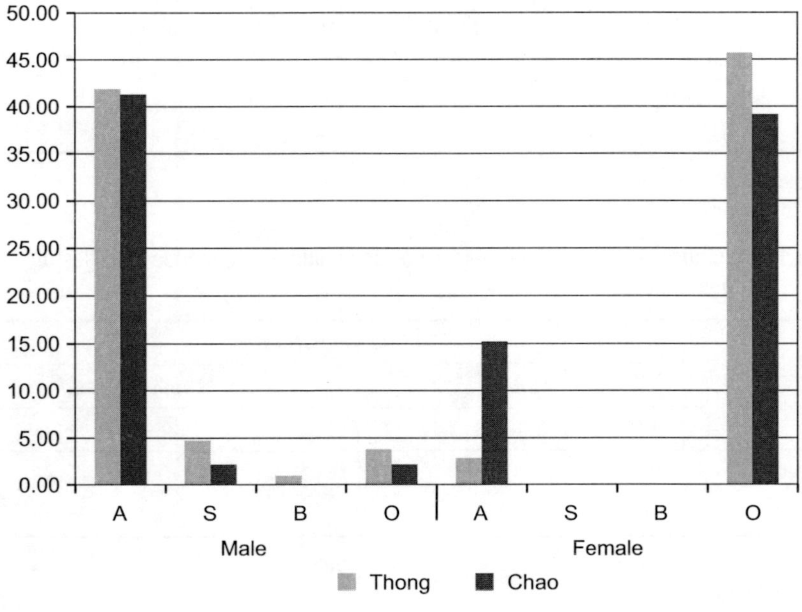

Table 4.15 Percentage of people, in class, involved in different economic activities of Thongre village

Class	*Main Occupation*							
	Male				*Female*			
	A	*S*	*B*	*O*	*A*	*S*	*B*	*O*
THONG	29.14	3.31	0.66	2.65	1.99	0.00	0.00	31.79
CHAO	12.58	0.66	0.00	0.66	4.64	0.00	0.00	11.92

A = Agriculture, S = Service, B = Business, O = Others
Source: Fieldwork 2010

According to Table 4.15, the percentage of *Thongs* is higher in every economic activity within the village. Females of both the classes are not represented in the government services. The percentage of males represented in agriculture is much higher in *Thong's* male population in comparison to the *Chao's* males within the village.

Fig. 4.8 Chart showing percentage of people, in class, engaged in different economies of Thongre

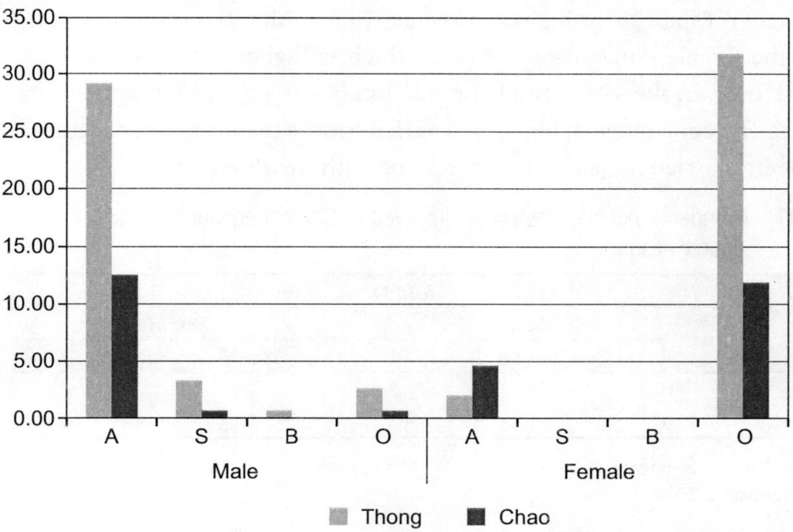

According to Table 4.18 majority of the Sherdukpen of Jigaon village are engaged in agriculture irrespective of class. The percentage, within the class, of *Chaos* males is higher in comparison to the *Thongs* males with a difference of nine per cent. Even in service the *Choas* male percentage is higher than the *Thongs*. However, in case of females it is nil in *Chaos*. In case of business the *Thongs* percentage is higher in comparison to the *Chaos* and in case of females it is nil in both the classes. In case of other economic activities in males, the

Table 4.16 Number of people, class and clan wise, involved in different economic activities of Jigaon village

Class	*Clan*	*Main Occupation*								*Subsidiary Occupation*							
		Male				*Female*				*Male*				*Female*			
		A	*S*	*B*	*O*	*A*	*S*	*B*	*O*	*A*	*S*	*B*	*O*	*A*	*S*	*B*	*O*
T	THONGCHI	10	5	4	-	3	3	-	15	6	-	-	-	16	-	-	-
H	THONGDOK	3	3	3	1	3	-	-	8	1	-	-	-	5	-	-	-
O N	THONGON	3	-	-	1	2	-	-	2	-	-	-	-	2	-	-	-
G	MOSOBI	3	-	-	-	-	-	-	2	-	-	-	1	2	-	-	-
Total		**19**	**8**	**7**	**2**	**8**	**3**	-	**27**	**7**	-	-	**1**	**25**	-	-	-
C	SINCHAJI	3	2	-	-	-	-	-	3	-	-	-	-	2	-	-	-
H	MEGEJI	2	2	-	-	2	-	-	4	1	-	-	-	4	-	-	-
A	MIJIJI	2	-	1	1	-	-	-	2	1	-	-	2	2	-	-	-
O	DINGLA	13	5	-	2	-	-	-	14	-	-	-	-	14	-	-	-
Total		**20**	**9**	**1**	**3**	**2**	-	-	**23**	**2**	-	-	**2**	**22**	-	-	-

A = Agriculture, S = Service, B = Business, O = Others
Source: Fieldwork 2010

percentage of *Chaos* is bit higher in comparison to the *Thongs* and so is the case of the female percentage of *Chaos* which is higher with respect to the *Thongs*. However, the same female population is also engaged in agricultural activities. The percentage of females in agriculture as their main occupation is from the unmarried females who are staying with their parents.

Table 4.17 Number of people, class wise, involved in different economic activities of Jigaon village

Class	*Main Occupation*							
	Male				*Female*			
	A	*S*	*B*	*O*	*A*	*S*	*B*	*O*
THONG	19	8	7	2	8	3	-	27
CHAO	20	9	1	3	2	-	-	23

A = Agriculture, S = Service, B = Business, O = Others
Source: Fieldwork 2010

Table 4.18 Percentage of people, within own class, involved in different economic activities of Jigaon village

Class	*Main Occupation*							
	Male				*Female*			
	A	*S*	*B*	*O*	*A*	*S*	*B*	*O*
THONG	25.68	10.81	9.46	2.70	10.81	4.05	0.00	36.49
CHAO	34.48	15.52	1.72	5.17	3.45	0.00	0.00	39.66

A = Agriculture, S = Service, B = Business, O = Others
Source: Fieldwork 2010

Fig. 4.9 Chart showing percentage of people, within own class, engaged in different economic activities of Jigaon

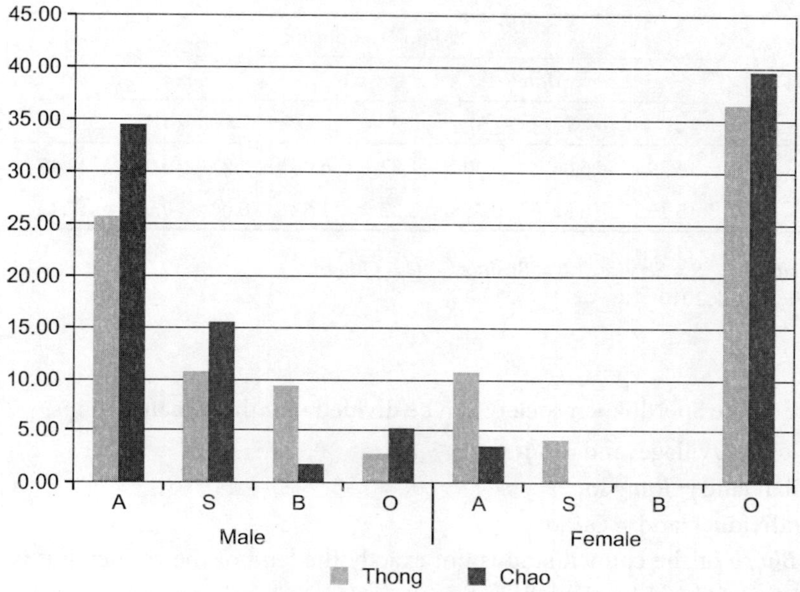

According to Table 4.19 the percentage of *Thongs* males engaged in agriculture is lower than the *Chaos* in Jigaon village as a whole. However, in case of male engaged in service is almost equal in both classes of the society within the village.

Fig. 4.10 Chart showing percentage of people, in class, engaged in different economic activities of Jigaon

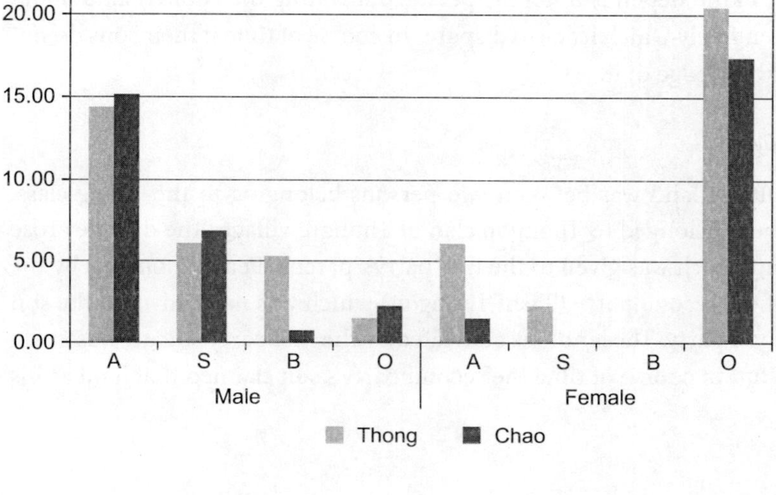

Table 4.19 Percentage of people, in class, involved in different economic activities of Jigaon village

Class	*Main Occupation*							
	Male				*Female*			
	A	*S*	*B*	*O*	*A*	*S*	*B*	*O*
THONG	14.39	6.06	5.30	1.52	6.06	2.27	0.00	20.45
CHAO	15.15	6.82	0.76	2.27	1.52	0.00	0.00	17.42

A = Agriculture, S = Service, B = Business, O = Others
Source: Fieldwork 2010

Land

The land in the Sherdukpen society can be divided into three main groups:

1. Council/village land = *Blu so*
2. Clan land = *Rung so*
3. Individual land = *Gu so*

The *Blu so* or the council land is not exactly the land of the council but is the area that falls under the village territory. Hence, in other words it can be called the territorial land or village land. The *Rung* land as defined by its name itself is the land of the clan. These are the lands on which their fore fathers had made a claim during their times and which is not yet divided among the members of that clan hence is called *Rung so.* Lastly the *Gu so* (*gu* = mine) is the individual land which is the individual property where the individual constructs his house and cultivates or gives the land to others for cultivation for free or for some payments. The payment can be in terms of cash or kind. The payment in cash depends upon consensus between the parties while the payment in kind depends upon the person cultivating the allotted land. Land is also given freely which leads to disputes in course of time if their sons do not have the knowledge of it.

Case Study No.1

This dispute of land was between two persons belonging to the *Thong* class. Both of them belonged to Thongon clan of Thongre village. The dispute arose on the land which was given to the first party's parent (Pema Thongon) by the parents of the second party (Tashi Thongon) which was not known to the son of the second party. The land was cultivated by the first party since it was given to them. But, in course of time the second party's son claimed that land as his property.

In this case the dispute was settled within the two families. Here it was the grandmother of the second party's son that clarified the matter. In this way the dispute was settled among themselves.

The land holding system is not class based. It depends on the member' of people of the class. If there are single *Thong*s and four or five *Chaos* then automatically *Chaos* will have more land in the society in comparison to the *Thongs*. There are *Thongs* who hardly have land and there are *Chaos* who possess large land areas. However it is the *Thongs* in general who possess more land in comparison to the *Chaos* within the society (see tables). Though, it is difficult to show the possession of land in terms of area as there is no system of area measurement within the society. So the data was collected in plot system.

Table 4.20 Class and clan wise possession of land within three villages

Class	*Clan*	*Number of Families*	*Number of Plots*	*Total number of Plots*
THONG	THONGDOK	44	210	592
	KHRIME	23	138	
	THONGON	13	78	
	THONGCHI	27	75	
	MOSOBI	12	44	
	WANJA	7	27	
	KARMA	7	16	
	YANGFAN	1	4	
CHAO	MEGEJI	27	74	134
	DINGLA	17	26	
	SINCHAJI	9	20	
	MIJIJI	8	14	
TOTAL		195	726	

Source: Fieldwork 2010

It is to be noted that the area of a single plot may vary as plot refers only to the patch of occupied land without any unit. So the plot sometimes may be as big as two to three plots or maybe small in comparison to other plots.

According to Table 4.20 the *Thongs* occupied major portion of land within the society. Thongdok occupied the highest number of plots while the least were occupied by Yangfan. In combining the three villages together it is found that the average plot of land which falls under each family of the *Thongs* is four and half plot compared to *Chaos* which is only two plots each family.

Fig. 4.11 Chart showing percentage of plots occupied by various clans within three villages

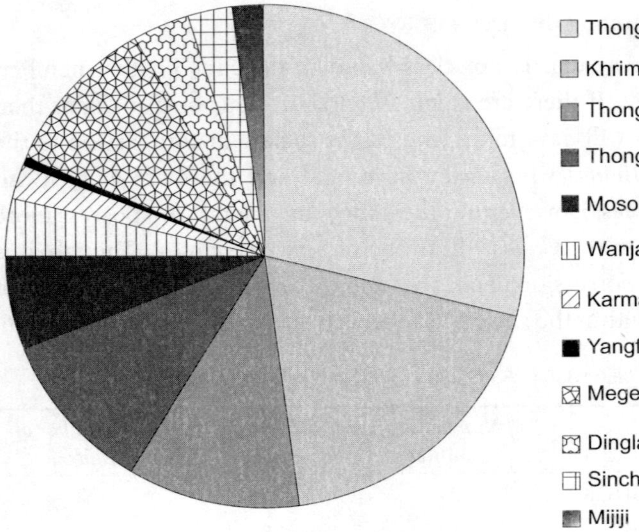

Table 4.21 Number and percentage of families owning land according to plot interval combining three villages

Class	*Plot Interval*	*Number of Families*	*Percentage of Families*
THONG	1–5	109	55.05
	6–10	15	7.58
	11–15	6	3.03
	16–20	2	1.01
	21–25	4	2.02
CHAO	1–5	60	30.30
	6–10	2	1.01
	11–15	-	-
	16–20	-	-
	21–25	-	-

Source: Fieldwork 2010.

It is found in general that more than 80% of the families fall in the first interval of plot division.

According to Table 4.22 the number of plots occupied by the *Thongs* in Rupa is much higher in comparison to plots occupied by the *Chaos*. An average of two plots falls under each *Chaos* family as compared to six plots for each *Thongs* family which is three times more than that of the *Chaos*. However, in Rupa there are three households who do not possess any cultivable land (see Appendix A Table No. A-1). There is one Megeji family which has not yet divided the land.

Table 4.22 Class and clan wise possession of land of Rupa village

Class	*Clan*	*Number of Families*	*Number of Plots*	*Total Number of Plots*
THONG	THONGDOK	19	142	410
	KHRIME	14	111	
	THONGON	7	59	
	THONGCHI	4	15	
	MOSOBI	9	36	
	WANJA	7	27	
	KARMA	7	16	
	YANGFAN	1	4	
CHAO	MEGEJI	11	26	53
	DINGLA	5	9	
	SINCHAJI	4	8	
	MIJIJI	5	10	
TOTAL		93	463	

Source: Fieldwork 2010.

Fig. 4.12 Chart showing percentage of plots occupied by various clans in Rupa village

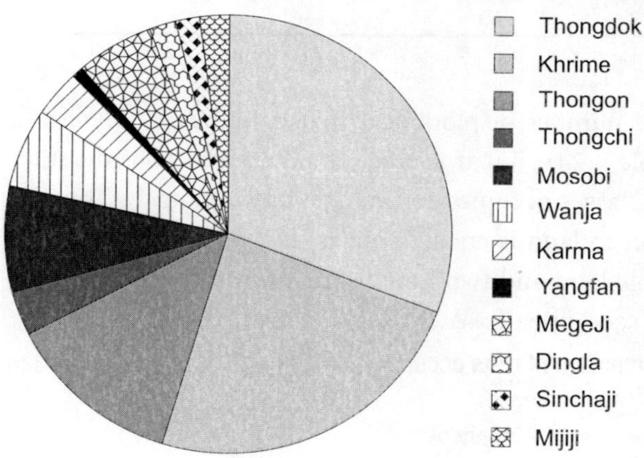

In Rupa, *Thongs* are seen to be holders in every plot interval category while the *Chaos* are holders in first interval of plot division only. However, the concentration of holders is highest for the first interval of plot division even in the *Thongs*. *Thongs* are dominating in population structure in Rupa and most of the plot belongs to *Thongs*.

Table 4.23 Number and percentage of families owning land according to plot interval in Rupa

Class	*Plot Interval*	*Number of Families*	*Percentage of Families*
THONG	1–5	45	47.87
	6–10	12	12.77
	11–15	6	6.38
	16–20	2	2.13
	21–25	4	4.26
CHAO	1–5	25	26.60
	6–10	-	-
	11–15	-	-
	16–20	-	-
	21–25	-	-

Source: Fieldwork 2010

Table 4.24 Class and clan wise possession of land of Thongre village

Class	*Clan*	*Number of Families*	*Number of Plots*	*Total Number of Plots*
THONG	THONGDOK	18	52	116
	KHRIME	9	27	
	THONGCHI	7	23	
	THONGON	4	14	
CHAO	MEGEJI	13	44	50
	SINCHAJI	2	6	
TOTAL		53	166	

Source: Fieldwork 2010

In Thongre village the number of plots occupied is higher by *Thongs* as compared to *Chaos* (Table 4.24). But if average is taken into consideration then each family of both classes occupies an average of two plots. In Thongre village, status with respect to land is equal. Besides, there is one family who does not possess cultivable land and two houses are cultivating in joint land which is not yet divided (see Appendix A Table No. A-2).

Fig. 4.13 Chart showing percentage of plots occupied by various clans in Thongre village

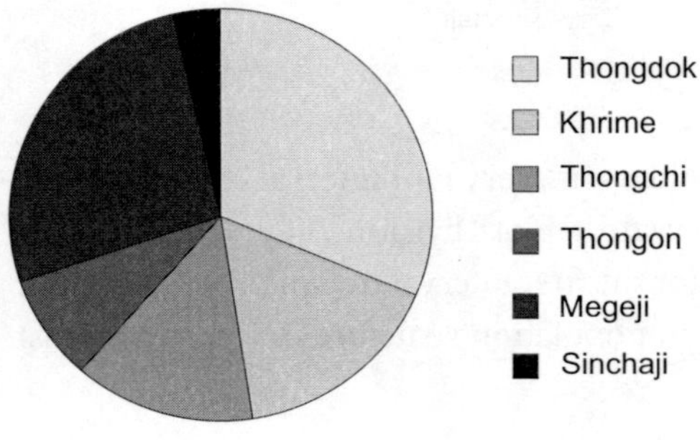

Table 4.25 Number and percentage of families owning land according to plot interval in Thongre

Class	*Plot Interval*	*Number of Families*	*Percentage of Families*
THONG	1–5	36	65.45
	6–10	3	5.45
	11–15	-	-
	16–20	-	-
	21–25	-	-
CHAO	1–5	14	25.45
	6–10	2	3.64
	11–15	-	-
	16–20	-	-
	21–25	-	-

Source: Fieldwork 2010

In Thongre, it is found that in both *Thongs* and *Chaos* the families are distributed in holders of first and second interval of plot division only and the concentration is highfor holders in first interval of plot division for both the cases.

Table 4.26 Class and clan wise possession of land of Jigaon village

Class	*Clan*	*Number of Families*	*Number of Plots*	*Total Number of Plots*
THONG	THONGCHI	16	37	66
	THONGDOK	7	16	
	THONGON	2	5	
	MOSOBI	3	8	
CHAO	SINCHAJI	3	6	31
	MEGEJI	3	4	
	MIJIJI	3	4	
	DINGLA	12	17	
TOTAL		49	97	

Source: Fieldwork 2010

In Jigaon, the number of plots occupied by the *Thongs* is higher than the *Chaos* in general. When an average is taken then the each *Thongs* family occupied nearly two and half plots. For the *Chaos* it is one and half plot for each family. Even in Jigaon there are three families who do not possess cultivable land (see Appendix A Table No. A-3).

In every village there are one or two families who do not possess cultivable land of their own. But it does not mean that there is scarcity of land. All the cultivable land throughout the village is located in and around the domesticated areas. So those who want to occupy new land for cultivation have to go far from the domesticated area. They do not do so usually because there are occupied areas around the domesticated area which are not cultivated or used by the owners, in which non-holders of land cultivate by paying some amount or for free, according to the convenient consents.

Fig. 4.14 Chart showing percentage of plots occupied by various clans in Jigaon village

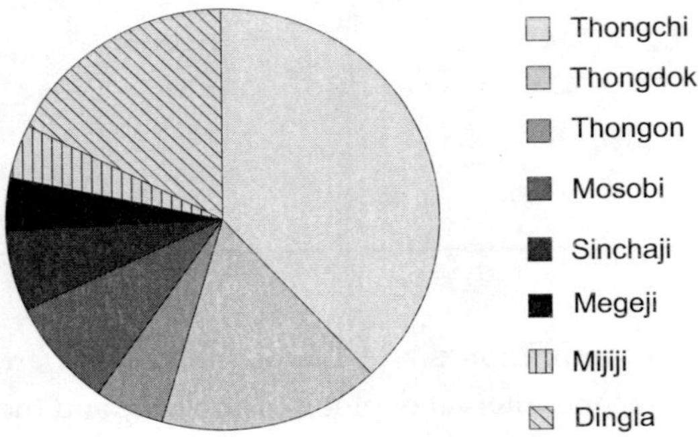

Table 4.27 Number and percentage of families owning land according to plot interval in Jigaon

Class	*Plot Interval*	*Number of Families*	*Percentage of Families*
THONG	1–5	28	57.14
	6–10	-	-
	11–15	-	-
	16–20	-	-
	21–25	-	-
CHAO	1–5	21	42.86
	6–10	-	-
	11–15	-	-
	16–20	-	-
	21–25	-	-

Source: Fieldwork 2010

In Jigaon, the families holding plots of land are found to fall in first interval of plot divisions only, for both *Thongs* and *Chaos.*

As cited by N.T. Khrime "Traditionally the land which is claimed by the people of the society is recognised by the *Chaos*. That is why *Chaos* are very important citizens. Right from the beginning it is divided. Some belong to the *Chaos* and some belong to the *Thongs*. So you[5] have to recognise it. Sometimes there are disputes but disputes are again settled by both the classes. The *Chao* elders have to affirm. *Thongs* can do anything they like. This is checked by the

Chaos. Despite rich in land, the *Thongs* are given respect and are regarded as it has been practised since generations. As in those days *Japtang* was regarded being 'a *Thong*' (a king), and that tradition is still followed".

As narrated by Kesang Megeji "Land holding capacity depends on an individual. On the territorial land, i.e. *Blu so*, a person or family is permitted to clear an unoccupied land area for cultivation. In this *Blu so* whoever comes and clears as much land for cultivation that much land comes under the possession of that person and will be considered his land. The *Thongs* usually have more land because we used to respect them, help them, whenever they asked for help. If he (*Thong*) takes the help of ten *Chaos* to clear a portion of land, all land cleared by these ten *Chaos* will be considered his land. Since this way could get large areas cleared for cultivation, that's why they have more land. So, it depends upon the person on how much land is cleared by him, as that much land will be counted under his possession and no one can make a claim over it".

Thus, occupying land in the society is very simple either by buying or by clearing a new patch of land which has never been used. The clearing of land is done from within the territorial land that is *Blu so*. That particular occupied land will be considered to be owned by the person who cleared and cultivated it for his living. Thus, such unutilised land becomes the property of the family who clears and cultivates it. Names of the people have been given below who had recently occupied new land for cultivation:

1. Dorjee Khandu Thongchi recently cleared a plot of jungle which he is cultivating. This land is now considered to be his land as he had cleared it and is cultivating it.
2. Kesang Dorjee Megeji acquired a plot of land by clearing the jungle and is cultivating it.
3. Sang Tsewang Dingla also acquired a plot of land by clearing the forest and is cultivating it.
4. Dor Gombu Megeji had occupied a land by clearing the jungle and is cultivating it.

But sometimes disputes arise in occupying new cultivable land by clearing the forests due to miscalculations of boundaries.

Case Study No. 2

This is the case of land dispute between Pema Megeji (*Chao*) and Tsering Thongdok (*Thong*) of Thongre village. The case arose in clearance of new cultivable area by clearing the forest. The dispute arose after the Megeji cleared up a plot of land adjacent to Thongdok land which was cleared a long time back where plants and bushes had overgrown again. The Thongdok made a claim that the Megeji had encroached on the area cleared by him (Thongdok). But the dispute got settled within the two families after thorough discussion and necessary rectifications made between them.

The Thongdok also agreed that it was a mistake and that he had miscalculated the area he had cleared earlier and in this way the dispute was settled.

As narrated by Y. Thongdok

"If *Thongs* own more land and *Chaos* do not have land for the construction of their houses then *Thongs* can donate land to the *Chaos* for the purpose. If *Thongs* do not have and *Chaos* have more land then the *Chaos* can do the same. Even some *Chaos* possess more land than some *Thongs*. From the very early times land was sold and bought. Suppose someone who has lots of land and his sister gets married and she is staying here (Rupa) then one can give a share of land to the sister. Earlier in hamlet (*pam*), the area where the cows were kept turned fertile because of the animal dung and if someone cultivated on it that was considered to be his land then on. In this way the lands were occupied for settlement and agriculture. No one could say anything about it or touch it. It is recognised by the people and the council". Allotting of land for long duration for free, for the purpose of cultivation also creates disputes within the society some times.

Case Study No. 3

This dispute of land took place between Thongdok and Khrime (both *Thong)*. The land was given for cultivation to the Khrime by the Thongdok. In due course of time the Thongdok wanted the land back as they wanted to cultivate it for themselves. But the Khrime did not leave the land and made a claim that it was his land. The case was directly referred to the *Blu*. The date was fixed by the council (*Blu*) for three or four times but the case could not be solved. As the case could not be solved having been politicalised the Thongdok party decided to go to the Gompa and take an oath. When the matter reached to this level the other party i.e. Khrime surrendered his claim and then the council B*lu* gave the decision in the favour of Thongdok.

Case Study No. 4

This is the land case that happened between two *Thongs* one is Thongdok and other is Khrime. There was a land where Thongdok used to cultivate. But later the Khrime claimed that that land belonged to him. When the case could not be resolved between them it was taken to the *Blu*. Even the *Blu* could not resolve it due to lack of evidential support. After three times of deliberations of council when it was not resolved the *Blu* left the case undecided. Later on if one of the parties fenced the land the other used to come and remove it. At long last the two parties came on consensus by dividing the land.

The lands have been sold and purchased since long times.[6] The price of land within the village is higher in comparison to the land outside the village or far from the village. The Sherdukpens used to exchange land also after consensus between the parties. For instance, when a person from a village has a land in a hamlet (*pam*) and in lieu of that he could ask the concerned person staying at hamlet (*pam*) for an exchange who possesses a land in the village (Rupa).

Plate 4.1 *Lingjik* and demarcation with stone wall

Demarcation of land was done by putting a stone (*lingjik*) in the land. While putting the stone (*lingjik*) a ritual was performed by sacrificing a goat or a pig propitiating the spirit. The ceremony was performed by the local priest (*Jiji*). The people attending the ceremony were the lone witnesses of that demarcation. There used to be no written records. It is believed that if anyone else came and claimed that land that person or his family members would face the wrath of death. Disputes sometimes arose regarding this, because the stone sometimes got buried in due course of time.

Case Study No. 5

It was the land dispute of land demarcation that took place between the *Chaos*. Both the parties are Megejis from Rupa village. The dispute arose when the owner of the land was putting a fence around the area. The other Megeji (of the adjoining land) came and claimed that the demarcated boundary of the first party land was not upto that place where he was putting a fence rather it was an encroachment on his land. By showing the demarcation mark of stone (*lingjik*) the claimer said the fence had crossed the demarcation point. Dispute arose on this but it was resolved between them with the help of one

Thong (Thongdok) who had the actual knowledge of the demarcation of that disputed land. Actually, the claimer of that demarcated land had put another stone away from the actual demarcation point.

There is no division of river but a particular portion where the river splits into two channels called *khroh* is owned by a particular clan and is used for fishing. Fishing in *khroh* is done by diverting the water course of one channel to flow into another. When the channel of the river, due to diversion of water course dries up the fishes are caught. A person not belonging to that particular clan was not permitted to go for fishing there. If someone wanted to go for fishing there, that person had to take permission from the clan who owned that *khroh*. That is why it is called *Rung khroh* like *Mosobi khroh*, *Thongdok khroh*, *Dingla khroh*, *Megeji khroh* and so on.

Agriculture

Agriculture has been the major economic activity of the Sherdukpens (Table 4.1). It continues to be the major source of livelihood. Men, women, children and aged persons are found engaged in one or the other agricultural activities. In busy agricultural season all have to contribute to extract the maximum product. There being only one agriculture season in a year, the Sherdukpen had to be more industrious. Due to extreme cold, nothing can be cultivated on the land in the winter. Slash and burn method i.e. *jhuming* was also practised but after nineties everyone got engaged in settled agriculture due to change in crop cultivation. In the past, maize was the main product as it was made into flour, flakes and wine. We can say that maize was the staple food of the Sherdukpens. Even in these days maize is planted but not to that extent as before, as people now are opting for profitable crops. Now-a-days, people are engaged in tomato (*Bilati*) production as it is more profitable looking at the present market demand. In cultivating tomato, chemical fertilisers, pesticides and insecticides are also used in large extent. Besides tomato cultivation in large quantities, chilly, potato, brinjal, beans, cabbage, cucumber, cauliflower, radish, pumpkin, etc. are also cultivated for household consumption only.

Agriculture is the main activity of both the sections of the society and both the classes indulge in the work equally. The only difference is that the *Chaos* help in the agricultural work in the fields of the *Thongs*. But it does not happen vice versa. It is not a compulsion for a *Chao* to go and work in the *Thongs'* field. It is so because the *Thongs* are in better economic condition than the *Chao*. It is the *Thongs* who provided for the needs of the respective *Chaos* in past days. So in lieu of that, the *Chaos* go and works for their respective *Thongs*. But there used to be some *Chaos* who worked as servants for the *Thongs* and stayed at

Plate 4.2 Agricultural field at Rupa

their houses and were called *yamchao*. It happened only when a *Chaos* after committing a crime is unable to afford to pay the penalty. Here, the respective *Thongs* used to pay his due and in return that *Chao* came and worked for his generosity. As they stayed together the *Chaos* looked after the *Thongs* property.

Plate 4.3 Agricultural field at Thongre

Plate 4.4 Agricultural field at Jigaon

In agricultural activities, the males are engaged in heavy work for instance they make fence, plough the field and the women folk do the sowing and weeding. The ploughing of the field is done by two persons. One moves the bulls and the other holds the plough applying force on it. The house which does not have ploughing bulls can borrow it from someone in exchange of their labour on their fields or it can be paid in terms of rupees. The payment of a pair of bull in term of rupees is ₹200–300 per day in the present day situation. In terms of exchange for labour, it is per person per bull per day. However, this kind of exchange was not found during the field work rather it was found that everyone made payments in terms of rupees. Now the use of plough has stopped at Rupa but people of Thongre and some of Jigaon are still found to be engaged in it. The reason for stoppage of using plough is said to be due to the decrease in the size of cultivable field. Ploughing is never done by any female, it is the work of the male. Even the *Thong* class indulges in it. Although it is not a taboo for a female to touch it but it is considered as a tedious job so it is done by the male folks.

The place to start agriculture is at *Thongdok rek*,[7] which is at Rupa, is ploughed first and then the rest will start ploughing for agriculture. This day is termed as *Thongdok rek phikpa*. On this day, a small ritual is performed in the name of wealth god (*Yangsrijom*) at *Changkong* (place where *Yangsrijom*

Plate 4.5 Man ploughing the field

is located) which is adjacent to *Thongdok rek*. On this day, the youth give bath to the *Yangsrijom* and burn incense and the *khikjiji* propitiates the ritual. After that the *Thongdok rek* is ploughed. In the past whole plot of field was ploughed but now they plough it for name sake. They plough it for four-five rakes only. But with the increase of population which has spread into different settlement areas, this tradition (*Thongdok rek phikpa*) has lost it's importance.

Plate 4.6 *Thongdok rek* with Changkong

Plate 4.7 *Changkong*

Plate 4.8 *Yangsrijom*

No other special ritual is associated with the initiation of agriculture. The only ritual associated with agriculture is, a Buddhist ritual, the propitiation of the rain god called *Lobsang*. *Lobsang* is performed by monks in Smuchi. The next day it is done in Brokpublong pam, Thongre pam, Chilli pam, Digsi pam, etc. wherever the people stay. After performing the ritual in all the pams at last they reach Changkong where there is a stone idol *Yangsrijom* where a monk performs prayer for a whole day. After that in the evening, young boys and girls carry water and they splash water in every household on people shouting *Sarphapso*. It is said and believed that after this there was rain. This ritual is done after sowing of seeds and if there has not been rain for long.

Now-a-days Jhum is not practised. But when it was done in the past maize, potato, brinjal, pumpkin, cucumber and red coloured rice (*dese*) were planted in Jhum.

Regarding horticulture, the Sherdukpens plant apples and walnuts, though they do not produce it in large quantity. Besides these, now few people are engaged in kiwi plantations which are sold in the nearby markets.

In addition to agriculture and horticulture, now-a-days people who have completed their higher education are engaged in government jobs and contractual work. Beside these, ministers sanction contracts to the villagers in which the people work in groups and share the amount equally. But in case, if a family has a voter list in that village and are unable to go for work they can entrust their share of work to another person but that family have to share half of their earning with the entrusted person.

Division of Labour

The rules of division of labour are not very rigid in the sense that a particular person would have to do only particular job. A grown up person has to do multipurpose works. However, some reservations have been made on the basis of age, sex, physical fitness. No division as such is seen in the society according to the class. Each and every individual works for themselves to earn their livelihood. It is not that a *Thong* won't work himself. He also works in his fields. Now this trend is coming up as the agriculture is done for the marketing purposes and so as to replenish the working force the hired labourers are introduced. They are generally brought from Assam and stay with the family they work for, for that agriculture period.

Animal Husbandry

Beside agriculture, animals and poultry are also reared by the Sherdukpens. The rearing of animals and poultry was not done for consumption as the

Sherdukpen did not take all these in their diet in the past. Cow is reared for milk and milk products like Butter (*Mo*) and cheese (*Tsroh*) and also for ploughing and for paying tax to the Akas and Mijis. Horse was reared for transportation, pig and poultry for performing rituals. However, rearing of animals has almost stopped. At present no one rears horses which was the means of transportation and which has been replaced by the modern mode of transport. Only few houses rear cows which are not taken for grazing as used to happen earlier. Cows are left on their own.

Cows were reared both by *Thongs* and *Chaos*. The cow shed is called *yambok*. The owner of cow shed is called *suspu* and the grazer is called *brokpu*[8]. A person who is interested or wants to rear 2–3 cows but does not have a shed may keep their cows in the shed of other after seeking permission, irrespective of class. But in the lieu of keeping the cows in others' shed one cow or a bull is paid to the owner in every three years. And then the *brokpu* will take all the cows together out of the village for grazing during the agricultural time. *Brokpu* can be from anywhere. *Brokpu* can be from both *Thongs* and *Chaos*. Besides, people from Rahung, adivasi (people from Assam), or Nepalis are brought to work as *brokpu*.

Owners of the cows during agriculture time have to send their cows out of the village. The time is consulted in the monastery for agricultural activities to start. Instruction is given by the council (*blu*) to let their respective animals to be sent out of the village. The *brokpu* takes the cows out and return before the onset of winter after the agriculture seasons are over. After giving instructions to *brokpu* for taking the animals outside, fencing (*Gag*) is made by the *thikkong chkok*[9] in Rupa and *Luser Chkok* in Shergaon. After the fencing is done whosoever's animal destroys the agricultural products in the village is imposed with a fine. After the agriculture season is over, information is sent to the *brokpu* to return to the village.

There are different routes to take the animal for grazing but it is not fixed class wise or clan wise. The taking of route for grazing depends on a friend's intimation or marriage alliance. One may ask his friends to join him for grazing the animal. So in this way the *brokpu* used to move together irrespective of class. *Megejis* and *Thongdoks* first will move to Manthingbaw, from there Sumuchi, then Brokpublong, to Didingpam then to Octom then Thongre. By that time the agriculture work is also almost over. But generally *Thongs* take the route of Chillipam, Limbakthang, Jigaon, Smachulii. This way going round grazing their reared animal, they reach Rupa. Even within the same clan also the route for grazing can be different. One of the *Thongdok* person cited "Even we, *Thongdoks* are divided into three groups. Pem Norbu Thongdok would go round from Dukhumpani to a place below Wangho village to Jungpam and back to Rupa. *Khrime* would start from Sumuchipam and go round with us to Brokpublong, Didingpam Octom, Thongre".

The rearing of pigs also goes with a reason. The rearing of pigs is done only to propitiate the god of wind. The ritual is called *Jongkhlong* but now it is not performed, as the society has converted to Buddhism. *Jongkhlong* is the worship of wind god by sacrificing the pig. Wearing the Aka dress, the pig is taken round the village beating it and letting it to cry. The Akas are considered to be furious and terrorizing. To show the same sentiment, their dresses are worn. The horoscope (*Mo*) is seen by the *khik jiji* whether in the east or west direction, the ritual of sacrifice have to be performed. The pork is not consumed. It is considered to be dirty to have its meat.[10]

Poultry

The keeping of poultry goes with a story that once Tsewang Ganggang's Queen fell ill. When omen was checked it was found that in plains there was a bird with long feathered tail and a comb on the head (showing a sign with the hand) which was to be let off in the queen's name. The letting off of the poultry in the name of somebody is termed as *chethar*. Then one person, may be a *Chao*, was sent with the description of the bird calling it *sorai.*[11] So that person carrying eatables in his traditional cloth (*bogre*[12]) and a jar made of cane paste with rubbery substance from inside (*hirbung*) left for Assam memorising the bird as sorai. When he reached Assam he saw a lady was sweeping her front house. At that moment, a strong wind blew and the jar (*hirbung*) fell down and got blown. The lady shouted, "Your jar (*hirbung*) is being blown away by the wind".

The person while collecting his jar (*hirbung*) forgot about the sorai. So when the lady asked him about the reason that had brought him to the plains he answer that the king had asked for the jar (*hirbung*). Then the lady replied, "We do not make this jar (*hirbung*)." The person went back to the king. The king asked, "What had you asked there?" He replied, "Whatever you had told me. I said jar (*hirbung*) and the lady said that they didn't have it". The king said, "It is sorai", and sent him back. This time he brought the sorai i.e. the poultry.

Then onwards, during winter, using a white cock (kept by the priest) a ritual is performed by *Mege, Mano, Rongla, Dingla*. After that the queen recovered from her sickness. That is why even if is not consumed the poultry is kept. There are different gods such as *Sungkhik, Srokhik, Lorgya Wangpu*, etc. who are propitiated with the offerings of the poultry sacrifices which is why Sherdukpens keep poultry. In this way the keeping of poultry came within the society to exist.

Trade

During the winter season the Sherdukpens used to go to Doimara (*Ruchong*) for 3–4 months for two main purposes. Firstly, because of extreme cold climatic conditions and secondly for trading as the society was not self sufficient in all the products.[13] It is also said that the society had a cordial relation with the people of the neighbouring state Assam, also because of which the Sherdukpens went to Doimara. Every member of the house young, old and child used to go to Doimara during the winters. A particular group (*Chkok),* was sent some time earlier, before the winter camps started, to clear the way upto Doimara. After that everyone would set off for the journey. While going for winter camp some family who had new born babies or small kids would engage load carriers (*Yungpo*) from among the youths, irrespective of class. "A higher class youth also may come and help the *Chao* family which has been practically witnessed by me".[14]

From here dried chillies, dried radish, spice (*jabrang*), maize, etc were taken which was exchanged mainly for paddy. Threads, clothes and utensils were also bartered for. Every clan of Sherdukpens was attached with some families of the plains referred as *duchu chanthing* (for the Kacharis) *or hindu chanthing* (for Assamese) with whom the exchange was done.[15] At last while leaving, the Kacharis used to offer endi clothes, tobacco, betel nuts, betel leaves, etc. The Assamese used to offer tea while Kacharis offered wine in a bowl held with a leaf to their kings from their hands once and touch their feet to be blessed. This offer was made to every adult male irrespective of class as they considered the attached clan as *sincha raja.*[16] "We used to bless and sometimes offer money if available. As they gave newly harvested betel leaves and betel nuts rituals were performed by us and them in the name of mountain god (*khiksaba*). So taking the name of the mountain god and saying, "we shall meet again and peace prevail with you" all the *sincha rajas* used to bless them".[17] Finally, the families of the plains would offer a towel (*sra mokhok*) to every person of their attached clan. Few families would also offer endi clothes. They sometimes also asked for some dao or *jijih* (tripod stand used in hearth) to be brought in return. And while treading back the people of the plains used to see the Sherdukpens off for some distance. Again according to their capacity the people (Sherdukpen) offered money to the elderly people and leaving them behind the Sherdukpens started their journey back. So the items asked for, by the families were brought for them during the next visit along with the products that were taken for exchange.

By mid-April, everyone came back and the old people used to take rest in Thongre while the youth carrying the products brought from the plains reached Rupa. Slowly, every individual would reach Rupa and get engaged in the fields by clearing the grass and ploughing. And when the rains started, instructions were given by council to *brokpu* to bring back the animals to their *brokso*.[18]

It is also said that Sherdukpens used to trade with Bhutanese and Tibetans. They used to buy beads from them. As the Sherdukpens did not have much handmade products so they were dependent both on the people of the plains and the people beyond the mountains. From plains, items especially endi clothes and from beyond the mountains beads, caps, milk products, etc. were procured.

Material Life

To focus on the differences between the classes through the material culture is quite difficult as the society has transformed a lot. It is through the well being of the family from where they acquire their comfort. So there is no restriction on the possession of property. However, it is said that in the past there were restrictions on using some stuffs like the *Chaos* never sat on carpets and on tiger skins and the *Chaos* never ate with silver spoons.

In the context of material life, there are no differences in the house patterns, dresses, ornaments, etc. though it is said that *Thongs* used to live in houses constructed by stones while *Chaos* resided in the wooden houses. But it is found that even *Thongs* lived in wooden houses and there was no difference in the structure of the houses.

House

It is said that traditionally there were three types of houses:

1. *Decha yam* (house made of stone).
2. *Panthing yam* (house made of stone, bamboo and wood).
3. *Tampla yam* (house made of bamboo and wood).

Before the place is occupied for house construction *lama* (monk) is consulted. The *lama* takes the soil and performs a ritual and tells the owner whether to construct house there or not. If the site is considered appropriate then the day is fixed to occupy it. On the fixed day five bamboos are put on the four corners of the house and one in the middle. The thread is tied around the four corners of the erected bamboos. The putting of bamboos also depicts the directions as well as the elements. Thereafter a pig is sacrificed and the blood is poured on the line of the thread. As the Sherdukpens did not take pork in earlier days so a sheep is butchered for the grand feast.[19] After this the foundation stones are laid.

Plate 4.9 Model of traditional houses: *Decha yam*, *Panthing yam* and *Tampla yam* (L–R)

But before the foundation stones are laid, if a tortoise shell is available, it is buried in the centre. If 5–6 shells are available then they are buried on all the points of the erected bamboo. The burying of the tortoise shell is done with a belief that the house would stand strong like the tortoise shell in all climatic conditions. The type of tortoise shell that is used is *mosergiripo*.[20]

After the completion of the construction, house warming is performed. In house warming the sister (*mringdimih*) brings sheep or yak for the feast. In return the brother gives her a brass utensil (*tao*) according to his capability and also endi clothes to her.[21] On this day, the constructors are paid according to the rates fixed by the village and food and drinks are offered to them.

Plate 4.10 *Panthing yam* at Thongre

Plate 4.11 Remains of *Decha yam* at Rupa

The workers involved in the construction of house are not based on class basis. There is a head worker under whose instructions the other workers work. The head worker can be from any class according to his knowledge and expertise. In the construction of house both *Thongs* and *Chaos* participate. It may also happen that if a *Chao* has expertise then the *Thongs* have to work under his instruction.

Plate 4.12 Plank arrangement

Plate 4.13 Roof setting

The Sherdukpen house was generally erected on a substantial stone foundation, five to six feet in height which acted as a basement. But sometimes the height of the wall from the ground varies with the fall of the slope. The shape of the house is rectangle but the size varies due to absence of measuring instruments. The basement is used for sheltering domesticated animals. Above this basement, a two storied house is constructed. The lower storey is constructed with thick wooden planks while the upper storey with matted bamboo platform and walls. The roof is covered with light planks supported by stones so as not to let it be blown away by the wind.

The lower storey consists of the living room having double compartments. The front part occupies almost three fourth of the space and called *Yamdok* while the back side only one fourth called *Rapse* which is the prayer room. The upper storey acts as a store room and is called *Zoh*.

However, in the present day context one can see differences in housing pattern. But these differences do no show the picture of stratification in terms of class division in the society as it is in monetary terms. Those who are well off, irrespective of class background, build big houses comprising of several rooms.

Plate 4.14 Main room (*Yamdok*)

Plate 4.15 *Rapse*

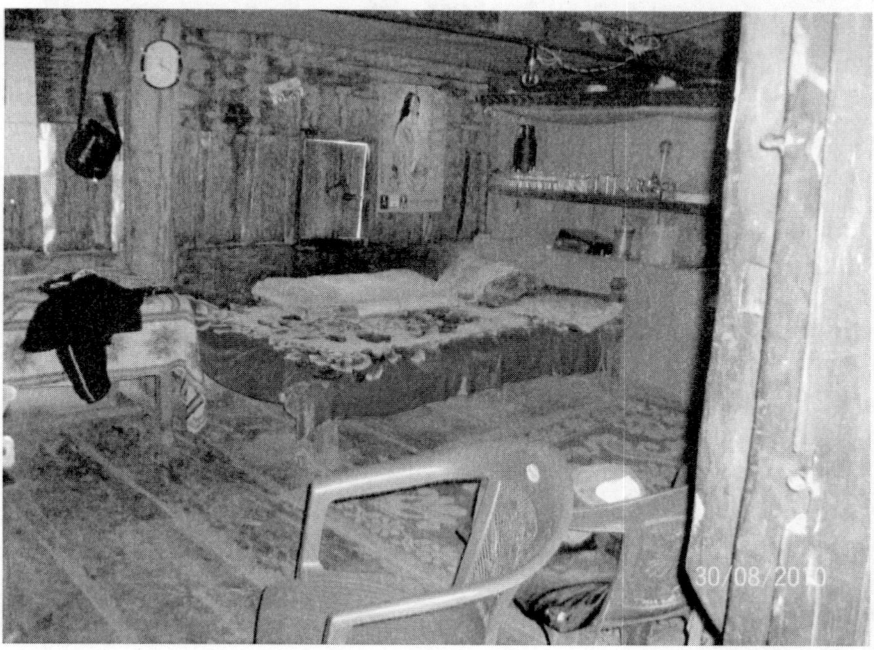

Plate 4.16 Upper storey of the house (*Zoh*)

Plate 4.17 Stairs leading to *Zoh*

Plate 4.18 Inter lock system in house

Dress and Ornaments

The dress and ornaments of the Sherdukpen is similar to that of their neighbouring tribes specially the Aka, Miji and Bugun. The male dress of the *Thongs* is different from *Chaos* whereas the females of both the class wear same dress. Though the *Thongs* have dresses different than that of *Chaos'* yet they do not wear it in day-to-day life. Only during the *Khiksaba* festival and during collection of Posa[22] they wore this Tibetan noble dress. In day-to-day life they put on the same dress as the *Chaos*. As cited by N.T. Khrime that "there is no difference but *Thongs* have got better ornaments so they wear it. *Chaos* do not have much ornaments and so they don't wear it. There is no restriction though. In this way it is identified that the better dressed are *Thongs* because they have them". But in the course of field work it was found difficult to make out through the dresses that a particular person is a *Thong* or a *Chao*. The reason is that nowadays people hardly wear their traditional dress.

Male Dress

The Sherdukpen men wear a sleeveless endi cloth wrapped diagonally called *Sape*. The two ends of the cloth are pinned onto the shoulders that reach down to the knees. The *Sape* forms the main constituent of the male dress of Sherdukpen. Over it red-shash (*mokhok*) having an embroidery at the border of the two ends is tied to the waist. Then sword with silver scabber engraved with designs (*adok chong-thok*) or knife with silver scabber engraved with design (*achan chong-thok*) is tucked in the shash (*mokhok*) on the left side. Over these, coat (*alphudung*)[23] is worn which is black in colour and is made of yak hair. The cap (*gurdam*) made from yak hair with tassels (*stok bomchan*) jutting down over the face, is mainly worn by the men. It is decorated with a white cockade (*chitpo bomchan*) and colourful band around its brim. A cloth (*bogre*) woven from natural fibers, is tied around the shoulders to form a fold

Plate 4.19 Sherdukpen couple in their traditional attire

at the back. This cloth (*bogre*) is used for carrying eatables and articles of frequent use. It is also used as a mat for sleeping in the jungles. It is the identity marker of the Sherdukpen people.

Plate 4.20 A Sherdukpen woman in her traditional dress

Female Dress

The women wear a collarless and sleeveless endi cloth, which covers them from the shoulders to the ankles termed *sinku*. The *sinku* is a loose parallel cloth which is tied with shash (*mokhok)* round the waist, making parallel plates. A full-sleeved embroidered jacket (*alung dedik*) is worn over the *sinku*. A shawl (*snap*) is tied around the neck by tying its two ends and leaving the rest part hung on the back side. The ladies tie their hair into a bun at the back, although most grown-up girls do not. Weaving is considered a feminine art and most of the women were able to weave clothes in a highly artistic manner.

Plate 4.21 *Thong* dress

Plate 4.22 *Thongs* in their attire

Thong Dress

The dress of the *Thongs* comprises of a cloak (*tspoh*) made of colourful silk, which is full sleeved and covers the whole body from shoulders to the ankles. Over the cloak (*tspoh*), red coloured shash (*mokhok*) is tied around the waist having similar embroidery with the common *Chao* male dress. Over the shash (*mokhok), a* belt (*korki*) is worn which is made up of brass. A sleeveless silk coat (*ringgo*) is worn over the cloak (*tspoh*). A black coloured cap (*chokjo*) is worn on the head. Two strips of cloth hang on the back side of the cap from its centre. On the left side a box beautifully engraved with designs and bearing a picture of Lord Buddha inside it (*jabgaw*) is hung with the help of an artistically woven strap. These dresses are imported from Bhutan or Tibet.

Ornaments

Besides the dress, there are ornaments which are worn by the people irrespective of class. Both the classes wear the same ornaments. The beads are traded from Bhutan and Tibet through Tawang. Beads are inherited by daughters who look after the parents or are also given to daughters-in-law if the mothers wish. In the absence of children, the beads are inherited by the brother(s) of the father. The price of the beads varies according to the material, size and age. The perception of originality is also done according to the weight of the beads–the heavier one is considered to be original. However, the number of beads are decreasing in the society due to closure of cross border trading. In the past days beads also represented the status of the family. Those who possessed more number of beads they were considered as rich in the society. Even beads were used in purchasing of land. There is no taboo for using the beads. Hence, no particular beads are associated with any particular person or section of the society. So it is common for the whole society. No special beads are there for a particular occasion; same beads are worn for all the occasions. However, the using of ornaments have decreased a lot though few ornaments still can be found specially the brooch (*zrok*) which is used to pin up the loose fitting clothes.

Some of the common ornaments used by the Sherdukpen male are:

1. *Dajawthok*: It is a chain made up of silver in two or four lines with a ring at two points. Pin is attached in these two rings which are used for pinning up the male dress (*sape*) at the shoulder.
2. *Champong gaw*: It is the silver pendant worn by males with the help of a thread or a piece of cloth.

3. *Phunye gaw*: It is a square silver pendant with a tiger teeth protruding out in opposite directions. It is also tied around the neck with the help of a piece of cloth or thread.
4. *Thring*: It is a brass bangle which is engraved with designs.

Plate 4.23 *Dajaw thok*

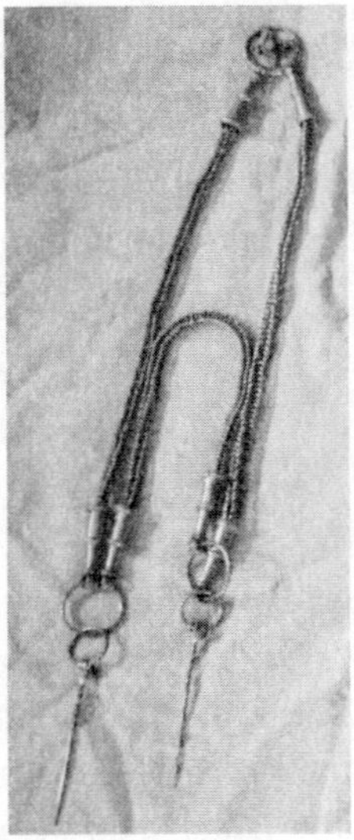

Plate 4.24 *Champong gaw*

Plate 4.25 *Phunye gaw*

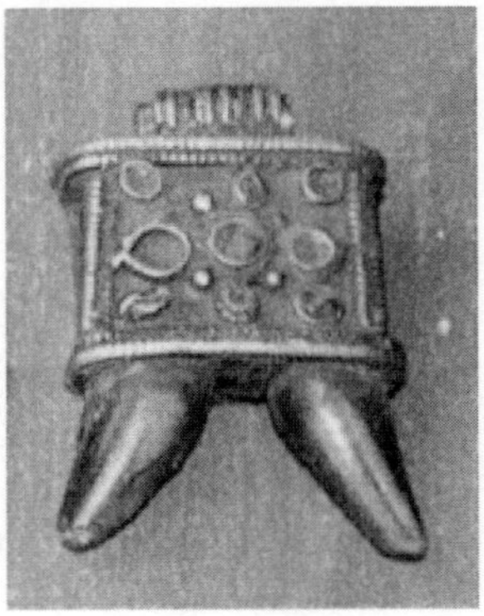

Though it is said that the *Thongs* possessed more ornaments than the *Chaos* but on seeing the photographs taken during 1944 when the Satraja went to Bilsiri for a meeting with J.P. Mills, it is found that the *Thongs* did not wear any ornaments, while above mentioned ornaments were worn by *Chaos* males only.

Some of the common ornaments used by Sherdukpen females are:

1. *Laso zrok*: It is a silver chain bearing pin and studded with beads.
2. *Pempla zrok*: It is a brooch made up of silver and beads. Its shape looks like two leaves attached from the base and is engraved with designs and studded beads.
3. *Hu zrok*: It is a bird shaped brooch made up of silver and beads. The body is engraved with the designs of small leaves studded with a bead representing its eye.
4. *Dorjee zrok*: It is a small flower design brooch made up of silver.
5. *Champong gaw*: It is a silver pendant worn by females also but with the help of a string of beads.
6. *Khik*: It is a necklace made up of string of beads and silver charms with a silver pendant (*madili*) which is moon shaped.

Plate 4.26 *Pempla zrok*, *Hu zrok* and *Dorjee zrok* (L-R)

7. *Gaw grobje*: It is a necklace of beads with a huge pendant square in shape. The pendant is engraved with designs and beads.
8. *Laso thring*: It is a thick silver bangle which is engraved with designs and beads.
9. *Nying thring*: It is a silver bangle engraved with designs and beads.

Plate 4.27 *Khik*

Plate 4.28 *Gaw grobje*

Plate 4.29 *Laso thring*

Plate 4.30 *Nying thring*

Endnotes

1. Informant N.T. Khrime, aged 68.
2. Informant K. Megeji, aged 35.
3. Tenga is a place along the valley to the east of Rupa. It is 6 km away from Rupa.
4. Bomdila is a district head quarters of west Kameng. It is 18 km away from Rupa and is situated to the north of it.
5. Here the respondent was referring to the investigator, the investigator being a *Chao*.
6. Informant S.K. Khrime, aged 65; W. Thongdok, aged 72; C. D. Wangja, aged 80.
7. *Thongdok rek* means field of Thongdok. But it does not mean that all the field of Thongdok is ploughed.
8. It is to be noted that *brokpu* is not an occupation. The term is used for a person who takes the animals out for grazing during the agricultural period. The person brought from outside to work as brokpu is a later concept. Earlier it was done by suspu . At present there is no brokpu as rearing of cows has stopped except in few houses having 2–4 cows and a bull. These animals also, when they are left in the jungle without being looked after during the agriculture season sometimes become the prey of wild animals.
9. *Chkok* is a group of people irrespective of class and involved in the work of the society. Thikkong is the name of the group.
10. Informant Y.D. Thongdok, aged 76.
11. "Soria" is an Assamese term for bird.
12. "Bogre" is a tradionally made cloth used by male members as a bag while leaving for outside or used as a mat for sleeping.
13. Informant Y.D. Thongdok; L.K. Megeji.
14. Informant Kesang Megeji, aged 35.
15. Informant Khandu Megeji, aged 58.
16. Informant Y.D. Thongdok; L.K. Megeji.
17. Informant Y.D. Thongdok; L.K. Megeji.
18. *Brokso* are the grazing lands; *brok* means grazer and *so* means land. While grazing, the animals are kept in an area by the *brokpu* at night. Due to their stay the soil became fertile and later was occupied for cultivation and converted to private property. These *broksos* were the hamlets (*pam*) where people went on later to cultivate and settle down.
19. Informant Y.D. Thongdok, aged 76.
20. Mosergiripo is a small size tortoise the bigger one is called Hudri.
21. If the mring dimih bring Yak the brother has to give more than two or three *tao*.

22. Sherdukpens claimed a tribute or payment from the plains which they collected annually. In February 1826 the Darang authorities resumed the right of direct collection and paid the Sherdukpens, ₹2,526/7 which was later reduced to ₹1,740.
23. *Alphudung* is a round necked coat and open in the front. It is available in sleeveless and full sleeve forms. It is thick and keeps warm during winter season. It is procured from Tawang.

5

Social Systems and Stratification

It is evident that the Sherdukpen society is divided into two main classes i.e. *Thong* and *Chao.* It is said that they used to live together helping each other. In this context it is to be kept in mind that each clan of *Thong* is attached with each clan of *Chao*. So these attached clans considered one another as brother clans. Marriage is a taboo between them. These attached clans supported each other in every possible manner. For instance, if some quarrel came up with *Thong* family the attached clan would come for their support. And if any *Chao* faced any sort of difficulties then their attached *Thong* family helped him (refer to Chart 3.3 to see which *Thong* is attached to which *Chao*).

One of the respondents[1] said "*Chaos* used to help and support the *Thong* in times of their difficulties. If someone comes and has a fight with a *Thong*'s son then *Chaos* had to come to their aid. They would enquire, "Why did you beat our *Thong*'s son?" *Chaos* are not the servant of *Thongs*, they are just like bodyguards to the king. And as the king, orders the bodyguard performs. And if *Chao* faced same sort of problems then the *Thongs* had to protect them. Likewise the *Chaos* also had to give their help to the *Thongs* in their bad times. For instance, if a *Thongdok* faces some difficulties then *Megeji* comes for their help.[2] Suppose, a child of a *Thong* became an orphan then the *Chao* had to look after it likewise if the same situation happened to the *Chao* then the *Thong* had to do the same".

In the day to day work also the *Thongs* participated equally as the *Chaos*. The *Chao* clan members used to go to help in the agricultural fields and other works of the attached *Thong* clan. But it is not a compulsion for a *Chao* to attend that work if his own schedule is busy.[3] It is also said that during the work the *Thong* would offer the best food and drinks to their *Chao*. Even if they (*Thong*) don't have much rice it is offered to the *Chaos* and *Thongs* themselves used to take porridge made of new soft leaves and bud of oak tree mixed with maize floor.[4]

"*Thongs* also do agricultural work. *Chaos* do not come to do the whole work. Even if they come also they do not work alone, *Thongs* also get involved. During agricultural season, there is no king and commoner. The kings have to come down and do the work. If the product is less in *Chaos's* house then the attached *Thongs* give some of the products to them (*Chao*). The same for the *Thongs*; if they are having problems, the attached *Chaos* give some of their products to their *Thong*. The work is individual but living is by sharing and caring for each other".[5] "If a *Thong* is going for agricultural work, the *Chaos* has to go as helping hand and in return get a share of that product. So *Chaos* were paid for what they did in return as kind".[6]

"There are some isolated cases where *Chaos* were treated badly. In conducting of council also *Thongs* and *Chaos* sit separately. If a *Thong* visited a *Chao* house, though it is not compulsory or practised now-a-days but earlier a small carpet with Dragon design (*Thikso-to*) was spread for him to seat and in front a stool (*tek*) was kept covered with a cloth (*sri-to*). They were seated either on the right or left side of the hearth (*khrukding*) so as to be paid due respect. But, after the conversion to Buddhism, first preference is given to the monk (*lama*) after which the *Thong* is seated. In the past even during the session of political intercourse the member, the Gaonbura used to sit separately as I have seen in Rupa during meetings. It is said that a *Chao* never sat face to face with *Thong* in those days. While talking also, a *Chao* had to show his respect to the *Thong*".[7]

"*Chaos* were not allowed to ride horses, only *Thongs* could. Sometimes the *Chaos* used to ride secretively but if the *Thongs* were watching they had to dismount. Actually even the *Thongs* were not allowed to ride on horses in the village. The reason is that, others would say, "everybody is a *Thong* here, why should he ride? Wherever or whenever they went outside the boundary or village they could ride but when they came back they had to dismount from the outskirts itself and walk. In any social gathering or programme the *Thongs* sat in the front".[8]

Yanlogs were the helping hands of the society but were not given the responsibility and involvement in the political decisions though they had helped the society for generations.[9] Earlier the *Yanlogs* were not allowed to enter the houses and the food was provided to them outside the house. Even food cooked by them was not accepted except for water, because they were considered to be of low class.[10] This is only in saying as in the present context the *Yanlog* class has been abolished. Till which year it was practised is difficult to ascertain as *Yanlogs* were found to be brought into the *Chao* class 80 years ago (see the case study of conversion of *Yanlog*).

Plate 5.1 *Chaos* holding the rein of the horse of their *Thong*

Family (*Yam-Jring*)

Family is the basic unit of the society. Family within the society is generally nuclear in structure with husband, wife and their progeny. The youngest son usually stays in the parent's house and is responsible for taking care of his parents. The family setup is patriarchal. As the father is the head of the family, the domestic affairs of the family generally are ruled by him. The decision taken by him is the final decision. The domestic chores are generally done by the females.

Each and every family pays revenue to the council (*Blu*) for festivals and occasions like *Chokor* and *Wang*. And the family which pays revenue is considered as *khomi*, and they have customary rights. The number of families in *khomi* increases after one gets married and starts living separately for more than three years. This duration is given taking into consideration that by that time the newly married family is well established.[11] In other words it can be said that *khomis* are the people who are drafted to *chkok*.[12] "It used to be done in the evening of the day after the division of betel nut is over during *Khiksaba*. After this the person has to contribute equally in whatever work ascribed or donation collected in the society".[13] But now the counting of family is done on *Chatpuniseh* (meeting).[14]

Role of Women

Traditionally in the household activities the women folks' contribution is more than the men. The womens' contribution is equal, if not more, in the agriculture operations. Except ploughing, which is done by the men folk alone, and is considered as a tedious job.[15] In the construction of house, the sister used to tie a scarf at the pole, at the initiation of construction, and used to bring local wine in vessels (*Chung*).[16] Women play an important role at the birth ceremony irrespective of class. Man and woman have equal right to divorce. The woman has a right to divorce the husband when she does not get proper attention and finds her husband is interested in some other female or is having an affair.[17] When divorced, woman can claim for compensation to an extent she likes.[18] Women are not secluded nor do they veil their faces rather they freely consume local wine (*Phog*), smoke and have betel in the company of menfolk. Both men and women dance together in marriages and festivals. No disparity marks the celebration of male or female at birth. The Sherdukpens, in general express love and affection for woman. Freedom for marrying is equally granted to the members of both sexes. It is only in the political field where women do not have any right to raise their voice or to participate or attend as a member in the traditional council. "She can attend only when the case is related to her".[19]

Property Inheritance

The decisions and rights for division of property rest with the parents. When the parents feel like dividing the property then it is informed to the clan members that they are going to divide the property among their sons. The property is divided in the presence of witnesses. Though, no record is made in written form. Everything will be done verbally. While dividing the property the house and a share of plot is kept in the parents' name which is termed as *gaizi*.[20] Then the rest of property is divided amongst the sons almost equally. The parents' share goes to the son, who usually takes care or looks after the parents till death. In this way generally it goes to the youngest son as he is the one who stays with the parents after the elder siblings leave the house after their marriage. In the society, it is said that the eldest son and the youngest son used to get more share of property in comparison to the middle son. But this is not the case in the present scenario. "It is said it may have happened as the eldest sons' contribution is more in comparison to the younger brother. Hence, when he leaves the parents' house the parents with love give him a share of plot for his living before the divisions take place. For the youngest it happens that, generally he inherits the parents share as he is the one who stays back at home and looks after them".[21] And regarding the middle son it is said that he is sent to be a monk.[22]

Case Study No. 1

This is the case study of property division taken from Dorjee Tsewang Thongon of Rupa village. All together they are eight brothers and sisters. Each brother got single plot of land as his share. But the parent's house was given to the three younger brothers. Beside this, each brother got a pair of cow. The brass plate and bowl were divided equally among the brothers by their parents. The sisters were not included in the share of property.

Case Study No. 2

This is the case study, taken from Sang Norbu Sinchaji, of property division among three brothers done by their parents. All three brothers got a plot of land and even the household brass articles were distributed equally. In this case the parent's house and land was given to the youngest son.

"As there is no measuring system therefore division of land is not performed by measuring the land. For instance in cultivable land if they have two kids they will just divide the land into two parts and allot one to each by saying that one could cultivate on that portion and the other on the other portion. The eldest does not get the house. It is the youngest who usually inherits the house. Giving of the brass articles or utensils depends on the parents. If the eldest son gets married and settles separately, the parents give some items for memento. Even gun is given either to the eldest or the youngest.[23] The middle son used to get very less share".[24]

Girls, while leaving the house after marriage are given gifts by parents or brothers according to their likes and wishes but the main things gifted are piece of endi cloth, brass plate (*bati*), mug (*chok*), tripod stand (*jijih*), one brass utensil (*tao* or *zaat*), etc. The stuff given are generally the ones which are needed first in settling down in a new house. Nowadays besides these many other things are also given to the girl. If her parents are well to do then even gold ornaments are also given. "The girl is set off with vehicle full of gifts".[25] Earlier they were let off with endi cloth and brass articles.[26] Beads are inherited by daughters who look after the parents or are also given to daughter-in-law if the mother wishes.[27] The girls do not inherit the land but the parents can give a plot of land to the daughter as a gift during her marriage which is termed as *phoggochiba*.[28]

Birth Ceremony

The rites and ceremonies are common to both with exceptional materials included in the ceremony on the basis of gender only. There is no difference in the ceremony on the basis of the class. No ceremony is performed on the day of birth of a baby. The only thing that is done on that day is that the monk (*lama*) is consulted by the family members for giving a name as well as to prepare the horoscope of the new born baby. For giving the name to a new born baby the monk (*lama*) refers a book called *kestar* and whatever comes up accordingly the monk pronounces. But it is not necessary that this has to be done on that day. It can be done on the *nini uhu satpa* day.[29]

Nini Uhu Satpa

A small ceremony which is performed on the third day is called *nini uhu satpa*. The referring of a book (*kestar*) can be done on this day if not done on the birth day. The *nini uhu satpa* is a traditional way of welcoming the new born baby in this world. In this ceremony three to four women are involved. The items needed here is one piece of fish,[30] small in size, nicely dried with whole body parts intact.[31] Then one piece of stick (*khongke*),[32] one piece of clamp (*kampo*), one cup of ash (*brop chaphulu*) and one cup of *Phogchu*.[33] These are the items generally needed in both the gender cases. But an additional item is used according to gender. Bow and arrow (*mig-li*) is used if the baby is a boy and spindle (*mongbi*) is used if it is a girl.

One lady holding the stick (*khongke*) and clamp (*kampo*) and another lady taking the ash (*bropchaphulu*), *phogchu* and bow-arrow (*mig-li*) in case of male baby or spindle (*mongbi*) in case of female in a winnow (*khaw*) go outside towards the east direction.[34] Putting the items out there they would say "before your birth your soul was like a god soul and as you have came to this world, you must stay along with us for long". The two women return after this. While returning, before entering the house, the one who is inside asks a series of questions and the two ladies respond to those questions from outside. The first two to three are general questions and the following questions are related to the works of male and female. The questions for the male are related to hunting, fishing, political affairs, etc. and for the female they are regarding household works, weaving, etc. But due to growth and change of modern education and economic system the questions have changed and usually are same for both boys and girls. This is because of ongoing modernisation process which has removed gender biasness in relation to occupations or work opportunities among the Sherdukpen.

A few of the questions which are frequently asked are given below:

In case of female:

Q- *Nini satpa oyni?* Did you see the sun rise?

A- Olo du (Yes)

Q- *Nambulu Chatpa oyni?* Did you see the moon?

A- Olo du (Yes)

Q- *Doho chekpa oyni?* Did you see the cleaning of vegetables?

A- Olo du (Yes)

Q- *Daung rapa oyni?* Did you see a bag being woven?

A- Olo du (Yes)

Q- *Lokan rapa oyni?* Did you see weaving?

A- Olo du (Yes)

In case of male:

Q- *Nini satpa oyni?* Did you see the sun rise?

A- Olo du. (Yes)

Q- *Nambulu Chatpa oyni?* Did you see the moon?

A- Olo du (Yes)

Q- *Su rekpa oyni?* Did you see hunting?

A- Olo du (Yes)

Q- *Nyu Jukpa oyni?* Did you see fishing?

A- Olo due (Yes)

At last the women from inside will say, "from now onwards do not go back and do have a long life". And then wine is offered to the women standing outside. After this various types of salad (*khaji*) are kept in small quantities on a plate in the name of the baby. Then with the dried fish one woman will put three drops of wine into the baby's mouth. At first it is put from the mouth side of the fish and then from the tail side. Lastly, wine (*phog*) and salads (*khaji*) are offered to the people attending the ceremony. The items for the ceremony have not changed but the eatable items have changed.

Hair Cutting Ceremony (Azang butho gozong chekpa)

It is done on the completion of one year of the new born baby. In the past it was done on the eighth day of the lunar calendar for the girl and on the tenth day for the boy. This is because the eighth day of the month is considered to be the day of Taradevi (*chenraji*) and the tenth day is considered to be the day of Padmasambhava (*Lopon Rimpoche*). But today, the day is fixed by the *lama*. The hair cutting is done by the maternal uncle. The hair is trimmed from the centre with the blessing words for the child. It is not compulsory for the maternal uncle to trim the whole hair of the head. Then a scarf (*khata*) is put by the maternal uncle's wife and a gift is given to the child. For his blessings, the uncle is offered with *phrom khaji* (yak/cow milk paneer) fish (*nyu khaji*) and the best wine (*phog*).

Marriage

Marriage in Sherdukpen society is considered very auspicious. It is the occasion of heartfelt joy and merriment. There is no difference in the marriage system in different classes of the society.

Rules of Marriage

In the Sherdukpen society, polygyny i.e. marriage in which an individual can have multiple spouses at a time is absent. The society practises monogamy i.e. marriage in which an individual can have only single spouse at a time. One person can remarry but after the husband or wife is deceased. In the Sherdukpen society both junior levirate i.e. marriage with the deceased husband's younger brother as well as junior sororate i.e. marriage with the deceased wife's younger sister is allowed. Though customarily allowed it is hardly practiced. In case of junior sororate it happens only when the matter is related to new born baby. Senior levirate and senior sororate do not exist in the community. In Sherdukpen custom, the elder brother enjoys the status of father–in-law for the wife of the younger brother. Similarly, the husband of the younger sister enjoys the status of the son-in-law in relation with his elder sister-in-law.

Cross cousin marriage is given first preference in the Sherdukpen society i.e. marriage with the father's sister's son or daughter and mother's brother's son or daughter is given priority. It is said that during the past if the aunt wants to give her daughter in marriage to one other than her brother's son, then she will first have to inform her brother before proceeding further.[35] Parallel cousin marriage is a taboo.

The marriage among the Sherdukpen is class endogamous and clan exogamous. These are the essential features. There is a strict restriction to marry within the clan and phratry. Both village endogamy as well as village exogamy is practised within the society. There is no restriction to marry from different tribes within the state. Marriage from outside the state's tribe is not considered as a taboo but the person has to pay a penalty to the council for such an act. Other than this, the outsider is accepted as the member of the society and will be placed in the class in which she gets married.

However, class exogamy is also practised. There is no taboo for it though restriction is considered because of difference in classes. The classes give preference for marriage within their own class. Intermarriage used to take place among the class. One of the respondents told "My father married a *Chao*. It was not very well. There was some criticism. There is no restriction but there was criticism".[36]

Interclass marriages used to take place in the past. The inter marriage happens due to personal choice but not with the choice of the parents. It depends on both the boy and the girl. The only thing is that when the relation comes to the knowledge of the parents then one party may verbally assault the boy or girl or even their parents. "Suppose I brought a *Thongs* girl, her parents would come and destroy things for example Nawang[37] of Membachur, but it was a common practice in earlier days".[38]

In past days marriages between Thongdok and Megeji also used to take place. It is to be noted that not all the Thongdoks can marry with someone from the Megeji clan. It is only the Thongdoks of Khleng Thong generation who can marry with the Megeji. It happened so because long time ago the Khleng Thong married a Megeji woman and settled at Khleng.[39]

Case Study No. 3

This marriage took place in the year 1954 between Megeji and Thongdok. The boy belonged to the Megeji clan while the girl was a Thongdok. The boy and the girl were in love but the parents and the clan members of the bride were against the relationship. The boy went and stayed at the girl's house for one year.

After one year the boy's father had a consultation with the family clan members and the attached clan to bring the bride home. The day, time and the direction through which the bride should walk while leaving the house was also consulted with the *lama*.

On the arranged day the boy's father and uncle took three sheep. One was given to the bride's house, one to the bride's clan and one to the bride's attached clan. Both males and females went to the brides' house to bring the couple back to the groom's house. The *phog chung* was carried in front of the procession.

By that time the bride had her food at her *mringdimi* house. The *mringdimi* dressed her up. Then the bride bowed three times in front of the hearth. The *mringdimih* put *khata* and offer *scam* (plate) and took her to her house.

In the bride's house the girl's clan and attached clan offer along *sinku* and *bati* (brass plate) by keeping in front of the bride. On leaving the house the song was sung by the *mringdimi* and *aacham rok*.

On reaching the groom's house one woman of the groom's house put three scarves on the bride when she entered the house. The three night rule was observed but here the food was provided from the groom's house itself.

Gobdoh (offering of wine with money) was done which was kept in front of aged women of the *mringdimi* of both bride and the groom and to *amubu* (aged women belonging to the other clan present there). Then distribution of wine was done by the bride which was prepared by her.

Table 5.1 Table showing instances of class endogamy, class exogamy and tribe exogamy of Sherdukpen

Sl. No	*Form of Marriage*	*Number of Cases*	*Percentage*
1	Class Endogamous	139	56.50
2	Class Exogamous	86	34.96
3	Tribe Exogamous	21	8.54

Source: Fieldwork 2010

It is found from Table 5.1 that the percentage of class endogamy combining the three villages, i.e. Rupa, Thongre and Jigaon, is highest while tribe exogamy is less practised. Tribe endogamy is a major rule within the society.

Table 5.2 Table showing instances of class endogamy, class exogamy and tribe exogamy of Rupa village

Sl. No	*Form of Marriage*	*Number of Cases*	*Percentage*
1	Class Endogamous	72	60
2	Class Exogamous	34	28.33
3	Tribe Exogamous	14	11.67

Source: Fieldwork 2010

The percentage of tribe endogamy is higher at Rupa in comparison to Thongre and Jigaon. Even in Rupa class endogamy is practised more than class exogamy even though Rupa is an urban set up.

Table 5.3 Table showing instances of class endogamy, class exogamy and tribe exogamy of Thongre village

Sl. No	*Form of Marriage*	*Number of Cases*	*Percentage*
1	Class Endogamous	38	54.29
2	Class Exogamous	26	37.14
3	Tribe Exogamous	6	8.57

Source: Fieldwork 2010

In Thongre village though the percentage of class endogamy is higher than class exogamy but in comparison to Rupa class exogamy is gaining momentum.

Table 5.4 Table showing instances of class endogamy, class exogamy and tribe exogamy of Jigaon village

Sl. No	*Form of Marriage*	*Number of Cases*	*Percentage*
1	Class Endogamous	29	51.79
2	Class Exogamous	26	46.43
3	Tribe Exogamous	1	1.79

Source: Fieldwork 2010

In Jigaon village the percentage does not show vast variation within class endogamy and class exogamy.

Types of Marriages

There are different forms of marriages or acquiring of mates prevalent among the Sherdukpen people. Some of the main forms are:

1. Marriage by negotiation (*Honk-tanbah*)
2. Marriage by capture (*Acham zomba*)
3. Cross cousin marriage (*Chhamuh*)
4. Marriage by Negotiation (*Honk-Tanbah*)

In this type of marriage, the boy's parents send two mediators (*achung jring*) to the house of the girl they choose for their son. One mediator (*achung jring*) belongs to their own clan while the other is selected from any other clan except the girl's clan. The mediator (*achung jring*), who belongs to the other clan places the proposal for the marriage. The proposal as well as all the talks are done by the mediator (*achung jring*) from the other clan so that he won't take the side of the either; the boy's or the girl's clan. He is, therefore, believed to be a neutral body. The duty of the mediator, selected from same clan, is only to watch that the mediator (*achung jring*) from the other clan does not take the side of the girl's clan.

While going to ask for the hand of the girl, they take a scarf (*khata*) and a jug of local beer (*phog*) to the girl's house. The scarf (*khata*) is tied to a post somewhere inside the house and the local beer is given to the girl's parents. The tradition of giving local beer and tying of scarf (*khata*) in a house is termed *Temreh*. If the girl's parents don't like to establish any relationship, they simply refuse the proposal and do not accept the beer.

If the girl's parents accept the proposal, then, the marriage takes place when both the boy and the girl attain the marriageable age in case of the negotiation that took place during the childhood. Once the relation is accepted, there should be no objections to it further. If either of the families of the boy or the girl objects to the betrothal before the actual marriage takes place, it pays a fine to the other with whom the relation was supposed to be established.

In between the period from the acceptance of the proposal and the marriage, the two families share whatever each family gets from hunting. The members of the two families also help one another during house construction and agricultural works.

If everything goes well and the boy and the girl attain marriageable age and the boy's parents want to bring the girl home, they send the mediator (*achung jring*), who was selected from the other clan, to the girl's house to ask whether they are ready to send the girl. If the reply is positive, then their horoscopes (*lu*) are compared by the monk (*lama*) and the day and time are fixed for sending and receiving the bride. Monk (*lama*) also decides the direction to which the bride should move while leaving her house and at what time she should reach the groom's house.[40]

When the day and time of the marriage is fixed, members of the groom's clan as well as phratry along with both the mediator (*achung jring*) go to receive the bride from her house. The groom himself or his parents do not join such group of members who go to bring the bride. During this period, the groom does not stay in his house. He stays with his friends, showing his shyness. The receiving troop takes one sheep (*ska*) and *yak* with them. In the horn and chest as well as at the back of the *yak,* a paste of butter (*mo*) is applied. The butter is applied as good sign. One young girl from the groom's clan carrying a vessel (*chungzung*) leads the troop. The vessel (*chung*) contains local beer with butter pasted on its mouth.

The *yak* and sheep (*ska*) are given to the bride's parents. The *yak's* meat is distributed to each and every clan member of the bride. It is also ascertained whether the meat contains too much or too less fat. If meat contains too much or too little of fat, then it is considered to be a bad sign. The sheep meat is eaten among the family members. Its liver is used to see the omen of the bride and the groom.

In the bride's house, members' of the receiving group sit near the door and the bride's group a little away inside the house. The bride with her friends sits in the small room behind the main room (*rapse*). At this time, the mediator (*achung jring)* delivers a lecture and after it, a scarf (*khata*) is presented to every member from the bride's side. The people present there are entertained by the members of bride's group with drinks and food. By that time, the girl gets ready and bows three times before the god in the *rapse* and comes out crying.

She takes permission from her father and mother, brother(s), sister(s) and other consanguineal members. While taking permission from each member, it is customary that each member presents her a gift. Even land is sometimes presented if the father wants which is termed as *phoggochiba*. Then the bride bows before the hearth three times saying, "I have eaten and cooked here till this age, but now I take your permission to leave you". She then comes out of the house. While coming out of the house, again gifts are presented to her by relatives. After walking down the stairs of the house she bows before the house and takes permission to leave the house also. She says, "till date my legs were towards the direction of the house but from now onwards, it won't be in this direction". She turns to the direction decided by the monk (*lama*) even if the groom's house is not in that direction. All sayings for taking permission are in the form of song. If the bride does not know the song, any woman can sing for her. Then she performs this ritual just walking a few steps and turns to the house of clan members for taking permission from them also. The clan members may also present gifts to her if they want. After taking permission from the clan members she reaches the groom's house by the time fixed by the monk (*lama*). By that time the bride's mother reaches the groom's house. When she reaches there, she is presented with a big vessel (*tao*) and endi cloth. The vessel (*tao*) is given as a symbol so that her tears do not fall on the ground consequent upon the sorrow of the separation of her daughter. Similar sentiment is attached to the presentation of the endi cloth which can help her in wiping of the tears.

As the groom does not remain in the house at that time, his father sends someone to bring him. He usually entrusts the work of bringing the son home to his (son's) friends. The friends bring the groom home at night. The bride at that time does not sleep alone. She is accompanied by other girls. The friends of the groom make him sleep with the bride. Then the father and mother light the room before dawn with fire and all members present (especially friends from both clans) are able to see the couple together. As everyone sees them sleeping together, the bride gets up shying and prepares local beer (*phog*) for the groom for the first time. From that very moment, they are considered husband and wife.

Case Study No. 4

This is the marriage that took place in the year 1984. Here the boy is Thongdok (*Thong*) while the girl is Thongchi (*Thong*). It is the marriage by negotiation where the parents of the boy selected the bride. The parents went to the bride's house and expressed their desire to the bride's parents and then the day was consulted from the *lama* to bring the bride to the boy's house. Here the clan member of the boy went to consult the day of bringing the bride. When the day was fixed the bride was brought to the groom's house by the Thongdok and Megeji clan members. Here the three days ceremony was performed where the food to the girl was provided by the girl's clan members. And on the third night the wine was distributed by the bride to the people who came to pay a visit.

Marriage by Capture (Accham Zomba)

If the boy's father likes a girl and wants to make her his daughter-in-law, then he arranges for her capture. But before capturing a girl, horoscope is compared and the day is fixed for the capture. If the horoscope matches, the boy's father tells his son's friends of his own clan to capture the girl whom he has chosen to make his daughter-in-law. The boy may or may not have any knowledge of it.

Then the boys tell the girls of their own clan who happen to be the friends of the girl to be captured. These girls take her (chosen one) to a lonely place on the day fixed for the capture. While capturing, the captors shout along with the girl's protesting shout so that the act of capturing is not doubted by the members of the girl's clan. In case, the members of the girl's clan happen to know the act of capturing, they protest and release the girl from her captors.

The girl is kept in the boy's house for three nights. The purpose of keeping the girl three nights is to persuade her for the marriage. She is given all hospitality and treated cordially. At the time of her stay the son (for whom the girl has been selected) does not stay at home. Then she is allowed to return to her home before the cock's crow of the third night.

However, on the day of third night, the boy's father engages two mediators *(achung jring)*, one from his clan and the other from outside the clan of both the parties. Here also non-clan mediator (*achung jring*) does all the talks with the girl's parents for reconciliation as their daughter had been kidnapped by them without their and their daughter's consent. During this time, girl's parents can reject the proposal. The girl's clan members also have the right to reject the proposal on the plea that such an act of captured negotiation was rejected by the groom's clan members in some past date.

After three nights when the girl is released she may agree or reject the proposal of marriage. If the girl accepts the proposal, then the day, time and the direction on which the girl should face while leaving her house is fixed by the monk (*lama*).

Case Study No. 5

This marriage happened in the year 1989. The boy was a Thongon and the girl was a Thongdok. It was a capture marriage. It was the choice of the boy's parents. The horoscope was matched and the day was fixed by the *lama* for capturing the girl. For capturing the girl five people went (including Thongon and Khrime). On the capturing day the girl was roaming with her friends. There was no one from the girl's clan at that time and she was captured easily. The three days ceremony was performed that is providing of food by the girl's clan member and distribution of wine by the bride at third night.

But after four-five days the girl ran away from that house and after three years she was captured again and the three days ceremony was also performed again.

Case Study No. 6

It was an act of capture performed in the year 2006. The boy was Megeji and the girl, a Lamaguru. Here the mother of the boy had selected the bride. The boy also had the knowledge of the capturing plan. The day was consulted with the *lama* for capturing the girl. For capturing the girl two Megeji members went to the girl's village (Shergaon).

At that time the girl after indulging in the work at her kitchen garden was taking rest at home. On reaching the girl's village the van was stopped on the road and one of the captors went to the girl's house which was away from the main road. On reaching the girls' house the captor acted as if he was too drunk and asked for her help to take him upto the road. The girl having no knowledge that she was being duped helped him. When she reached the road near the van she was lifted and brought to the boy's village where she was made to perform the three days ceremony. During her stay she was accompanied by the groom's sister. On the third day two *achung jrings* (Megeji, Thongchi) were sent to the girl's house for *temre*. Wine was distributed by the girl on the third night to the people attending the ceremony.

Case Study No. 7

It was an act of capture performed in the year 2005. Here the boy belonged to Megeji and the girl, a Wangja from Doimara. Here the girl was chosen by the eldest sister-in-law of the boy. The sister-in-law asked the girl's aunt regarding her desire, who had got married and lived in the boy's village. The girl at that time was studying there staying in her aunt's house. The girl's aunt said that she would convey the message to the girl's uncle who stayed at Rupa. The uncle said the matter had to be conveyed to the girl's parents at Doimara. The boy's sister-in-law went to Doimara and expressed her desire to the girl's mother. The girl's mother accepted the relationship. After the sister-in-law of the boy reached the village the capturing day and time was consulted with the *lama*.

For capturing six men were arranged (five Megeji and one Thongon). The act of capturing was performed early in morning at 5 a.m. The girl was lifted while she was sleeping. The door of the house was kept open by her aunt in advance. The three days ceremony was performed i.e. food was provided by the girl's clan members and on the third day three *achung jrings* were sent for *temre.* Wine was distributed by the girl to the people attending the third night ceremony.

Case Study No. 8

This is the act of capturing done in the year 1984. Here the boy was a Megeji while the girl was a Thongchi. It was the choice of the boy's father. The day was consulted with the *lama*, for capturing. Both the Thongdok and Megeji youths went to capture the girl. The girl at the moment was working in the porch from where she was captured to the boy's place. The three days ceremony was performed where the food came from girl's clan member and family side for the girl. Two *achung jring* (one Megeji and one Thongon) were sent to the girl's house on the third day. On that night the entire village came to put scarves on the newly wedded couple and wine was distributed to the people attending the ceremony by the bride.

Case Study No. 9

This is the case of capture marriage held in the year 1965. Here the boy is Khrime (*Thong*) and the girl is Thongdok (*Thong*). The girl was the choice of the parents and the clan members. The day of capturing the girl was consulted with the *lama*. When the day was fixed four or five boys of the boy's clan went for the capture. The capture was done from the house itself when the girl was busy in her household work. For three nights she was kept under strict vigil. The food was provided to the girl from the girl's clan members. On the third day *achung jring* was sent to the girl's house for *temre*. Then at night wine was distributed to the people attending the ceremony which was prepared by the bride herself.

As a custom, after three nights the girl has to return to her parental home but here she could not go as the next day it was the time for their winter migration to Ruchong (Doimara).

Case Study No. 10

This was a marriage by capture in the year 2003 the boy is Megeji (*Chao*) and the girl is Khrime (*Thong*). In this case the boy liked the girl and he conveyed his desire to his parents who also accepted the proposal. The day was consulted with the monk for the capture which fell on the picnic day of Losar festival. At Losar[41] picnic the girl came to Rupa as she was from Chillipam. The girl, after the picnic, went to visit her cousin. At that time three women had come to that house to celebrate Losar (New Year). Afterwards those three women insisted upon the girl to come along with them to the house of the boy. The girl without any thought went to that house. But this was a pre planned capture. She realised this only when she reached the boy's house. There she stayed for three nights and during her stay food was provided to her from her clan members. *Achung jring* was sent to the girl's house on the third day but the distribution of wine to the people was not performed by the bride. After the three nights stay she was dropped at her house by her brother-in-law.

Case Study No.11

It was on 24 December 2002, everything was pre-planned for the capture of Karma Dema Megeji of Chindi Top, who had no idea and was totally unaware of it. She was asked by her paternal aunt to accompany her for shopping from the cooperative shopping complex. Karma was not prepared for shopping but thought of purchasing a camera roll for the coming Christmas day.

Both Karma and her aunt reached the shopping complex and her aunt pretended to purchase goods. There was a Maruti van waiting outside, but Karma was totally unaware of it. A man came out of the van and he had a brief conversation with her aunt. Then her aunt requested Karma to accompany her upto Tenga to purchase something else. Aunt told her that they would come back soon by the Maruti van. Karma did not object and they went. Again in Tenga her aunt pretended to buy things. After a while aunt again requested Karma to accompany her upto Rupa as she had left her baby in the village. In fact the aunt belonged to Rupa. Karma could not doubt anything as she also overheard her aunt saying to someone that they would come back soon after feeding the baby. Karma's sense alarmed her when she reached Rupa, but by then she was kidnapped.

For three days she was kept under vigil of the groom's relatives. In these three days she tried to flee but could not. On the fourth day she accepted the proposal and the formalities of negotiation started for the marriage.

Case Study No.12

This is the case of remarriage of the boy, by capturing the girl in the year 2009. Here the boy is Khrime and the girl is Lamagum. The bride was chosen by the parents. In this capturing of bride four women were involved (two Thongdok, one Megeji, one Khrime). Day was consulted with the *lama* for capturing the girl. On the day of capture the girl was on her way to her friend's house to collect utensils for wine preparation. On her way the capture party talked to her and offered her some betel. When she came near the van unaware of the plan she was captured. The three days ceremony was performed where she was provided food from her clan members and family. On the third day two *achung jrings* were sent to the girl's house for the *temre*. On the third night the girl distributed wine to the people attending the ceremony. But she was not allowed to go back after the third night according to the customs.

Cross Cousin Marriage (Chhamuh)

If the boy wants to marry the daughter of his mother's brother with the girl's consent then the marriage takes place. It can also be said that this is a negotiation type of marriage where the bride is the mother's brother's daughter. If the relation proceeds further then their horoscopes are matched and the same rituals are performed as mentioned in negotiated marriage.

Plate 5.2 Marriage ceremony

Bride Price (ru)

The taking of bride price in the Sherdukpen society is unique as the price is taken after the death of the bride. It is believed that if the bride price is taken

Plate 5.3 Bride offering wine and tea

before or during marriage it would be just equivalent to selling her and there would be no rights on her after this. The bride price is not taken during her life to keep the right on her. If she is facing trouble and is being tortured by her husband a case can be filed in the *Blu* (village council) against her husband. The bride price is also not taken by the father of the girl in usual case as he may not be alive at the time of her daughter's death. It is given to that person who takes the authority of the girl. Generally it is her brother who takes the authority. But the person who takes this authority has to look after her in times of her trouble. If the person is dead at the time of the payment of bride price then his son receives it as the authority passes on to him. Generally the bride price is paid by her sons. This price is called *ru* meaning the price of the mother.

The bride price is paid in the form of silver bowl (*nying*) and brass pot (*zaat*) which are designed with beautiful carvings, made by the Tibetans (*rajapo*).

The value of both silver bowl (*nying*) and brass pot (*zaat*) is considered to be equal. Silver bowl (*nying*) is more decorative than brass pot (*zaat*) and therefore both are considered to be of equal value irrespective of their sizes. The determination of actual size of silver bowl (*nying*) and brass pot (*zaat*) is unique. The circumference of the mouth of the silver bowl (*nying*) has to be ten times of the circumference of an egg. Similarly, the circumference of the mouth of the brass pot (*zaat*) has to be ten cubits. In case of lesser size of the both, the groom's side (husband if the wife dies first or son if mother is alive and father dies) has to make good of the shortage by paying compensation in terms of a cow. There is a specification about the cow. If the size is less by one time of the egg circumference or one cubit then a calf (without horn) is given. If the size is less by two according to above measures then a grown up calf (whose horn is about to come out) is given as compensation. But if the size is less by three according to above measures an adult calf with new horns is given to the bride's family. The age of the cow to be compensated goes on increasing with decrease in size of silver bowl (*nying*) or brass pot (*zaat*). However, in case of larger size of silver bowl (*nying*) or brass pot (*zaat*) than the specification, the compensation is paid from bride's family side. But in today's society the price is in terms of rupees which is ₹10,000 for *Thong* and ₹5,000 for *Chao*.

Widow Marriage

Widow marriage is accepted in Sherdukpen society. If a widow marries then one-fourth of the bride price is given by her husband's side and the rest is paid by the deceased husband's side. It will take place only if the woman bears a child from her deceased husband. Generally one-fourth price of the bride is given as a help from the second husband's side. It is not necessary that such help is to be given. But if the women does not have child from the first husband then the full amount as a bride price has to be paid by the second husband.

Case Study No. 13

This is a case of widow marriage of a woman done by negotiation in the year 2007. Here the boy is Thongdok (*Thong*) while the girl is Thongchi (*Thong*). It was the parents' desire to make the widow their daughter-in-law. So the boy's parent sent three women (all family members) to the girl's house for negotiation. There the parents of the girl also accepted the proposal. After that the day and time was consulted from the *lama* to bring the girl home. When the day was fixed both Thongdok and Megeji went to receive the bride. On that same night the wine distribution ceremony was performed in the groom's house by the newly wed bride to the people attending the ceremony.

Achung jring was sent to the girl's house on the third day as usual.

Divorce

Any of the spouses can initiate the divorce process in the Sherdukpen community on mutual understanding. One who initiates it has to pay fine to the other. The fine may be in the form of mithun, horse, yak, sheep, and ornaments and landed property also. The important grounds for divorce are frequent quarrels, domestic unhappiness and extra marital affairs.

Case Study No. 14

This is the divorce which took between Tenzin Khrime (husband) and Wangmu Thongon (wife) (name changed). It took place on the grounds of extra marital affairs. It is said that the wife was having an extra marital affair. In due course of time the affair of the wife with another person came to the knowledge of the husband and the parents. Because of which the husband, parents and the clan members objected the relationship and let the wife to go back to her parental house. No fine has been imposed as the case has not yet been taken up by the *Blu* (council).

Case Study No. 15

This is a case of divorce which took between Sonam Megeji (husband) and Nima Dingla (wife) (name changed). It took place on the grounds of extra marital affairs. It is said that the wife was having an extra marital affair. In due course of time the affair of the wife with another person came to the knowledge of the husband and they had a fight. Because of the fight the wife left for her parental house. After three months the husband sent three women (one Thongdok, two Meggeji) for reconciliation with the wife's family, but they refused. Again after three days four women (three Megeji, one Thongdok) were sent for reconciliation. On their way to the girl's house, the women met the girl's mother. The counsling party counsled the mother to send her daughter back but the proposal was rejected again. The matter reached the council (*Blu*), where, at first the council told the husband and wife to reconcile. But both of them disagreed and asked for a divorce. As the divorce was mutual both were penalised with a fine of ₹ 750 each.

Case Study No.16

This is the case study of divorce where the boy is Thongon and the girl is from Khrime. Here the boy accused the girl of being alcoholic. It's the boy who asked for the divorce but the girl wanted to reconcile. Even then, the boy rejected the proposal of reconciliation. This case did not reach the council (*Blu*) and was solved by the clan itself. The boy was penalised with his share of land to be given to the girl as they already had a son.

Pre-Marital Relation

A person can have a pre-marital relation. If a girl becomes pregnant she is forced to disclose the father's name and then the boy is compelled to marry her.

If a girl claims a person to be the father of the unborn baby and that person rejects it, then it is decided by the village council (*Blu*) in its meeting (*chatpuniseh*) which is conducted after every five years though now it is conducted after every three years. In this meeting, the face of the child is matched with the person whom the girl claims to be the father. If the faces resemble the person has to pay a penalty towards the council for an act of indiscipline. And if not then the girl has to pay the same towards the council.

Fine System

The fine system is a very old tradition of the Sherdukpen custom. It is imposed on every offender irrespective of class and gender if the degree of guilt is same. For example, it will be imposed on a girl if she is not able to reveal the name of the person who impregnated her. If a person is caught to be the father of that child and he accepts his guilt then he has to pay the fine. Here the fine is paid to the council (*Blu*). The amount of fine is, however, not fixed and varies over the years.

In the case of divorce, if the boy is found guilty then, he has to pay the bride price (*ru*) as well as anything that she demands. It depends on her adamant nature as well as her family members. If the girl is found guilty even then also she will get the bride price (*ru*) but with less penalty.[42]

"In past days in a divorce case if a girl left you not much fine was imposed only one or two brass items may be. If the girl had committed the offence and did not want to reconcile then the boys did not have to pay anything to the girl. If the boy left the girl then whatever the girl brought along with her during the marriage she would take back with her and along with that she could make further demands. But in mutual divorce, minimal fine was to be paid to the council (*Blu*)".[43]

"In the past a minimal fine used to be given if inter class marriage took place. Here the penalty was given to the *Thong*. For instance if a *Chao* girl got married to a *Thong* boy then the *Chao* had to pay a minimal fine to the *Thong* and if a *Thong* boy married a *Chao* girl the *Chao* had to pay that minimal fine again to the *Thong*. In both case it was the *Chao* who had to pay the penalty. The penalty was in the form of horse, mithun, cow, etc."[44]

There is another fine relating to the marriage matter. The fine is imposed on a person, if he/she marries a non-Arunachalee. Before nineties, this system of paying fine was not there. One could marry any person. The fine is paid to the village council (*Blu*) when meeting (*chatpuniseh*) is held.[45] This fine was introduced as marriage between the Sherdukpen with the Nepalese, Bhutanese and Tibetan started taking place. Girls usually stayed within the society after the marriage which created a problem on certificate issue and property rights. For boys it was done so as to let them marry from within the society.[46]

Disposal of Dead

Traditionally the ritual of the disposal of the dead is unique in Sherdukpen society. In olden days before the conversion of the society to Buddhism the Sherdukpens disposed off the dead bodies in *bo-log* (*Bo* = cave/hole, *log* = slope). *Bo-log* is a hill slope bearing holes/caves. It is said that in those days even if a person died in Doimara (*Ruchong*) the dead body was brought to Rupa and disposed it at *bo*. While bringing the dead body from Doimara (*Ruchong*) the person(s) carrying the dead body could only rest at one place termed *ji-i-duchok*. The custom of resting at this particular place is because of a tale which is as follows:

There were two friends. One of them came to Rupa to drop goods. So the friend while going back, from a distance saw his friend sitting in *ji-i duchok*. On reaching *ji-i duchok*, when he put his hand on his friend's back, suddenly that friend turned into a fly. The friend holding that fly in his hand thought that he had seen his friend but wondered what happened to his friend who was no longer there. Then cutting a bamboo tube he put that fly in it. He then went running to Doimara. On reaching there he saw his friend dying. He let the fly through the nose or ear of his friend and after sometime the friend survived.[47]

Because of this belief, that the deceased person's spirit could be at *ji-i duchok*, the body is brought straight to that place without taking rest anywhere in between. Disposing off the dead body in the *bo* also goes with a rule that the *Thongs* are disposed at a higher raised platform than the *Chaos*.

After the conversion to Buddhism the dead body is disposed off by cremation and burying. It is said that *Thongs* used to cremate and *Chao* went for burial.[48] But under present situation it is not so. Whatever comes after the consultation of text by the monk, it is done accordingly. It is also said that if a *Thong* residing in another village passes away and it has to be cremated then permission has to be taken from the Rupa council (*Thoji Blu*) for Rupa jurisdiction.[49] The reason for this is that in cremation the air gets polluted by its smoke.

But again it is said that the disposal systems were made free according to the monk (*lama*) after consulting the book. So, the disposal was not according to the class of the society but according to the text consulted by the monk (*lama*).[50]

However, a distinctive mark is seen in the matter of touching the dead body. The *Thongs* never touch the dead body. It is the *Chaos* who touch it for their respective *Thongs*. The reason for this is not known to most of the people. They just say that it was a custom which was followed since long time back and is being followed till today. One person justified it by saying that "Touching of dead bodies only by the respective *Chaos* was due to their love and affection for their attached *Thongs*. They did not even allow other *Chaos* to do so because they did not want to share their affection".[51]

When a person dies all the threads are removed from his/her body. It is done so because it is believed that the deceased has to go in a pure and clean state as and how it came to the world. And those threads are considered to be dirty. The body is positioned depicting the baby inside the womb. The face is washed and then a coin is put inside the mouth. Few drops of ghee, wine (*phog*) and water is also poured into the mouth.[52] The dead body is then covered with new endi cloth. A brass plate or basket (*bangchung*) is kept on the head side for donation. Local wine is kept in a silver cup. Food is also offered to the deceased. Offering of water, wine (*phog*) and food to the deceased is done three times a day by the sister (*mringmu*).[53] It is done after the monk performs the ritual which continues for seven days. The food is also offered in the fire for three times.

The day and time is checked by the monk (*lama*) to take the body for disposal relating to birth date, time, month and year.[54] Due to the concept of rebirth, at that time his or her rebirth is also told and whether it will be in human or animal form. The dead body is carried by two persons only while leaving the house. The head portion will be on front side and will move in the direction as directed by the monk for a few steps and will turn to the cremation ground irrespective of that direction. Anyone can attend the cremation ceremony. While coming back, the people do not enter the house directly. The members who are at home will burn incense (*posi*) and prepare warm water wherein incense (*posi*) is also added. The water is poured for the people who attended the cremation to wash their face. The washing of the face is done with the belief that they have become impure so they should clean themselves before entering the house and also with a belief that such incident should not happen in the house again. After this, ritual is again performed at home.

Mringmu has to wash all the clothes of the deceased after his or her cremation. These cleaned clothes are kept at a place nicely after arranging and it is termed *pepong*. In front of these arranged clothes silver cup (*nying*) is kept filled with rice. Then, the name of the deceased is written on a paper and fixing it on a stick is kept standing on the silver cup which is termed *mikgyong*. After this again, all the stuff as put in front of the dead body are arranged likewise in front of the *pepong*. It is done as this pepong represents the deceased person. The offering of water and food is done as usual. The *pepong* is kept at home till the sixth day. On the sixth day from the day of the death of the person the *pepong* is taken to the monastery (*lagong*). The *pepong* is carried by the *Mringmu* led by the monk followed by the family members in their traditional attire. The *pepong* is positioned in the monastery (*lagong*) and the mid day and evening meals are offered there by the family of the deceased to the people attending the ceremony. The ritual is performed there by the monk. On the seventh day a flag (*ji-i pho*)[55] is hoisted in the monastery (*lagong*). Lamp (*chemi*) is lighted beneath the flag by the *mringmu*. Thereafter three rounds are made by the family members around the flag from left to right and the family members bow three times in front of the monk and then towards the flag. After this the *lamas* perform rituals in front of the flag which is termed *ramne*. It is done by pouring water (water mixed with naphthalene) going round the flag for three times by one *lama* and another *lama* will stand aside by holding incense and scarf in his hand.

Plate 5.4 *Ji-i pho*

Plate 5.5 *Tormo*

Tormo is prepared in which *mikgyong* is fixed. The *tormo* is placed on a brass plate. The *mikgyong* is then burnt with incense (*posi*). As the ash of the *mikgyong* falls in the plate it is mixed with *tormo* which is placed in the monastery (*lagong*). After burning the *mikgyong*, the *mringmu* will spread the *pepong* and will take the clothes out of the monastery (*lagong*).

After this, the *mringmu* is offered with few clothes, plates, etc. and some money as a thanksgiving which is termed as *gobdo*. Money with scarf is also offered to the monk.

Chhok is distributed among the people attending the ceremony in the monastery (*lagong*). Again ceremony is performed on the 14th, 21st and 49th day wherein the ritual is performed by the *lama* with lamp offering at the monastery (*lagong*). *Chhok* is distributed to the people attending and a flag is hoisted. On the 14th and 21st day flag is hoisted at the mountain. The ceremony is done again on the completion of one year at the monastery (*lagong*).

For accidental deaths, the dead body is not allowed to be brought to the village. The dead body is disposed outside the village with the belief that such incident might happen again or more people may die if the dead body is brought into the village. But this notion is not applied now-a-days. Besides this during *Khiksaba* the dead body is not allowed to be disposed through cremation within the village. As *Khiksaba* is considered a pure period and disposing of a dead body in the village would create impurity in the air by its smoke. However, burial is allowed in this occasion.

Kinship Terminology

In kinship terminology the Sherdukpen society have very limited terms. Except the terms for father and mother the rest terms are used as classificatory as well as for reference. The classificatory term for the father is *Abo* and in descriptive, in *Thong* it is *Achi*, in *Chao* it is *Boyo* and in *Yanlog* it is *Apo*. It is said that the *Yanlogs* have to use their own term of reference even if they are incorporated into the main class of the society. The term for mother is same for all. Besides this the *Thong* use the term *Tsloh* for father's elder brother, *Ache* for father's younger brother. But the classificatory term is *Khnyi* and descriptive as *Akhi* to father's sisters and mother-in-law. The *Chaos* use the term *Bokhao* for their father's elder brother, *Aku* for their father's younger brother and *Anyi* for their father's sister and mother-in-law (see genealogical Tables 5.1 and 5.2).

The classificatory term for the son, is *Duh*, for daughter *Dimih*, for grandson and granddaughter *Chuduh* and for great grandson and granddaughter it is *Bakdu*. Leaving these, the rest of the terms are common like *Abu* for son, brother and brother related; *Anu* for daughter, sister and sister related. The term *Ara* is used for husband or brother-in-law as well as with whom matrimonial relationship can take place. The term *Azu* is used for wife or brother's wife and *Aazu* for wife's sister or with whom matrimony can take place. The term *Azang* is used for maternal uncle as well as for father-in-law. It is to be kept in view that the terms *Azang*, *Anyi* and *Akhi* can be used for the entire groups of persons with whose son or daughter, marriage alliance is possible (see Charts 5.1 and 5.2).

If we analyse the society through the terminology then with those few terms we can say that they are stratified in some way but one important thing to be noted here is that each *Chao* clan which is associated with *Thong* clan use the same term to refer to each other accordingly. The associated clan consider themselves as brother clan. Hence the terminology used by them to refer or address each other is also according to the family relationship. If the *Thong* father and *Chao* father are considered to be brothers then their kids will call each other by the existing terminology accordingly. The *Chao* will address their related *Thong* with the *Thong*'s terms and vice versa. For instance if the *Thong* father is elder to the *Chao* father then the kids of *Thong* will call the *Chao* father as *Aku* and the kid of the *Chao* will call the *Thong* father as *Tsloh*. The kids will address each other as *Abu* (brother) and *Anu* (sister) likewise for all the related person (see Chart 5.3).

Chart 5.1 Kinship terminology for the *Thongs*

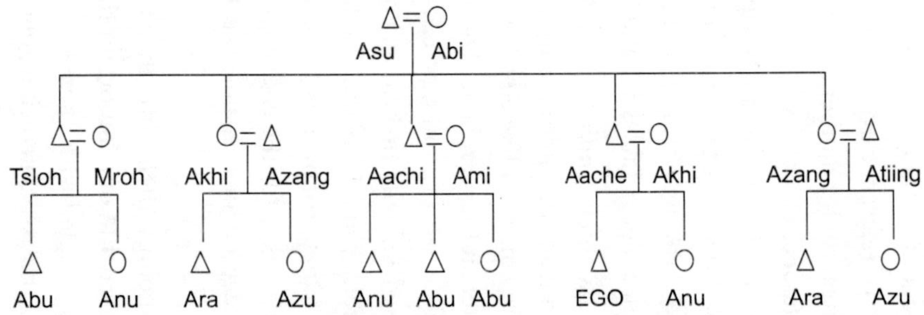

Source: Fieldwork

Chart 5.2 Kinship terminology for the *Chaos*

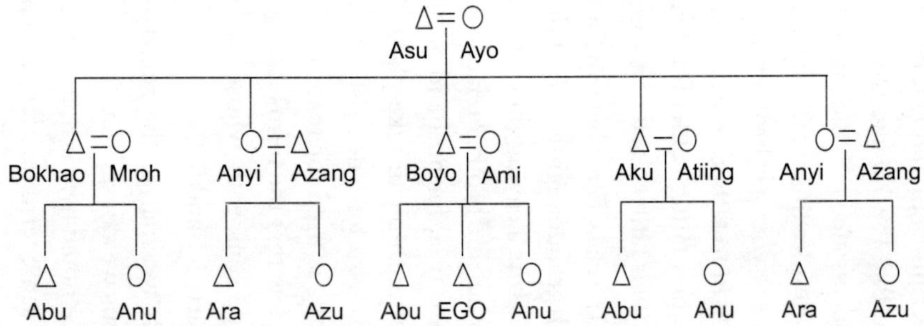

Source: Fieldwork

Chart 5.3 Kinship terminology for the attached clan

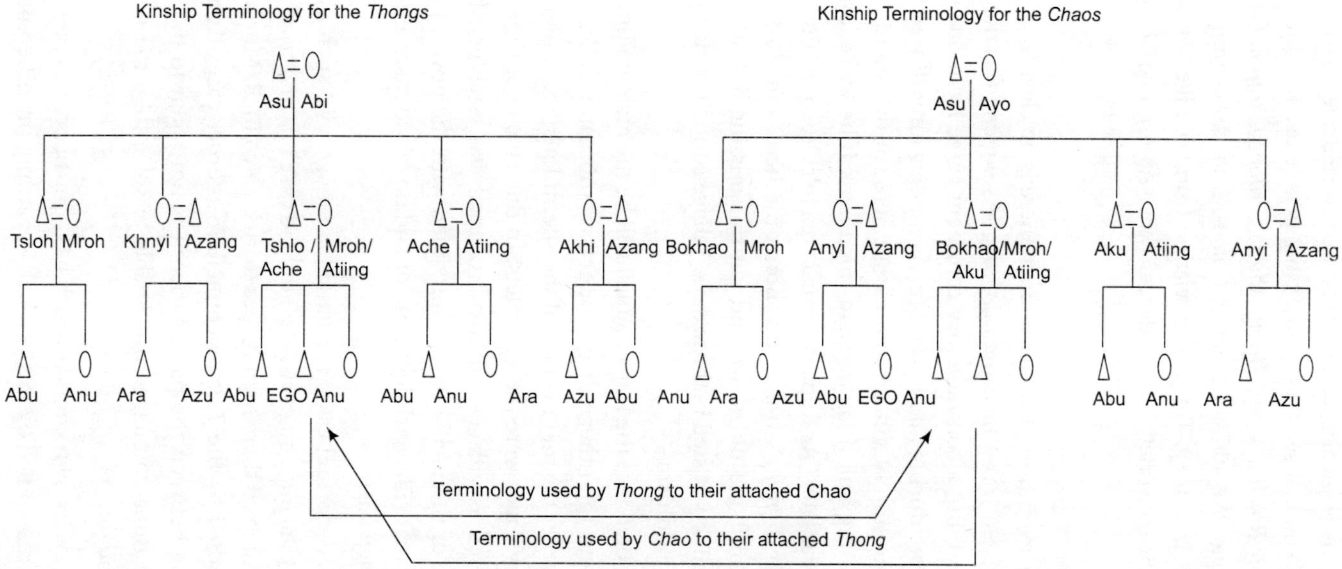

Source: Fieldwork

"One thing the original *Chao,* and not the converted ones, never address *Thongs* as *Thong*. But you can see these Musaksing people use to address *Thongo*. For example, *Thong Rinchin Motu, Thong Abudok, Thong Chumbi*. But, we originals never say *Thong*. We address them as *Chloh-Mroh, Ache-Atiing* and for *Chao, Bokhao-Mroh Aku-Ating*. This is our relation (*raram*). Like *Yanlog* we don't say Thongo. But the converted *Yanlog* address *Thong Abu, Thong Chandu* likewise".[56]

Political Life

Regarding the evolution of village council there is no clear idea. However, it is said that it existed from the time of *Japtang*. As *Japtang* was the king (*Thong*), he was its head. But a contradictory comment came from one respondent as "it was not there during *Japtang's* reign. As *Japtang* himself was a ruler, a king, there is no question of village council out here (in the Sherdukpen society). There is a missing link if *Japtang* had ruled here. If he was a king then where did he disappear later? As Rupa is a small area to rule, so the question of village council during *Japtang*'s time, does not come here. But we have the village council and until and unless we find out this missing link it's difficult to say that village council existed in those days. Village council came to exist after the influence of Buddhism".[57]

It is to be noted that the Rupa council will be the main council for the Rupa jurisdiction and the other village council as sub council. This is due to the reason that earlier the main village of the Sherdukpen was Rupa and Shergaon and all other villages were their hamlets. In due course of time these hamlets were considered as villages and a sub council was established to look after the discipline of these villages. It is provided with the power to dispense the petty cases of that village while the major and unsolved cases are dealt by Rupa council (*Thongji blu*).

For instance, normal cases are settled at village level such as to go against local holiday (*Duchin*), quarrels, etc. For land case it is first tried at village level and if it is not solved there then it goes to *Tukpen* council. Murder and divorce cases are handled by the *Tukpen* council. In murder cases if there is mutual understanding between the parties then it is not taken to the council (*Blu*). If in case the Rupa council is also unable to solve then the help of modern judiciary is sought.

Shergoan has its own council which has control over its jurisdiction. Thus, all the cases are handled by this council. Regarding the different councils, it is said that the *Thongs* were two brothers. The elder one stayed at Rupa, while the younger went and settled down at Shergoan. So, two separate councils came into existence.

The women were not allowed to join the council meetings. It was so because they were thought to be weak in thought and mentality.[58] But if the case concerned a lady that particular lady will be present in the proceeding of the council.[59] But on the other hand it is said that the women are not allowed even if the case is related to her. Rather mediator (*Khlapoh*) is arranged who will hear and convey the grievances in between.[60] In the present context, the women due to their noninvolvement in the traditional council have a sad feeling. They are eager to attend the council meeting(s). If not as a participating member but only to let them hear and witness the proceedings.[61]

The village in the Sherdukpen community is controlled by a council called *Blu*. It is normally headed by the *Thong*. All can attend the proceedings. "*Chaos* are also given chance to talk, it is not that they cannot talk, they participate on argument like a parliament assembly".[62] The decision is given by the *Blu*. Execution is carried out by the *Thong*. Actually it's not all the *Thong* that performs the duty of the execution, there will be a Gaon Bura locally called *Thik-Akhao* (*thik* means village and *akhao* means elder). "In earlier ages three elders *Thondok, Thongo*, and *Khrime* used to represent as *Thik-Akhao*. So they executed the meeting; any mistake *Blu* will try to prevent it".[63] The office of *Thik-Akhao* is not hereditary but is for life time. Beside *Thik-Akhao*, there are council members termed as *Jungme (Jung* means meeting/gathering and *me* refer to native people; *Jungme* means meeting member). There are other members attached to the council and they are called *Kachin*. The *Kachins* are the people who work for the council and look after the village discipline. Beside these members, it is said that there are other members called *Jungme Barse* who are not council members but take part in the proceeding process.[64] But on enquiring further it was found that all the members (*Jungme*) in collective sense are termed as *Jungme Barse.*[65]

The *Thik Akhao* usually were from *Thongs* only. But in a village where there is no *Thong*, the *Chaos* can also be the *Thik-Akhao*. The *Thik-Akhao* is chosen from any clan belonging to *Thongs* class. "But it is not compulsory, so to say if no *Thongs* clan reside in a particular village the *Thik-Akhao* post can be held by a *Chao* member also. It can be said that preference is given to *Thongs* being of the ruler's family. The Jigaon once had a Sinchaji Gaon bura. He was a good and an able ruler".[66] Some criteria are taken into consideration for the selection of the *Thik-Akhao* such as his activeness, wisdom and knowledge of rules and regulation of the society. "The *Thik-Akhao* should have a good knowledge of the society and ability of judgement."[67]

"Earlier the *Thik-Akhao* was selected by the villagers and the information was sent to the people for gathering (*jungba*) at Gompa[68] where it was declared officially".[69] "The *Thik-Akhao* is elected by the existing *Thik-Akhao* and the council members after a thorough discussion. The selection of *Thik-Akhao* can be made from both *Thong* and *Chao* but preference is given to *Thong* first. But if an eligible *Thong* is not there then an eligible *Chao* is selected with regard to his knowledge of the society and awareness of rules and social regulations as well as his capability".[70] But nowadays everything is politicalised.[71] Traditionally, it used to happen that the members (*Jungme*) were selected by the villagers and the village head (*Thik-Akhao*) was selected by the members (*Jungme Barse*).[72] There is no fixed duration for the office of *Thik-Akhao*.

Jungme: The *jungmes* are the council members who included only *Thongs* in past days but now *Chaos* are also allowed to be the members. The membership is for lifetime. The member is selected on the basis of his activeness and he has to be a well versed person.

Kachin

Kachin is not in real sense the member of the council but takes the work of the *kachin* being the member of the clan. The membership of *kachin* is not done by selection or election. It is according to their respective turns. The number of *kachins* will be equal to the number of the clans within the society. Hence *kachins* include both *Thongs* and *Chaos*. The term of *kachin* is three years. After the term is over the *kachin's* work is handed over to another person of different family of their own clan. The turn will come back to the same family after the rest of the families of the same clan have completed their turn. Though this may take long time and may not come to the same family in the next immediate generation.

The work of the *kachin* is to remind the people every night to be careful of fire and water. If any person(s) goes somewhere he/she/they should be careful while on the way. Moreover, *kachin* needs to ensure that no one should indulge in stealing; to keep their surrounding clean and maintain discipline. He has to inform the people about the date of meeting or social work one day in advance. If anyone violates the law, the *kachin* has to inform it to the council (*Blu*) who are supposed to take action as per their customary laws.

Types of meetings:

1. *Damchik*: Damchik is a meeting in which all the clans of the society are included to have a general consensus. This meeting is conducted to make new law in the society.
2. *Chatpuniseh*: The *Chatpuniseh* meeting is conducted every three years. Earlier it used to be conducted in every five years but now the duration has been shortened. For quick dispersal of cases, the duration has been

shortened. This meeting is conducted to dispose the whole three years cases and also the previous pending cases.

Chatpuniseh is fixed after consulting whether the day would be good or bad. Earlier the day used to be fixed by the *khik jiji*. But after the conversion to Buddhism the day is fixed by the *lama*. The consultation is done because it is said that if the meeting is held on the bad day then there may be occurrence of quarrel as per their belief system.

Besides these two main meetings the council will conduct meeting according to the urgency and need within the society. The proceedings may take one or many days. It depends upon the dispute of the conflicting parties.

Penalty

The punishment in the society can be given in the form of penalty or physical assault. Penalty is given to a person according to the degree of crime done by him. So there are different values or units of penalty imposed on a person accordingly. But whether this penalty is or was different for different classes within the society is the question that comes to the mind as the society is always headed by the higher class only. One of the *Chao* people responded, "Regarding penalty I don't have any idea of earlier days but at present fine is imposed irrespective of the class. Both classes have to pay same amount of fine if their misdeed is same".[73] The fine system was same for all irrespective of class.[74] The money collected by the council (*Blu*), through the imposition of fines is used during religious festivals like *Wang*, *Chokor* and *Khik-saba*.

There are different reasons where the fines are imposed on persons. For instance when he/she breaks the discipline of the village, commits crime, etc. Fine is also imposed if fishing is done without the owner's permission in the *khroh* (portion of river splitting into two), or honey is collected from cliff (*chhok*) without prior permission.

There are few holidays called *Duchin* within the society on which the people do not indulge in agricultural work, fishing and hunting, forest cutting, etc. There are four *Duchin* days in Sherdukpen society according to Chinese calendar. These are *Cha sarjat* (8th day) *Chaso* (10th day) *Chasangkhu* (15th day), *Tongchin* (30th day). However, in Chaso, the 10th day, it rests upon the person's wish to indulge in the restricted work. It was not considered as *Duchin* in olden days. It is prevalent among Monpas and is now followed by the Sherdukpen but not in a strict sense. And if somebody is found to have breached this rule, fine is imposed on that person. If somebody goes against these then they have to pay fine in their village council (₹ 1500).

Punishment in the form of physical assault may be inflicted if there is a naughty or indisciplined person. But it is not done at first instance. First the council (*Blu*) will make him/her understand. And even if he/she does not take it seriously and continues with indiscipline then only the council (*Blu*) will hand him over to the youth (*Junyu blu*). The youth (*Junyu blu)* will beat him with a stick at the meeting place tying his hands and legs to the flag pole (*darsing*). In case of females such punishment is given by female members.

Religious Life

Before the advent of Buddhism, the Sherdukpens believed in the existence of numerous gods and demons all around them. These were held to personify the powers and forces of their highland landscape and were believed to be responsible for all the calamities threatening their welfare. So the Sherdukpen propitiated these supernatural beings by performing rites in which sacrifice of animals formed an important part. This age old traditional belief system is termed as *Chipo*. When Sherdukpen took Buddhism they stopped practicing these rites.

Like the Monpa, the Sherdukpens are also followers of the Gelugpa sect of Tibetan Buddhism. However, pre-Buddhist, animist spiritualist elements also co-exist with the Sherdukpen's Buddhist beliefs within the society. Sherdukpen priests include the *Jiji* (local priest or shaman), and the Buddhist monks from the neighbouring monastery. After embracing Buddhism the society engaged the Buddhist priests called *lamas* to perform rituals for the welfare of the society as well as the family. The religious structure, like monastery (*Lagong*), shrines (*Mane*), stupa (*Chorten*), long flag (*Dadar*), *Phan* (Small flags of clothes or strips of papers), can be seen in the Sherdukpen villages.

Jijis are the traditional priests/shamans of the Sherdukpen. There are two types of priests/shamans (*jiji*)—one is *khik jiji* and another is *Chand jiji*. The *khik jiji* is selected by the council and he learns the priesthood. The *khik jiji* will be from the *Chaos* only i.e. *Dingla* and *Megeji*. The *Dinglas* used to be the head priest. The priesthood in *Dingla* is given to the original only and not to the converted one. The simple priest/shaman (*Chand jiji*) is believed to be the one chosen by the spirit. It is said that he is imitated and taught in series of visions by the spirits with whom he is considered to be married. There are three spirits with whom these *jijis* are attached and are called accordingly. These are *Largyawangpu*, *Zerchigombu* and *Jumuwangsing* so it can be said as *Largyawangpu jiji*, *Zerchigombu jiji* and *Jumuwangsing jiji*.

The priests/shamans (*Chand jiji*) do not consume garlic and onion. It is a taboo for them to take these stuffs. There is a legend cited by Verrier Elwin (1958: pp. 269–270) which gives an explanation to such act as society believed, as:

Plate 5.6 *Monk*

Plate 5.7 *Khik jiji*

> When the world was made and men first created the great god *Lopung Chungba* made *Jumuwangsing*, the god of the forests. After his son had gone away deep into the jungle, *Lopung* wondered how people would know him for he was afraid that he might injure people. So he created the *jiji* (priest) whose name was *Bonsarap* and sent him to serve and help mankind.
>
> On his way the *jiji* met *Konchosum* (the Lord Buddha) who asked him, "who are you and why have you come here?' I am a priest replied the *jiji*, 'and I have come to sacrifice to the gods and spirits and save mankind from distress'. But *Konchosum* said, "You cannot stay here, for you are a sinner. I am righteous and I teach righteousness. I take the life of no living thing. I injure no living thing. But you kill every kind of creature. You must go away.
>
> As they were talking *Jumuwangsing* came to the place and said to *Konchsum*, ""It is true that you are righteous and a teacher of righteousness. You take the life of no living thing. But I am not like you. I am a spirit of the forest and I eat meat and drink blood. If you are not willing to give me my food, at least allow the *jiji* to give it to me."
>
> *Konchosum* was wise and merciful and he said, 'very well you may do as you wish'. Then he said to the *jiji*, 'Have you a book of sacrifice?' 'No' said the *jiji*. 'Then how can you sacrifice? How can you know what to do? I know every kind of goodness because I have the sacred books'.
>
> The *jiji* went to *Jumuwangsing* and told him what *Konchosum* had said. The god of the forest replied, "it is not too difficult to live a good life. Follow the law of goodness: do not eat onions or the flesh of deer or pig or fowl. There are certain kinds of fish you must avoid. Do this and I will come to you in dreams and tell you what to do."

It is believed that if the priest/shaman (*jiji*) consumed these stuffs then he will lose his mental stability and will act like a mad person.

The principal festivals of Sherdukpen are *Losar*, *Chokor*, *Wang* and *Khiksaba*. *Losar* is the Buddhist New Year following the Chinese calendar. It generally falls in the month of February-March. It lasts till fifteenth day of the lunar calendar.

Chokor, is celebrated for the well being of the society and to keep away the malevolent spirits away from the villages. It is a Buddhist ritual and procession is held on this day carrying the religious text, idol or piture of lord Buddha. It is generally celebrated in the month of May-June as per lunar calendar. The celebration starts a month ahead by reciting religious/holy script by the monk (*lama*) in the monastary and the day is fixed by the monk (*lama*) for the procession. During this holy month, all forms of hunting and fishing are stopped. It is said that in past days during the *Chokor* festival the *Thongs* used to ride on horses, during the procession, with the rein held by their respective *Chaos*.

Plate 5.8 Carrying of religious text during *Chokor* festival

Wang, is a blessing offering ceremony done by the head priest for the people on religious occasion. It is also a Buddhist ritual. *Khiksaba* (*khik* = mountain, *saba*=ritual) is a bon religion festival where the local priest (*khik jiji*) propitiates the mountain god. It is a post harvesting festival where the agricultural products are offered to the mountain god. It is done for one whole week. During this whole week the entire power of the village council (*Blu*) rests in the hand of *khik jiji*. The council becomes powerless and all the work and function is controlled by the *khik jiji* which the people have to obey irrespective of class. This whole week is considered very sacred. Hence during this week disposal of dead body through cremation or birth giving is not allowed within the village. It is believed that these two works will create an impurity in the environment. So both these functions have to be carried out outside the village. No picture of stratification can be depicted from religion. All the rules and rituals are same for all the classes.

Endnotes

1. Informant Y.D. Thongdok, aged 76, village Rupa.
2. It is because the Thongdoks are attached to Megeji.
3. Informant D.G. Megeji, aged 39.
4. Informant S.P. Khrime, aged 44.
5. Informant Y.D. Thongdok, aged 76; S.P. Khrime, aged 44; and D.K. Sinchaji, aged 52; K.T. Megeji aged 31; D.G. Megeji aged 39 Thongre.
6. Informant S.K. Khrime, aged 65.
7. Informant K.T. Megeji, aged 31.
8. Informant N.T. Khrime, aged 68.
9. Informant S.K. Khrime, aged 65.
10. Informant R.K. Karma, aged 64.
11. Informant Y.D. Thongdok, aged 76; N.W. Thongon, aged 74; R.D. Thongdok.
12. *Chkok* is a group of people irrespective of class. There are seven Chkoks within the Sherdukpen society. These groups are used in the social works or functions of the society even individually whenever necessary.
13. Informant Y.D. Thongdok, aged 76.
14. Informant R.D. Thongdok, aged 50.
15. Informant K.T. Megeji, aged 31.
16. Informant P.D. Megeji, aged 73; N.W. Wangja, aged 64.
17. Informant N.W. Thongon, aged 74.
18. Informant K.T. Megeji, aged 31.
19. Informant S.K. Khrime, aged 65.
20. Informant Y.D. Thongdok, aged 76.
21. Informant D.K. Thongdok, aged 55; Y.D. Thongdok, aged 76; R.D. Mosobi, aged 41; P.D. Megeji, aged 36.
22. Informant D.K. Thongdok, aged 55.
23. Informant K.T. Megeji, aged 31.
24. Informant K.T. Megeji, aged 31; D.K. Thongdok, aged 55; Y.D. Thongdok, aged 76; P.D. Megeji, aged 36.
25. Informant K.T. Megeji, aged 31.
26. Informant K. Megeji, aged 31.
27. Informant S.K. Khrime, aged 65; Y.D. Thongdok, aged 76; K.T. Megeji, aged 31.
28. Informant Y.D. Thongdok, aged 76; N.W. Thongon, aged 74.
29. Informant N.W. Thongon, aged 74; Kesang, aged 37.
30. Any kind of fish caught from the nearby river except the flat head variety. Fish available in the market can also be used.
31. The whole body part is kept intact because it signifies life. There will be no life if the parts are taken out. The fish also represents the baby and an

emotion is attached along with this that the baby should look pretty and beautiful like that fish.

32. Stick used in frying corn which is T-shaped.
33. *Phogchu* is the waste product after the local wine is sieved. *Phog* means wine and *chu* means the waste product of *phog*.
34. It is done so because the day begins with sun rise from there hence for the long life of the baby.
35. The information is given to the brother because cross cousin marriage is given preference and to let him not have any hard feelings for the relation that is going to take place.
36. Informant N.T. Khrime, aged 68.
37. Nawang (pseudonym) belong to *Chao* who had an affair with a *Thong* girl. Both were having an affair and were going to get married. On the marriage day, which was taking place at the boy's house, the family members of the girl came, scolded and abused the boy as well as the parents of the boy and took along the girl with them.
38. Informant K.T. Megeji, aged 31.
39. The *Thong* of Khleng was given the title of Thongdok. For detail, go through Khleng Thong story given at chapter-3.
40. The direction of leaving is because of the belief in spirits and demons present at all directions and the bride may go to their mouth. The time of reaching the bride house is with the belief that if entered early or even late, there could be frequent quarrels in the new life and the life of the child born would be born short.
41. Losar is the New Year, celebrated in the month of February or March by the Sherdukpens following the Chinese calendar.
42. Informant C.D. Wangja, aged 80.
43. Informant K.T. Megeji, aged 31.
44. Informant Y.D. Thongdok, aged 76.
45. Informant T. Thongdok, aged 39.
46. Informant D.K. Thongdok, aged 55; R.K. Wangja, aged 52.
47. Informant Y.D. Thongdok, aged 76.
48. Informant N.T. Khrime, aged 68.
49. Informant P.D. Megeji, aged 73.
50. Informant Y.D. Thongdok, aged 76; P.D. Megeji, aged 36; K.T. Megeji, aged 31.
51. Informant D.K. Khrime, aged 70.
52. A coin is put for expenditure of the deceased, the ghee for energy and wine to replenish his thirst.
53. *Mringmu* means sister. The sister (*mringmu*) engaged in the ritual will be from the attached *Chao* clan for the *Thong*. It is the duty of the engaged sister to look after the ritual.

54. The dead body is not taken out on Saturday and Sunday. It is considered as a taboo with a belief that more incidents may occur if the dead is disposed on these two days.
55. *Ji-i pho* means flag of death. It is white in colour and is imprint with '*om mane peme hu*'.
56. Informant K.T. Megeji, aged 31.
57. Informant R. Thongchi of Jigaon.
58. Informant D.K. Thongdok, aged 55.
59. Informant S.K. Khrime, aged 65.
60. Informant T.C. Megeji, aged 32.
61. Informant T.C. Megeji, aged 32; P. L. Thongon, aged 36; N.W. Megeji, aged 37.
62. Informant R.D. Thongdok, age 50; N.T. Khrime, age 68; K.T. Megeji, Age 31.
63. Informant N.T. Khrime, aged 68.
64. Informant C.D. Wangja, aged 80.
65. Informant R.D. Megeji, aged 63.
66. Informant N.T. Khrime, aged 68.
67. Informant Y.D. Thongdok, aged 76.
68. The lawn of the Rupa Gompa is the place of official gathering. It is said that the Rupa Gompa in actual is not a Gompa but a fort.
69. Informant C.D. Wangja, aged 80.
70. Informant S.K. Khrime, aged 65.
71. Informant Y.D. Thongdok, aged 76.
72. Informant R.D. Megeji, aged 63.
73. Informant K.T. Megeji, aged 31.
74. Informant Y.D. Thongdok, aged 76.

6

Stratification and Emerging Realities

It is a universal fact that no society or culture remains static. It undergoes various changes. The changes may happen due to adoption of the cultural traits of others or may happen by losing some of the traits on its own. The changes may be rapid or go at a slow pace. The degree of change, thus, would depend upon the magnitude of shake the conditions of human life received under particular circumstances (Mann, 2004: p. 13). These changes within the society lead to social changes where a society behaves in a different manner from its earlier form.

There are various factors which lead to changes within the society. For instance innovation and cultural contact are the two classical factors which bring changes within the society. But with the advancement of civilisation in the field of science and technology, new education system, modern political system, market economy, etc. have brought tremendous change in the life styles of the people. With the advancement in the educational sphere, the political view and the marketing sector the people are becoming more or totally inclined towards modernisation.

The tribal society which is considered of having primitive or subsistence economy, with simple technology, traditional way of education and political system is being influenced by the so called civilised or modern factors. This had let to the emergence of the concept of sanskritisation and westernisation by M.N. Srinivas (1966). Sanskritisation, was found to be a widespread cultural and social process among the Hindus in different parts of India. It is also reported to be occurring among some tribal groups such as Bhils and Oraons (Srinivas, 2003: p. 2). In this process, the people of lower group adopt the beliefs and practises of the higher group to raise their cultural status. Among the tribals they come under the fold of caste system to raise their status. Westernisation on the other hand is the process where the people adopt the traits of western culture in their life style.

There are numerous papers, presented in relation to changes or transition or transformation in Sarkar's (2003) edited book by C.R. Sathyanarayanan, B.K. Basu, M. Hazra, Md. A. Mohidden and G.V. Ramana, G.K. Bera, R.P. Athparia, B. Das, J. Chakraborty, S. K. Chaudhuri, N. Saha, G.C. Ojah, K. Mukhopadhyay, S. Bagchi, S.P. Lala, R. Biswas, R. Prasad, R.K. Sinha, M. Sahay, D.K. Samanta, R. Sarkar. S.K. Nandy. All of them talk about the changes that are taking place in various tribes all over India. And all these changes are due to the impact of governmental programmes and its acts, education and culture contact in different courses of time. The process of acculturation and assimilation is also highlighted which is transforming their way of life completely or partially.

Tremendous changes have come in the Sherdukpen society after the Government of India initiated various developmental programmes, such as, education, administration, medical facilities, political system, etc. Introduction of market in the society also had a great impact by the introduction of many products in the society which were earlier unknown to them or for which they had to depend on the neighbouring state.

There have been changes in Sherdukpen society, from earlier times till present, and these changes within the society can be discussed accordingly. Starting with the social structure as already mentioned earlier that the society has been divided into two classes i.e. *Thong* and *Chao*. But later when some families from Bhutan were permitted to settle within the society, they were not included in the main class but were placed under another class termed as *Yanlog*. However in due course of time the *Yanlogs* were adjusted to the main class of the society.

The introduction of the *Yanlog* in the main class was done after passing a resolution in *damchik* meeting. It is difficult to ascertain the time of this meeting as the conversion took place eighty years ago according to case study number 2. This meeting (*damchik*) is referred to because in this meeting new law was introduced with the consensus of all clans of the society. "This *Damchik* meeting was necessary to conduct as the original *Chaos* boycotted the decision of inclusion of *Yanlogs* in the *Chaos* protesting that if the *Yanlogs* were given the status of *Chaos* then the *Chao*s also should be allowed to move upward by giving the status of *Thongs*. So in this *Damchik* meeting the *Thongs* consoled the *Chaos* by reasoning that the *Yanlogs* were being given the status of *Chaos* not to supersede them but only for their help and to increase the clan population."[1]

The council passed the resolution for inclusion of the *Yanlogs* within the main class of the society keeping in view that:

1. Since they (*Yanlog*) had resided in the place long enough they couldn't go back to their native places and also that many girls of the main clans had got married to *Yanlog* men, who were not considered to be equal in status with the main clans, they could be accommodated into the main fold.
2. They had been utilising the resources of the society and helping the society whenever need arose and whenever their help was required since generations. Thus they had to be incorporated within the main frame of the society.

According to the council decision after the meeting (*damchik*) the *Yanlogs* were eligible in the following clans, as per the resolution, of the *Chao* as given in the table below:

Table 6.1 Table showing to which clan of *Chaos* the *Yanlogs* can be incorporated

Sl.No.	*Yanlogs*	*Chaos*
1	Ibi	Dingla
2	Sarmu	Megeji
3	Sertipa	Mijiji
4	Dungkhar	Sinchaji

Source: Council resolution 1990

But to beget a title, the permission was to be taken from the clan (*Rung*) in which one was to be incorporated. Regarding conferring of titles to the *Yanlogs* it was decided upon by the clan elders.[2] The clan (*Rung*) elders held meetings and argued on the merits and demerits. And if in that meeting they reached consensus then only that clan title was given to those *Yanlogs*. The meeting was conducted and attended by the original clan members and not by the converted ones. Here the council could not interfere nor could the village head, though intimation was given to the council after the title was conferred to a particular person.

Case Study No. 1

This is the case study of conversion. This case took place around 1978. The person belonged to Ibi clan who was conferred the Dingla title by the *Blu* (council). So this Ibi family took a yak to Rupa at Manthingbao for the ceremony. There at Manthingbao Asu Dingla and people of Khrime clan were present. The animal was slaughtered for the feast at Manthingbao. Before the feast the concerned person holding the heart of the butchered animal in his respective hand took a pledge at *Prawding Sri* (stone foundation) along with his son saying that "I am going to work for the society as a member of this clan and will perform the same duty for the attached clan. And in future if I ever made a mistake or happen to lie, that I may be forgiven for the same".

Plate 6.1 *Prawding Sri*

Plate 6.2 *Manthingbao*

Case Study No. 2

This is the case study of conversion where the *Blu* called the Ibi family which was conferred with the Dingla title. In this case the pledge was not taken and even the feast was provided by the *Blu* itself. This incident is said to have taken place 80–90 years ago.

Case Study No. 3

This case study is about a *Chao* (Sinchaji) who is using the *Thong* (Thongchi) clan with their name instead of Sinchaji itself. It happened that there was a widow of a Thongchi person, who later got married with one of the Sinchaji person. This widow already had a son from her deceased husband (Thongchi). The in-laws of the widow told the Sinchaji to stay along with them and to look after the property belonging to the deceased and son who was also given the right to use Thongchi as surname for himself as well as for his children.

"Even when the *Yanlogs* were given a title of any clan they could not use kinship terminology to address their relations. For instance the *Chao* address their father as *Boyo* but the converted still call by their term as *Apo*."[3] But conferring of titles was not limited to *Yanlogs*. There are instances when the outside people have also been incorporated. In this instance Dawa Thongdok (name changed) said that "a person in Birpur was brought by Tashi Khrime (name changed) long time back to look after the cows called *Koli* (may be because of his dark complexion the name was given), who was let to marry a Rahung girl and had been adjusted in *Chaos* clan called *Dingla*. Now he is adjusted in yet another group (*Chekok*) and is working accordingly for the society.

Though it is said that *Yanlog* would be incorporated in *Chaos* clan only but there are few cases where they have been incorporated within the *Thong* clan also. Pema Thongchi (name changed) cited that "there are instance where *Yanlog* are in *Thong* clan in Jigaon. They had been in *Sinchaji* at first for generations and have worked with us in every *Chokor* and *Khiksaba* festival. They help us, the *Thongchi* clan, and in recognition we have given them the title *Thongchi*. But in *Thongchi* we called our father *Achi* they cannot use this term. They consider *Thongchi* as royal clan and this royal clan has some privilege like putting of royal dress during *Khiksaba* but the converted *Thongchi* do not wear it. So there are some demarcations in it".

But it became a great concern for the youth as the people at first entered as *Yanlog* and then easily got an access into different clans of the society. The term *Yanlog* was used only for the people who came from Bhutan and settled at Sherdukpen area long back. As per the resolution only four clans were recognised as *Yanlog* i.e. *Ibi*, *Sarmu*, *Sertipa* and *Dunkhar*.

But later, besides these people, some others also came under the banner of *Yanlog* such as Nepali, Tibetan and Bhutanese. These people, especially due to marriage alliance, stayed within the society. They used the resources and helped the society by providing material needs and running the petty errands where the involvement of group (*Chkok*) was not found necessary. After working as a *Yanlogs* for three to five years these people used to get absorbed in the main clan of the society. Once they were incorporated in the main class they were considered as *Khomi* (people drafted to *Chkok*) who would have customary rights. The *Yanlog* stage became a doorway through which a person could enter into the society with the right to all the privileges as per rule. To prevent this, the youth under the banner of ASYWA (All Shertukpen Youth Welfare Association) conveyed the message to the council (*Blu*). This apprehensive intervention by the youth put a hold on the conferring of titles to the outsiders by the council (*Blu*) since 2008.

Tremendous changes have taken place in relation to the material culture. The so called traditional houses are being almost completely replaced by modern houses. Traditional houses do exist but in very few numbers. The roofs are covered by tin sheets in some of the existing traditional houses. The house constructions still depend upon the economic conditions of the family irrespective of class as earlier. Though stone house construction can be seen even now, unlike the stone houses and the wooden house built earlier which were usually double storied the houses built now differ in their structures. The concept of bedroom, sitting room, dining room and kitchen has come up. The number of rooms also depend upon the economic status of the family. Generally the houses have a bedroom, prayer room, sitting room and a kitchen. Instead of the stone houses, semi pucca type (SPT)/Assam type houses and reinforce concrete cement (RCC) houses are becoming common. Even the stone house walls are plastered with cement inside and in some cases even on the outside.

According to Table 6.2 the number of stone house type are more in *Thongs* while in *Chaos* the number of Assam type houses are more.

But all together the most prevailing house type within the society is stone house, SPT/Assam type house and traditional house. But in Rupa only the distribution of dwelling houses is almost uniform within the village (see Table 6.3).

Table 6.2 Class and clanwise number of houses combining Rupa, Thongre and Jigaon

Class	*Clan*	*House Type*				
		RCC	*Non-Traditional Stone House*	*SPT/ Assam Type*	*Wooden Traditional House*	*Wooden House*
THONG	THONGDOK	6	15	11	8	6
	THONGON	5	4	2	-	2
	THONGCHI	2	9	8	4	5
	KHRIME	5	8	3	5	2
	MOSOBI	1	4	3	3	2
	WANGJA	2	2	1	1	1
	KARMA	1	-	3	3	-
	YANGFAN	-	-	-	1	-
Total		**22**	**42**	**31**	**25**	**18**
CHAO	MEGEJI	4	6	9	8	5
	DINGLA	-	4	11	3	1
	SINCHAJI	1	2	1	5	1
	MIJIJI	-	-	2	3	1
Total		**5**	**12**	**23**	**19**	**8**

Source: Fieldwork 2010

Table 6.3 Class and clanwise number of houses of Rupa village

Class	*Clan*	*House Type*				
		RCC	*Non-Traditional Stone House*	*SPT/ Assam Type*	*Wooden Traditional House*	*Wooden House*
THONG	THONGDOK	5	6	3	3	1
	THONGON	5	1	-	-	1
	THONGCHI	-	2	2	-	1
	KHRIME	4	5	2	2	1
	MOSOBI	1	4	1	3	1
	WANGJA	2	2	1	1	1
	KARMA	1	-	3	3	-
	YANGFAN	-	-	-	1	-
Total		**18**	**20**	**12**	**13**	**6**
	MEGEJI	3	3	3	3	2
	DINGLA	-	1	3	-	1
	SINCHAJI	1	-	1	2	-
	MIJIJI	-	-		3	1
Total		**4**	**4**	**7**	**8**	**4**

Source: Fieldwork 2010

Table 6.4 Class and clanwise number of houses of Thongre village

Class	*Clan*	*House Type*				
		RCC	*Non-Traditional Stone House*	*SPT/ Assam Type*	*Wooden Traditional House*	*Wooden House*
THONG		1	7	3	5	4
	THONGON		3	1		
	THONGCHI		2	2	1	2
	KHRIME	1	3	1	3	1
Total		**2**	**15**	**7**	**9**	**7**
	MEGEJI	1	3	4	4	3
	SINCHAJI		1		1	
Total		**1**	**4**	**4**	**5**	**3**

Source: Fieldwork 2010

In Thongre village stone houses are more prominent than other types of houses. However, within that also it is the *Thongs* who possess more numbers of it while for *Chaos* it is almost uniform.

Plate 6.3 Assam type house

Plate 6.4 Modified stone house

Table 6.5 Class and clanwise number of houses of Jigaon village

Class	*Clan*	*House Type*				
		RCC	*Non-traditional Stone House*	*SPT/ Assam Type*	*Wooden Traditional House*	*Wooden House*
THONG	THONGDOK	-	2	5	-	1
	THONGON	-	-	1	-	1
	THONGCHI	2	5	4	3	2
	MOSOBI	-	-	2	-	1
Total		**2**	**7**	**12**	**3**	**5**
	MEGEJI	-	-	2	1	-
	DINGLA	-	3	8	3	-
	SINCHAJI	-	1	-	2	1
	MIJIJI	-	-	2	-	-
Total		-	**4**	**12**	**6**	**1**

Source: Fieldwork 2010

In Jigaon, the most prevailing type of house is the SPT/Assam type throughout the village as well as among the classes.

Plate 6.5 RCC with tin roof

Plate 6.6 Wooden house with tin roof

Being religious, before the construction, the *lama* is consulted to see if the land is appropriate for the construction or not. However, no sacrifice is made as was done earlier. Due to the adoption of Buddhism sacrifice has been stopped. No feast is given before the house is constructed; only house warming is still performed. Bringing of sheep or yak by sister for the house warming has stopped. The meat and wine which is easily available from the Rupa market is brought by the owner to throw a party on house-warming day.

Besides these, even the traditional household articles are gradually getting replaced by new ones. The brass utensils and earthen pots which were brought from the nearby state i.e. SPT/Assam especially, have been replaced by the utensils of different materials found in the market. Though, it has not ceased to be used totally, firewood has been replaced by cooking gas. The grinder mill (*choskor*) is not made use of anymore though some houses still have grinders (*ranthok*). This is because the grinder mill is constructed near the river or stream. The water is brought by a channel and let to fall on the paddle of the grinder which is attached with the grinder stone through a wooden log. Due to the constant rise in the water level it used to get damaged. People also do not bother as they hardly use it.

As the concept of kitchen came the shelves and showcases also came into existence. Some people arrange the cups, spoons, plates, glass neatly on the shelves of these showcases. The modern plastic buckets are used to store water and plastic mugs to draw water. Using of modern technology is rampant in the society especially mobile phones. The young and middle aged people will be seen going around holding it in their hand. Most of the houses have television with private cable connection such as Dish TV, Tata Sky, etc. Some families also own bikes and cars.

Plate 6.7 Kitchen

Plate 6.8 Display of household stuff in showcase

Plate 6.9 Sitting room

Plate 6.10 Sitting room

Electrification has replaced the traditional way of lighting the house which was done earlier with the help of pinewood. Pipe line water supply has stopped the fetching of water from the nearby streams or rivers. Though even now-a-days some people go to the river for washing clothes and bathing according to the availability of water and few bathrooms constructed at respective homes. The same goes for the sanitation facility. Those who do not have sanitation facility they go in the open in nearby shades of bushes or big stones by the river bank.

Plate 6.11 Kitchen separate from house

Plate 6.12 Kitchen attached with house

Plate 6.13 Doors leading to rooms

Plate 6.14 Sanitary facility

Even the food habits have changed. Now rice is the staple food which is easily available in the market and cooperative stores. Varieties of meat are consumed as compared to earlier times when people did not eat or consume domesticated animals and poultry birds.

Regarding inter-dining, though there was no such discrimination among the *Thongs* and *Chaos* but the *Yanlogs* were discriminated against in this matter. The food to the *Yanlogs* was provided outside the house if they happened to visit the village.[4] But now no such rule is followed as this stratum of people have been included within the main class of the society. They are treated as the other main people of the society. Now everyone inter dines with each other.

Even in dressing and use of ornaments tremendous changes can be seen. The Sherdukpen male hardly wear their traditional dress. Only during the local festivals men adorn themselves in their traditional attires which again are not worn by all the male members. Those who do not wear the traditional dress simply carry an endi cloth as a shawl around the shoulder with their trousers and shirts or suits with modern shoes. Even in day to day life they wear shirts or sportings and pants with slippers and put on additional jackets and sweaters during winter. The young generation males will put jeans, pants, shirts or T-shirts with slippers or shoes of various fashions. During winter they put an additional sweater and fashionable jackets.

Plate 6.15 Menfolk in modern dress

For females also the case is almost the same but during festival they maintain their traditional attire. The only change regarding the traditional dress is that the endi cloth has been replaced by silk cloth. More transformations have been brought in the female dress patterns. Earlier the female dress used to be a long frock but now it has been divided into two parts i.e. blouse and skirt with plates already stitched intact with it. They say that it is more convenient wearing this as it is simpler and there is no headache of arranging the plates. The traditional red colour jacket has been replaced by the Assamese colourful jacket. The use of *Difik* (cloth put below the knee) has been abandoned by the Sherdukpen people. Otherwise the dressing of Aka and Sherdukpen is almost similar.

But in day to day life the females wear blouse or tops, wrappers and trousers brought from the market. Only few old ladies can still be seen in the traditional dresses. The younger generation girls are more inclined towards the modern wear vogue like salwaar-kurta, jeans, tops, shorts, T-shirts, etc. with fashionable shoes and sandals. Adorning themselves with earrings, necklaces, bracelets, lipstick and nail polish is a common view.

Plate 6.16 Womenfolk in modern dress

Plate 6.17 Women in modified traditional dress

As the traditional beads are losing their importance, during marriage now beads do not play any important role. The young and educated generations are not attached to such kinds of beads and they don't have any idea nor are they aware of the classification and traditional value of the beads. Especially the young girls don't like the designs and the sizes of the ornaments. They are more inclined towards the fashionable items. Wearing of beads can hardly be seen in the society. Only during some occasions people wear them that too only those who participate in the ceremony.

Social life is also influenced by the changes that have come into the society. For instance, in the marriage system the acquiring of mate from within the class is losing its rigidity. Earlier three divisions existed in the society i.e. the *Thong*, *Chao* and *Yanlog*, now only *Thong* and *Chao* exist. The *Yanlogs* were brought under the *Thong* and *Chao* class by the consent of the heads of each clan members. Later the council abolished the *Yanlog* class. But in the mind set of some people it still exists but not to a great extent. The younger generations hardly have the idea of this term. But they know that there were people who came from Bhutan and settled at Sherdukpen area.

In the marriage system also there are vast changes. Now-a-days the youths are more inclined towards love marriage. Because of the increasing number of marriages in this form the rate of inter-class marriage frequency is also increasing. Even marriages with other tribes have become common. This may be the result of contact with outsiders in the process of work as well as interaction of the people who are going outside for their higher studies wherefrom they find their mates. The traditional custom of marriage where the bride is provided with food from her relatives during her initial three nights' stay at the groom's place is not followed in the inter-tribe marriages. Since the bride does not belong to the Sherdukpen tribe hence the mediator (*achung jring*) is not engaged.

Case Study No. 4

This marriage took place in the year 2006. The boy was Megeji (*Chao*) and the girl was Mijiji (*Chao*). The girl was studying at Bomdila college and the boy was studying monastic way of life at Bomdila. There they came to know each other and they fell in love. The parents of both the boy and the girl had no idea of the affair. Both of them lived together at Bomdila. After two months of having an affair and living together the boy took the girl to his village. The parents of the boy did not object the relationship and let them stay together. The three days ceremony was performed. *Achung jring* was sent to the girl's house on the third day for *temre* and the girl distributed wine to the people attending the third night ceremony.

Case Study No. 5

This is the case of a love marriage that happened in the year 2003. Here the boy is Thongdok (*Thong*) while the girl is Thongchi (*Thong*). Both the boy and the girl were in love but the parents of both the sides were against the relationship. So both boy and the girl eloped to Brokpublong to the boy's uncle's house. They stayed there for nearly ten days. Then the parents of the boy sent the boy's friend to bring both the boy and the girl home. After they came back the three days ceremony was performed where the girl was provided food by the girl's clan members and parents. On the third day three *achung jrings* (all khrime) were sent to the girl's house and at night distribution of wine was done by the bride.

Case Study No. 6

In this case the boy is Thongchi from Thongre village while the girl is Khrime of Chillipam. This marriage took place in the year 1987. The boy had a sister who was married among Chillipam. He would go to visit her occasionally where he met this girl and fell in love. The boy let his sister know about his desire. The sister then had a talk with the girl's parent who also did not object to the relationship. Here the boy himself went to the girl's house and brought her along with him to Rupa as he used to work there at that time. After few days they went to the village where the three days ceremony was performed and on the last night wine distribution was done by the bride.

Case Study No. 7

This marriage took place in the year 2000. The boy belonged to Thongchi clan while the girl was Thongdok. Both the boy and the girl liked each other but the parents of the girl were against this relationship. However, there was no objection from the boy's side. Both the girl and boy eloped to Sinchung to the boy's brother's house. After their stay for nearly twelve days at Sinchung one of the brothers of the boy came to Sinchung to take him back to his village. The three night ceremony was done but the food was not provided from the girl's clan and family as they were against the relation. So the food was provided from the boy's house itself. But on the third day *achung jring* was sent to the girl's house for *temre* and distribution of wine was done by the bride.

Case Study No. 8

This marriage took place in the year 2010. The boy was Thongchi (*Thong*) from Thongre and the girl was Megeji (*Chao*) from Birpur. The boy and the girl fell in love and the boy told his parents about his desire to marry the girl. The parents accepted the relationship. The mother and a woman (Thongon) went to the girl's friend's house with the proposal. Then the friend went to the girl's house to convey the message. The girl's parent also accepted the proposal. Then the *lama* was consulted and three women (Megeji, Thongdok, Thongchi) from the boy's village went to get the girl by capturing her. The girl was brought to the boy's village and the three night ceremony was done. Food was provided from Megeji and Thongdok clan for two days. On the third day food came from the girl's family and the wine distribution was done by the bride on that night.

In this case *achung jring* (Krime, Thongon) was sent on the third day for *temre.*

Case Study No. 9

This marriage took place in the year 1985. The boy was Thongon (*Thong*) and the girl was Megeji (*Chao*). In this case boy's parents were against the relationship. So the boy went and stayed at the girl's house. There was no objection from the girl's parents. Almost after one year three women (all Thongon) came to the girl's house to take both the boy and the girl along with them to the boy's house. The three days ceremony where the bride does not perform any manual work and where the food comes from the girl's clan and family was not done. From the day of her arrival she performed her household work. On the third day, two *achung jrings* (Khrime, Thongon) were sent to the girl's house for *temre* and distribution of wine was performed by the bride.

Case Study No.10

This is the marriage that took place in the year 1960. Here the boy is Thongdok (*Thong*) while the girl is Sinchaji (*Chao*). Both the boy and the girl were in love with each other. The parents of the boy were against the relationship as the girl was of lower class. But the boy in love didn't listen to his parents and went to stay in the girl's house. There also the girl's mother told the boy not to come and stay in their place as he was a *Thong* and they were *Chaos.* But the boy did not listen and stayed there for nearly one year by helping them in their agricultural work. After one year the boy's parent sent three women (all Thongdok) to the girl's house for reconciliation and to bring the boy and the girl home.

Case Study No. 11

This marriage took place in the year 2003. The boy was Sherdukpen while the girl was Hrusso. The boy was studying at Bhalukpong where he met this girl with whom he fell in love. When the parents of the boy and the girl came to know about their relationship they were against it. So both the boy and the girl eloped to Banderdewa to boy's sister's house and stayed there for one month. After one month both went back to Bhalukpong and stayed at their respective houses and gave their class exams. After that the boy came to join the school in Rupa as he failed in his class exam. He had to go back to Bhalukpong after he failed again. There he once again met the girl he loved and they fled to the girl's uncle's house at Elephant. Then nearly after one month the girl's father and mother gave their consent to the relation. So they shifted to the girl's parent's house. The boy stayed there for nearly four years, as the boy's parents were strictly against the relationship. But after four years the boy's parent also accepted the relationship. Then both the boy and the girl shifted to the boy's village and stayed there. In this case the ceremony was not performed.

Case Study No. 12

This is the case of inter tribe marriage which took place in the year 1974. The girl is from Monpa tribe of Dirang. Both the boy and girl were in love and the parents were also not against the relationship. When the bride reached the groom's house the three day ceremony was performed. But here as she was an outsider the food was provided from the groom's house only. On the third day *achung jring* was not sent to the girl's house as she was from another tribe. But that night wine was distributed by the bride to the people who attended the wedding ceremony. On the next day of the third night the girl went back to her place with the husband, husband's family members and clan members. There the Monpa ceremony of marriage was performed and they came back after two days.

Case Study No. 13

This marriage took place in the year 1984. The boy is Thongchi while the girl is Monpa from Kalaktang side. The girl used to come to Rupa frequently to his brother's place who was working in the medical department. Here she met this boy with whom she fell in love. At that time the boy's mother was admitted in the hospital. The boy and the girl came to Thongre village after an affair of one month. The ritual of three nights was performed and on the last night offering of wine to the people was done by the bride. In this case the *achung jring* was not sent as the girl belonged to another tribe.

The food was provided from the boy's house itself.

Case Study No. 14

This is the case of love marriage. Here the boy is Sherdukpen while the girl is Monpa. The girl use to visit her sister who got married in Sherdukpen itself. There she met this guy with whom she fell in love. But the parents of both the boy and the girl were against this relationship. Finding no other option both the boy and the girl eloped to Rupa and there they stayed in the lodge. After two days the boy's elder brother went to coax them into coming back home. Then they went together to the village and there the three days ceremony was done. During her three days stay she was accompanied by the boy's sister-in-law. On the third night the distribution of wine by the daughter-in-law was performed.

Only the difference is that the food during the three days stay was provided from the boy's home itself. And no *achung jring* was sent to the girl's house as she was from another tribe.

It can be observed through the Table 6.6 that the frequency of inter marriage has been increasing in every decade. The growth in frequency of inter marriage of Rupa and Thongre almost go along together (see Tables 6.7 and 6.8) and with higher rate. While the growth in frequency of inter marriage, in Jigaon (Table 6.9), is slow in comparison to Rupa and Thongre.

Table 6.6 Decade wise frequency of inter marriages for all the three villages

Decades	*Number of Frequency*	*Percentage*
2000–2010	43	40.19
1990–1999	21	19.63
1980–1989	17	15.89
1970–1979	15	14.02
1960–1969	8	7.48
1950–1959	2	1.87
1940–1949	1	1

Source: Fieldwork 2010

Fig. 6.1 Graph showing frequency of inter marriages decade wise

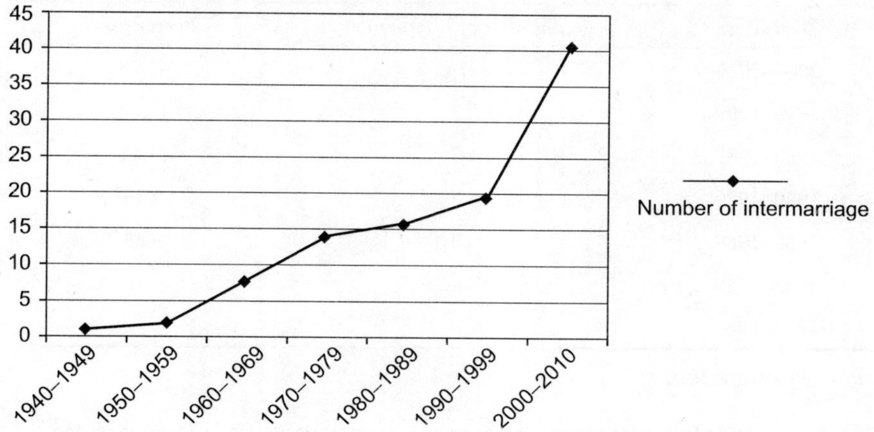

Table 6.7 Decade wise frequency of inter marriages for the Rupa village

Decades	*Number of Frequency*	*Percentage*
2000–2010	21	43.75
1990–1999	11	22.92
1980–1989	7	14.58
1970–1979	7	14.58
1960–1969	1	2.08
1950–1959	0	-
1940–1949	1	2.08

Source: Fieldwork 2010

Fig. 6.2 Graph showing frequency, decade wise, of inter marriages in Rupa village

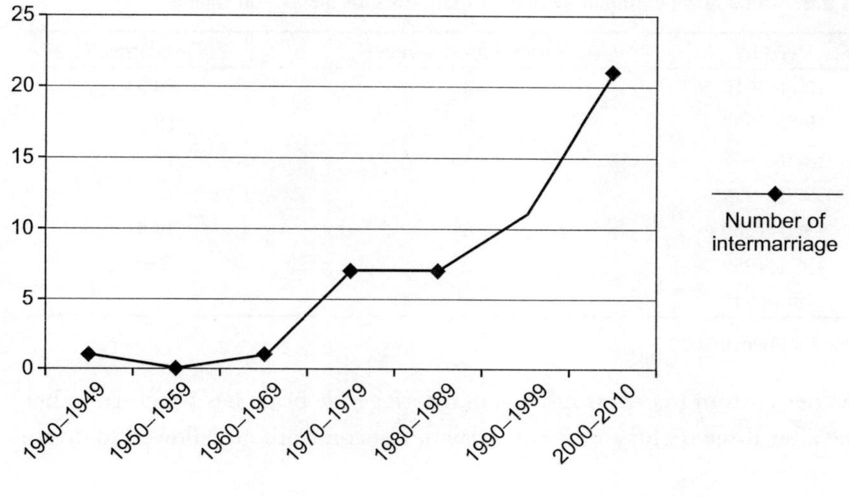

Table 6.8 Decade wise frequency of inter marriage for the Thongre village

Decades	*Number of Frequency*	*Percentage*
2000–2010	14	43.75
1990–1999	5	15.63
1980–1989	7	21.88
1970–1979	3	9.38
1960–1969	3	9.38
1950–1959	-	-
1940–1949	-	-

Source: Fieldwork 2010

Fig. 6.3 Graph showing frequency, decade wise, of inter marriages in Thongre village

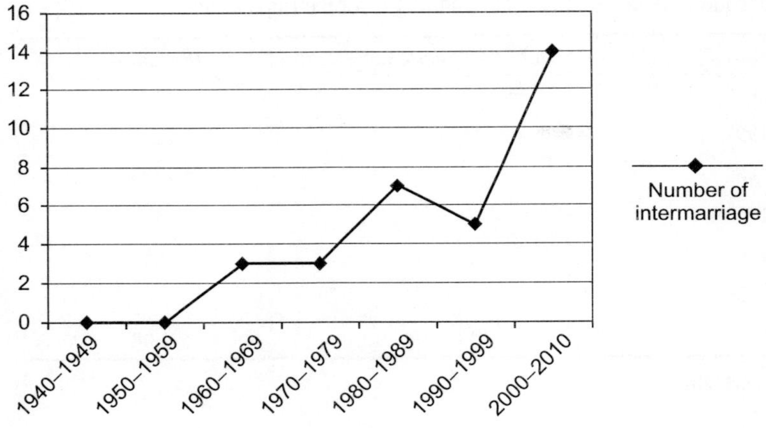

Table 6.9 Decade wise frequency of inter marriages for the Jigaon village

Decades	*Number of Frequency*	*Percentage*
2000–2010	8	29.63
1990–1999	5	18.52
1980–1989	3	11.11
1970–1979	5	18.52
1960–1969	4	14.81
1950–1959	2	7.41
1940–1949	-	-

Source: Fieldwork 2010

As per custom in capturing type of marriage the bride has to return to her home after three nights in the early dawn. But some are not allowed to do so.

Fig. 6.4 Graph showing frequency, decade wise, of inter marriages in Jigaon village

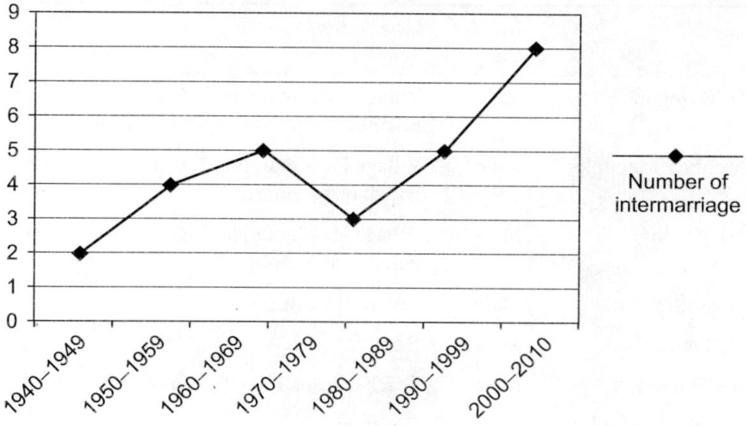

Earlier marriages between Thongdok (not all but the generation from *Khleng Thong*) and Megeji used to take place. "But now it has been stopped by the council as in one hand it is said that *Thongdok* and *Megeji* are brothers and on other hand they are marrying each other".[5] However, regarding this it is also said that the marriage between them declined in course of time and now it is stopped because of conscience of the people.[6]

The traditional village council *(Blu)* is still functioning and deals with most of the matters related to the society. It has not lost its importance within the society. But sometimes people seek the help of modern judiciary law for some cases such as, compensation related to divorce and land case which the council (*Blu*) could not settle. Councils (*Blu*) have emerged in course of time at various villages. They settle all the cases first at the village level except for the cases of murders and divorces. If unable to solve the cases at their level, it reaches Rupa/*Tukpen* council (*Thonji blu*). The selection of village head/ Gaon bura (*Thik-akhao*) is also influenced by the political leaders now-a-days. The Gaon bura (GB) is working as *Thik-akhao* and is heading the traditional council (*Blu*). As the Gaon Bura is a government appointed person hence the selection of the so called village head (*Thik-akhao*) also gets influenced by the person who comes to power through election system. In a traditional council (*Blu*) where members (*Jungme*) used to be from *Thongs* only whereas now members from *Chaos* can also represent such bodies.

If we go through the history of modern political system, in the Sherdukpen society, it was dominated by men only. From the beginning till date the representative in the state Assembly were from *Thongs* only such as P.K. Thongon, R.K. Khrime, D.K. Thongdok and presently T.N. Thongdok. The list of influential and prestigious persons, according to 1986 survey is as follows:

Table 6.10 Influential people from Rupa

Sl. No.	Name	Gender	Occupation
1.	Shri P.D. Thongon	Male	Village Headman No. 1, Cultivator, Businessman, Gram Panchayat Member
2.	Shri Chumbi Thongdok	Male	Village Headman No. 2, Cultivator, Gram Panchayat Member
3.	Shri R .D. Khrime	Male	Village Headman No. 3, Cultivator, Gram Panchayat Member
4.	Shri P. Mosobi	Male	Saw Mill Business
5.	Dr. P.K. Khrime	Male	Doctor
6.	Shri A.D. Thongdok	Male	Teacher Rupa High School
7.	Shri Wangchu Thongdok	Male	Contractor
8.	Mrs. Pema Chum Thungon	Female	Teacher Rupa Primary School

Source: Census of India 1981: Survey Report on Village Rupa.

With the introduction of Panchayat system, the women are getting opportunity to get involved in the modern political set up. The present ZPM is a woman from the Sherdukpen community. Though, the women are representing in good numbers as Gram sabha members but still they do not have the right to represent in the traditional council. The present young women consider it as a drawback. They also want to take part in the proceedings. Even if that is not possible they should be allowed to simply sit and see the proceedings. Even if women conducted meetings at the monastery ground (which happened rarely), they were scolded.[7]

Changes can be seen in occupations of the people within the society. With the coming up of new administrative set ups, the people are going for work in the government offices. Some become daily wage earners, some became contractors, some get involved in supply of vegetables, some are running shops, etc. there is an occupational shift though a good number of people are still engaged in agriculture. With the introduction of modern education system the people are sending their children to the schools.

According to the Table 6.11 the main occupation of males is agriculture while least are involved in other occupations. The number of female students is much higher than the number of male students among the *Thongs* in Rupa.

The Table 6.12 is showing that the people of Rupa are distributed in different occupational activities especially among the *Thong* males and females. The number of female students is more than the males as compared to *Chaos* of Rupa (for detail see Appendix B Table No. B–1).

Table 6.11 Class and clan wise occupational table combining three villages

Class	*Clan*	*Main Occupation*								*Subsidiary Occupation*								*Dependents*			
		Male				*Female*				*Male*				*Female*				*Students*		*Others*	
		A	*S*	*B*	*O*	*A*	*S*	*B*	*O*	*A*	*S*	*B*	*O*	*A*	*S*	*B*	*O*	*M*	*F*	*M*	*F*
T	THONGDOK	38	16	10	3	4	2	-	53	6	1	2	-	44	-	-	-	30	37	11	8
H	KHRIME	13	9	9	3	5	2	1	21	6	-	-	-	20	-	-	3	13	16	7	6
O N	THONGON	12	10	3	1	3	5	-	12	1	-	-	-	8	-	-	-	13	14	3	3
G	THONGCHI	22	6	5	1	4	4	-	29	7	-	-	-	29	-	-	-	18	27	4	2
	WANGJA	5	7	3	-		4	-	10	2	-	-	1	7	-	-	-	7	10	3	1
	MOSOBI	9	3	4	-	1	2	-	10	3	-	-	1	8	-	-	-	11	9	2	2
	KARMA	5	3	-	-	-	-	-	7	-	-	-	1	5	-	-	-	4	7	2	1
	YANGFAN	1	-	-	-	-	-	-	1	-	-	-	-	1	-	-	-	-	-	-	-
Total		**105**	**54**	**34**	**8**	**17**	**19**	**1**	**143**	**25**	**1**	**2**	**3**	**122**	-	-	**3**	**96**	**120**	**32**	**23**
C	MEGEJI	24	17	2	1	8	1	-	35	5	-	1	-	27	-	-	-	27	16	9	10
H A	DINGLA	18	7	-	2	-	-	-	19	-	-	1	-	19	-	-	-	19	11	2	3
O	SINCHAJI	7	6	-		2	-	-	7	-	-	-	-	5	-	-	-	8	9	1	-
	MIJIJI	3	4	2	1	2	-	-	5	2	-	-	2	5	-	-	-	7	10	1	-
Total		**52**	**34**	**4**	**4**	**12**	**1**	-	**66**	**7**	-	**2**	**2**	**56**	-	-	-	**61**	**46**	**13**	**13**

Source: Fieldwork 2010

Table 6.12 Class and clan wise occupational table for the Rupa village

Class	*Clan*	*Main Occupation*								*Subsidiary Occupation*								*Dependent*			
		Male				*Female*				*Male*				*Female*				*Students*		*Others*	
		A	*S*	*B*	*O*	*A*	*S*	*B*	*O*	*A*	*S*	*B*	*O*	*A*	*S*	*B*	*O*	*M*	*F*	*M*	*F*
T	THONGDOK	11	10	7	1	1	2	-	22	3	1	2	-	16	-	-	-	16	15	6	4
H	KHRIME	8	7	8	1	2	2	1	11	4	-	-	-	10	-	-	3	10	8	6	2
O N	THONGON	4	10	3	-	1	5	-	6	1	-	-	-	2	-	-	-	6	9	3	3
G	THONGCHI	2	1	1	-	1	1	-	3	1	-	-	-	2	-	-	-	1	5	1	1
	WANGJA	5	7	3	-		4	-	10	2	-	-	1	7	-	-	-	7	10	3	1
	MOSOBI	6	3	4	-	1	2	-	8	3	-	-	-	6	-	-	-	7	7	2	1
	KARMA	5	3	-	-	-	-	-	7	-	-	-	1	5	-	-	-	4	7	2	1
	YANGFAN	1	-	-	-	-	-	-	1	-	-	-	-	1	-	-	-	-	-	-	-
Total		**42**	**41**	**26**	**2**	**6**	**16**	**1**	**68**	**14**	**1**	**2**	**2**	**49**	-	-	**3**	**51**	**61**	**23**	**13**
C	MEGEJI	5	14	2	-	1	1	-	14	2	-	1	-	7	-	-	-	15	9	6	1
H	DINGLA	5	2		-	-	-	-	5	-	-	1	-	5	-	-	-	5	4	2	1
A	SINCHAJI	2	4		-	-	-	-	3	-	-	-	-	2	-	-	-	6	5	-	-
O	MIJIJI	1	4	1	-	2	-	-	3	1	-	-	-	3	-	-	-	3	8	-	-
Total		**13**	**24**	**3**	-	**3**	**1**	-	**25**	**3**	-	**2**	-	**17**	-	-	-	**29**	**26**	**8**	**2**

Source: Fieldwork 2010

Table 6.13 Class and clan wise occupational table for the Thongre village

Class	*Clan*	*Main Occupation*								*Subsidiary Occupation*								*Dependent*			
		Male				*Female*				*Male*				*Female*				*Students*		*Others*	
		A	*S*	*B*	*O*	*A*	*S*	*B*	*O*	*A*	*S*	*B*	*O*	*A*	*S*	*B*	*O*	*M*	*F*	*M*	*F*
THONG	THONGDOK	24	3	-	1	-	-	-	23	2	-	-	-	23	-	-	-	10	19	3	4
	KHRIME	5	2	1	2	3	-	-	10	2	-	-	-	10	-	-	-	3	8	1	4
	THONGCHI	10	-	-	1	-	-	-	11	-	-	-	-	11	-	-	-	6	5	1	-
	THONGON	5	-	-	-	-	-	-	4	-	-	-	-	4	-	-	-	5	5	-	-
Total		**44**	**5**	**1**	**4**	**3**	-	-	**48**	**4**	-	-	-	**48**	-	-	-	**24**	**37**	**5**	**8**
CHAO	MEGEJI	17	1	-	1	5	-	-	17	2	-	-	-	16	-	-	-	9	6	2	7
	SINCHAJI	2	-	-	-	2	-	-	1	-	-	-	-	1	-	-	-	1	3	-	-
Total		**19**	**1**	-	**1**	**7**	-	-	**18**	**2**	-	-	-	**17**	-	-	-	**10**	**9**	**2**	**7**

Source: Fieldwork 2010

Table 6.14 Class and clan wise occupational table for the Jigaon village

Class	*Clan*	*Main Occupation*								*Subsidiary Occupation*								*Dependent*			
		Male				*Female*				*Male*				*Female*				*Students*		*Others*	
		A	*S*	*B*	*O*	*A*	*S*	*B*	*O*	*A*	*S*	*B*	*O*	*A*	*S*	*B*	*O*	*M*	*F*	*M*	*F*
THONG	THONGCHI	10	5	4	-	3	3	-	15	6	-	-	-	16	-	-	-	13	17	2	1
	THONGDOK	3	3	3	1	3	-	-	8	1	-	-	-	5	-	-	-	4	3	2	-
	THONGON	3	-	-	1	2	-	-	2	-	-	-	-	2	-	-	-	2	-	-	-
	MOSOBI	3	-	-	-	-	-	-	2	-	-	-	1	2	-	-	-	4	2	1	1
Total		**19**	**8**	**7**	**2**	**8**	**3**	-	**27**	**7**	-	-	**1**	**25**	-	-	-	**23**	**22**	**5**	**2**
CHAO	SINCHAJI	3	2	-	-	-	-	-	3	-	-	-	-	2	-	-	-	1	1	1	-
	MEGEJI	2	2	-	-	2	-	-	4	1	-	-	-	4	-	-	-	3	1	1	2
	MIJIJI	2	-	1	1	-	-	-	2	1	-	-	2	2	-	-	-	4	2	1	-
	DINGLA	13	5	-	2	-	-	-	14	-	-	-	-	14	-	-	-	9	7	-	2
Total		**20**	**9**	**1**	**3**	**2**	-	-	**23**	**2**	-	-	**2**	**22**	-	-	-	**17**	**11**	**3**	**4**

Source: Fieldwork 2010

According to Table 6.13 the people of Thongre aremainly concentrated on agriculture for their economic occupation. Even in Thongre the number of *Thongs* females as students is higher than the males (for detail see Appendix B Table B–2).

According to Table 6.14 in Jigaon village the people are distributed in almost all the occupational activities. However, there is absence of *Chao* female involvement in business undertakings (for detail see Appendix B Table B–3).

Another source of income of the villagers is the contract schemes, such as construction of retaining walls, culverts, water tanks, and stairs, etc. given to them. In these kinds of contract schemes the villagers get involved in the work by themselves. The amount is divided as per individual involvement in the work. But the issue is that all the villagers are not benefited by these types of schemes as these are politicalised. The ruling party people are able to extract and enjoy its benefits.

Before the timber operation was banned most of the villagers especially of Jigaon were involved in it for their living. They used to extract huge benefits from the timber operations. But after it was banned by the Supreme Court the villagers had no option but to concentrate on agricultural activities again. Even in agricultural activities tremendous changes can be seen. Earlier maize was cultivated in huge quantity as it was the staple food. But after people came to know about the benefits that could be gained from cultivation of other agricultural products the villagers started cultivating other vegetables like cabbage and potato in huge quantities since early nineties, reducing quantity of maize production.

In agriculture the use of plough has decreased to a great extent. Some opt for ploughing and some do not. Instead, the use of hired labour is the new scenario which is coming up in the society. The labour, including both males and females are brought from the plains of the neighbouring state during the agricultural season for which they are paid monthly with the provisions of food and accommodation.

And now, after the introduction of tomato cultivation and its profit prospects almost all the cultivators are shifting their attention on tomato production. Cultivation of other agricultural products has been reduced to kitchen gardens only. Hybrid seeds are used for the tomato cultivation. The seeds are provided by the investors who come from the plains of Assam. The investors generally come to the village and take a person into confidence who would be responsible for taking in confidence the other families from the village for the production. Then these investors provide all the essential materials from seeds to fertilisers, insecticides and pesticides to the person whom they entrust from the village or they provide the stuffs according to the need of the land holder. However, these aids are not provided for free. Every record is maintained by the entrusted person, which would be adjusted later on during the harvesting of the product.

Plate 6.18 Trellis for tomato plants

Plate 6.19 Tomato plants

Plate 6.20 Man spraying fungicide

Plate 6.21 Man spraying fungicide wearing mask

Plate 6.22 Types of fungicide use in tomato cultivation

A person is entrusted by the investor as it is difficult for him, being an outsider to build up the villager's confidence. So it is the entrusted person's work to build up this confidence in the cultivators from the village. So at the village level it is the work of the entrusted person while the investors will deal with that entrusted person of the village. In return the entrusted person will get a share of one rupee per kg of tomato that he provides to the investor. In this way the villagers earn huge profits by marketing tomatoes which are supplied to different regions. The villagers are enjoying cultivating tomatoes with its profit margin as well as their savings from not going out to sell the products themselves. They are also aware of the fact that the fertility of soil is decreasing year to year as every year the amount of fertilisers need to be increased. Even with this knowledge they are not giving any serious thoughts to it as at present they are mainly concerned with the monetary benefits of cultivating this product.

Indulgence in hunting and fishing has decreased a lot as the meat is available in the market and as everybody is busy in his new economic activities. Hunting and fishing is done in leisure time only. Fishing is done mostly during picnic celebrations. Hunting has become a game for pleasure only, done mostly during the agriculture off season or when there is time for it.

Besides agriculture, floriculture is also initiated by two or three houses in Rupa, where they plant roses especially. But these plantations are not for large scale commercial purposes. It is only for decorative purpose of their houses.

Due to education and provision of health centre in the Rupa village the people hardly opt for traditional healing systems. The practise of such traditional healing has declined tremendously. If a person is not feeling well or fall ill they consult the doctor in the nearby health centre or simply go to the pharmacy and take medicines after consulting the pharmacist. The traditional healing system is almost getting extinct as the new generation opts for allopathic treatment. The treatment through modern medical system is not limited only to Rupa village. The nearby medical centers at Bomdila, the District Headquarter, and an Army Medical Center at Dahung, are also consulted according to the convenience. Those who can afford, search for better medical facilities in the country.

Education is also playing an important role in the transition of the society. It is the education that is giving better opportunity to rise in the modern society and to achieve a social status in the modern administrative system irrespective of the class differences within the society. Private schools are coming up in the locality. The concerned parents or those who can afford are sending their children to these private schools with the faith that their children will receive better education in these schools.

According to the Table 6.15 the *Thongs* have the highest number of persons who have completed their graduation and above. Most *Chaos* are found to have competed only the higher secondary level.

It is visible from the Table 6.16 that the people of Rupa are opting more for higher education. Good number of people have reached the higher secondary level (see Appendix C Table C–1).

According to the Table 6.17 the level of education of Thongre village is mostly upto secondary level in case of both the classes. The highest number is at the middle level (see Appendix C Table C–2).

In Jigaon the level of education shows a decreasing rate after the middle level. The highest number is at primary level (see Appendix C Table C–3).

The education is also bringing the change in the mind set of the society mainly within the present generation. The ideological concept of *Thong* and *Chao* is losing its grip from the minds of the younger generation. It is only a psychological set up which they have imbibed from their older generation. Sometimes conflict arises regarding the *Thongs* and *Chaos* issue. But in this conflict the whole class people do not get involved. It is the conflict between the parties or the households wherein tension arises. Economy of the household or person is another factor which breaks the notion of class within the society. But this notion of division arises in the mind set when a person or family of high class feels that they are being superseded by a particular person or family of a lower class.

Now-a-days no such class wise arrangement for sitting is done in any religious function or ceremony. Arrangement is done according to parental status like the grandfather group, father group at one side the grandmother

Table 6.15 Class and clanwise education status combining Rupa, Thongre and Jigaon

Class	*Clan*	*Non-Lit*		*Lower Primary*		*Primary*		*Middle*		*Secondary*		*Higher Secondary*		*Graduate and Above*	
		M	*F*	*M*	*F*	*M*	*F*	*M*	*F*	*M*	*F*	*M*	*F*	*M*	*F*
THONG	THONGDK	5	18	2	8	19	28	30	14	19	18	7	9	15	4
	KHRIME	3	12	1	3	8	10	12	8	10	5	8	8	10	3
	THONGON	3	6	4	3	12	5	8	9	3	3	4	3	8	7
	THONGCI	7	11	4	3	12	14	12	17	10	9	10	6	1	3
	MOSOBI	2	7	1	-	8	2	3	4	5	5	5	2	4	3
	WANGJA	3	4	-	-	4	2	3	6	7	6	-	2	5	5
	KARMA	1	2	-	1	3	2	3	3	3	3	3	1	1	1
	YANGFAN	1	1	-	-	-	-	-	-	-	-	-	-	-	-
Total		**25**	**61**	**12**	**18**	**66**	**63**	**71**	**61**	**57**	**49**	**37**	**31**	**44**	**26**
CHAO	MEGEJI	6	14	5	3	16	5	13	18	16	14	14	5	4	4
	DINGLA	2	8	5	1	17	9	9	10	6	4	5	2	1	-
	SINCHAJI	3	2	-	1	4	6	4	5	6	4	2	2	-	-
	MIJIJI	1	3	-	-	9	2	4	7	1	3	2	2	-	1
Total		**12**	**27**	**10**	**5**	**46**	**22**	**30**	**40**	**29**	**25**	**23**	**11**	**5**	**5**

Source: Fieldwork 2010

Table 6.16 Class and clanwise education status of Rupa village

Class	*Clan*	*Non-Lit*		*Lower Primary*		*Primary*		*Middle*		*Secondary*		*Higher Secondary*		*Graduate and Above*	
		M	*F*	*M*	*F*	*M*	*F*	*M*	*F*	*M*	*F*	*M*	*F*	*M*	*F*
THONG	THONGDOK	2	11	1	2	6	3	10	7	9	9	7	7	11	3
	KHRIME	3	8	1	2	3	4	6	4	7	3	7	4	9	3
	THONGON	2	3	3	3	5	4	3	3	2	1	3	3	8	7
	THONGCHI	-	-	-	1	1	2	2	4	1	2	1	-	-	1
	MOSOBI	1	5	1	-	4	2	2	2	5	4	4	2	4	3
	WANGJA	3	4	-	-	4	2	3	6	7	6	-	2	5	5
	KARMA	1	2	-	1	2	2	3	3	3	3	3	1	1	1
	YANGFAN	1	1	-	-	-	-	-	-	-	-	-	-	-	-
Total		**13**	**34**	**6**	**9**	**25**	**19**	**29**	**29**	**34**	**28**	**25**	**19**	**38**	**23**
CHAO	MEGEJI	3	3	4	3	5	3	4	8	9	3	10	3	3	3
	DINGLA	2	2	2	1	1	3	2	3	1	2	2	2	1	-
	SINCHAJI	2	-	-	-	3	2	2	4	3	2	1	2	-	-
	MIJIJI	-	3	-	-	3	-	3	5	1	3	2	1	-	1
Total		**7**	**8**	**6**	**4**	**12**	**8**	**11**	**20**	**14**	**10**	**15**	**8**	**4**	**4**

Source: Fieldwork 2010

Table 6.17 Class and clanwise education status of Thongre village

Class	*Clan*	*Non-Lit*		*Lower Primary*		*Primary*		*Middle*		*Secondary*		*Higher Secondary*		*Graduate and Above*	
		M	*F*	*M*	*F*	*M*	*F*	*M*	*F*	*M*	*F*	*M*	*F*	*M*	*F*
THONG	THONGDOK	2	4	-	6	8	17	17	7	9	8	-	1	1	1
	KHRIME	-	5	-	1	4	6	6	4	3	2	1	3	1	-
	THONGCHI	4	3	1	-	1	5	5	5	4	1	2	1	-	1
	THONGON	1	-	1	-	4	3	3	4	1	2	-	-	-	-
Total		**7**	**12**	**2**	**7**	**17**	**31**	**31**	**20**	**17**	**13**	**3**	**5**	**2**	**2**
CHAO	MEGEJI	3	9	-	-	10	1	7	8	6	10	3	1	-	1
	SINCHAJI	1	1	-	1	-	1	1	2	1	1	-	-	-	-
Total		**4**	**10**	**-**	**1**	**10**	**2**	**8**	**10**	**7**	**11**	**3**	**1**	**-**	**1**

Source: Fieldwork 2010

Table 6.18 Class and clanwise education table combining Jigaon village

Class	*Clan*	*Non-Lit*		*Lower Primary*		*Primary*		*Middle*		*Secondary*		*Higher Secondary*		*Graduate and Above*	
		M	*F*	*M*	*F*	*M*	*F*	*M*	*F*	*M*	*F*	*M*	*F*	*M*	*F*
THONG	THONGCHI	3	8	3	3	10	7	4	8	5	6	7	5	1	1
	THONGDOK	1	3	1	-	5	8	3	1	1	1	-	1	3	-
	THONGON	-	2	-	-	3	-	2	2	-	-	1	-	-	-
	MOSOBI	1	2	-	-	4	-	1	2	-	1	2	-	-	-
Total		**5**	**15**	**4**	**3**	**22**	**15**	**10**	**13**	**6**	**8**	**10**	**6**	**4**	**1**
CHAO	SINCHAJI	-	1	-	-	1	3	1	-	2	1	1	-	-	-
	MEGEJI	-	2	1	-	1	1	2	2	1	1	1	1	1	-
	MIJIJI	1	-	-	-	6	1	1	2	-	-	-	1	-	-
	DINGLA	1	6	3	-	6	6	7	7	5	2	3	-	-	-
Total		**2**	**9**	**4**	**-**	**14**	**11**	**11**	**11**	**8**	**4**	**5**	**2**	**1**	**-**

Source: Fieldwork 2010

and mother group on another side. The youths are involved in the work. Till mid-nineties during the Chokor festival the *Thongs* sat on the horse and the reins were held by the *Chaos* during the procession. Now this practise is not followed.

Women's Welfare Association Rupa

The Women's Welfare Association of Sherdukpen, was formed by Pema Chom Thongon and Yese Dema Thongdok. It was registered in the year 1988. The purpose of the association is to work for the upliftment of the women and also for the welfare of the society. Their biggest contribution is the opening of a primary school in the name of Tukpen School in the year 1989. After that there was no looking back. Under their guidance sixteen Self Help Groups (SHG) have been formed till date. In every work and programme conducted by the women's welfare association the SHGs are included so that they are not left behind and also learn something . From time to time they conduct health camps. An eye check-up camp was conducted in the year 2009. A training programme was conducted on Kiwi pickle making, which was sponsored by NABARD. The Women's Welfare Association tying up with the Army's women association of the area conducted a beautician course. Every year they conduct Aids Awareness Programme within the society. Selling of alcohol in the hotels was banned by the association. Besides these, the association also contributes donations for the following purposes:

1. To help the sick people who are unable to go for medical treatment.
2. For monastery renovation.
3. For the prize trophies for sports conducted on the Republic Day and Independence Day celebrations, etc.

Presently the association is actively, engaged in establishing a Rural Tourism Scheme at Shergaon village through the Department of Tourism.

All Shertukpen Youth Welfare Association (ASYWA)

The All Shertukpen Youth Welfare Association is a recent development in the Shedukpen society. The association got registered in the year 2003. The association was formed with the view to serve its members in particular and the Sherdukpen community as a whole. The society is purely voluntary and is formed with the following objectives according to their by-laws:

1. Bridging the divide.
2. Empowering women.
3. Social, economical and cultural consciousness with time.
4. Unity among the Sherdukpen people.

Plate 6.23 WWA office

Plate 6.24 Tukpen School

5. To create environment friendly society.
6. Educational awareness through association.
7. To raise standard of living of Sherdukpen people with cooperation.
8. To create awareness on health and hygiene.
9. To encourage child and women welfare schemes.
10. To fight against social evils and unethical judgments.
11. To help victims affected by natural calamities.
12. Campaign for handicapped children and old aged people.
13. Preservation of culture, custom and tradition.

Endnotes

1. Informant S.K. Khrime, aged 65.
2. The clan elders will be from both classes of attached clans. The clan elder in which the Yanlog is going to be introduced should be from the native. The converted members do not have this right as they are the converted one.
3. Informant K.T. Megeji, aged 31.
4. Informant R.K. Karma, aged 64.
5. Informant K.T. Megeji, aged 31.
6. Informant W.T. Thongdok, aged 72; D.K. Thongdok, aged 55.
7. Informant P.L. Thongon, aged 36.

7

Conclusion

The Sherdukpen society has undergone tremendous changes from the past till date. Regarding their history it is difficult to validate as it is based on oral tradition. No written documents or materials are available by which the history of origin can be ascertained. However, the character *Japtang* is prominent in the history of migration of Sherdukpen. It can be said that *Japtang* had migrated to the Sherdukpen region but whether he settled down in the area is still a question, as there are no historical evidences to supplement such stand. Singh (2000: p. 436) in his paper Buddhist Folk Tradition and the History of the Sherdukpens stated that "the tradition cannot be accepted". He (ibid.) also said "it is not a tradition of the Sherdukpen people. It is a Buddhist tradition developed to explain the origin of the tribe with the purpose of attracting them to the Buddhist faith". However, it is claimed that there are remains of house structures in some areas where *Japtang* is believed to have settled during his course of migration, such as in Lower Dzong and Salari. Even in Haimendorf's writings on early history of Sherdukpens he has cited that "Tribal history traces their origin to a Tibetan prince Gyaptang by name, who is believed to have migrated from Beyalung, the place of his birth, and to have established himself first at But[1], today's Monpa village, where the ruins of the fort are still to be seen" (*State Gazetteer*, 2010: p. 105). Hence the existence of this character is not debatable. Folktales tell that the higher class *Thongs* are the generation of *Japtang*. And the *Chaos* are the retinue who accompanied *Japtang* in the course of migration. It is difficult to ascertain whether the *Chaos* really accompanied *Japtang* in the course of migration from Tibet. In all the folktales *Japtang* is the descendant of the Tibetan King. But all the folktales hint that he left Tibet due to political reasons and there is no mention that from there itself he was accompanied by any retinue. Even when he entered into the Indian Territory, he was on a constant move for a better settlement place due to constant feud with the neighbouring tribes. Even on such constant moves, there is no mention of any retinue having accompanied him. It can be said, that he may have been all alone during those periods. Through a different story it has come to light that he had settled at different places such as Jerigaon and Khoina but from there also he had to move as disputes arose with the surrounding tribes. Two reasons were found from the folktales why he had to flee from these areas which are:

1. A man named Lhabe of Khoina was trying to avenge his son's death that got killed by *Japtang.*
2. He married a lower caste lady which was not acknowledged by the surrounding tribe.

Whatever may be the reason but it tells that he had to flee from there for his life. In this it can be concluded that he must have been alone by that time or may have been accompanied by two or three people. Chakravarty (1973: p. 6) cited that "The Sherdukpens say that the Tibetan king sent his third son to this area with the intention of checking the depredations of the war like Akas". But upon whom were these depredations inflicted? If it was on the so called Sherdukpens and the third son (who, most probably could be *Japtang*) was sent by the Tibetan king to check this disturbances then who are the actual Sherdukpens?

Whatever might be the reality there is a general acceptance that *Japtang* had three sons who were designated into three clans as *Thongdok*, *Thongon* and *Khrime* to preserve the sanctity of the class by inter-marriage within the class. Later on these three clans were sub-divided into different sub-clans or categories. Though they were divided into sub-clans but they used the parent clan name to denote themselves. For example, the *Thongdoks* are divided into five categories such as Thongdok Bukhao, Thongdok Chung, Karma, Yangfan and Khleng Thong. All these sub-divided categories can denote themselves as *Thongdok*. Within all these categories *Karma* and *Yangfan* are being used as a surname while the rest three are using *Thongdok* in denoting their surname. The *Thongchi* came from *Thongon* and *Mosobi* and *Wangja* came from *Khrime.* The sub-clans *Thongchi*, *Mosobi* and *Wangja* are also used in denoting the surname of the people. It can be said that *Karma*, *Yangfan*, *Thongchi*, *Mosobi* and *Wangja* are the sub-clans of the *Thongs*.

Intermarriage between these sub-clans is not permitted and is considered a taboo because all belong to same clan. The issue of *Khleng Thong* who used to write *Thongdok* is an undisputed one. There is a general acceptance that the *Khleng Thong* was a bastard (*duflo*) of *Japtang* conceived by a Chinggi woman during his (*Japtang*) course of migration. However a variation in the story regarding this issue came to light with the publication of The History of Migration of Shertukpen Monpa, by Urgen Jatso as:

1. *Thongdok*, *Thongon* and *Thongchi* are brothers but of different mothers while *Khrime* is the cousin who came from Bhutan and lived with *Japtang*.
2. *Japtang* initially belonged to *Wangja* clan as offered by his father. Later his grandfather renamed the clan to *Thongchi* clan. By that time *Japtang* already had two sons. One retained the *Wangja* clan name while the other went with *Thongchi* clan name. (see Chart 3.1)

In these above two mentioned statements according to Folktale No. 4 the first version of the story is closer to the story that goes within the society. However the only difference is that *Thongdok*, *Thongon* and *Khrime* were not the sons of *Japtang*. But Japtang himself was assigned with *Thongchi* clan by his grandfather and was the brother of *Thongdok* and *Thongon*. *Khrime* was the cousin of *Japtang* who came from Bhutan and stayed with him later.

Regarding the *Chaos* it is said that the *Dinglas* are the aborigines of *Jerigaon* and *Khoina*. *Sinchaji* also accompanied *Japtang* from Khoina. *Megejis* are the native people of the present Rupa and were under the rule of a king named *Tsewang Ganggan*. There is no sub-clan within the *Chaos*. About *Yanlogs* also there is a general acceptance that they were the later migrants who came from Bhutan and were provided a settlement place in lieu of their knowledge of smithery. At the initial stage they were provided settlement place only and were not counted as full fledged citizens or members of the society.

If this is the case then how did a person who migrated later gain a higher status in the society? It can be justified by the folktales which associate *Japtang*'s relations with the Tibetan king *Sangchen Gampo*. He was respected and accorded a higher status. As stated by Lucy Mair (1972: p. 58) "in many of the simpler societies, persons belonging to certain lines of descent are regarded as superior to others, are entitled to receive formal marks of respect, and may sometimes have other privileges."

The issue of stratification of the Sherdukpen society is neither on economic basis as in case of class nor is it on occupational basis as in case of caste. Here the division is based on the perception of the ruler and the subject, as in the case of Tibetan society which is divided into two main classes—the nobility and the commoner (Palakshappa, 1978: p. 73). As a ruler it is perceived that the economic condition of the ruler and its generation is better than that of the subject. But the truth is that the economic condition within the society is based on the caliber and capabilities of a person. So the person who works hard earns more and has better economic status. "*Thongs* were considered superior in status by *Chaos* only".[2] *Thong* literally means king whereas it is difficult to ascertain the literal meaning of *Chaos*. Everyone has a different connotation on this term such that the *Chaos* are ministers, warriors, body guards, friends or subjects. Because of these connotations the *Thongs* are superior in status to the *Chaos*.

The *Thongs* were economically well off as they were the descendents of king's family who used to collect tax from the plains of Assam i.e. *Posa*. So they were more than self sufficient. They could afford the expenditure for calling people for their help and in return could provide for food and drinks. But for the *Chaos* who were not as well off economically as the *Thongs* this was not possible. Their only source of livelihood was agriculture which was done for self sufficiency.

Agriculture is the main economic activity in almost all the Sherdukpen villages, except for Rupa which is the circle head quarters. A shift from the traditional mode of economic activity, in Rupa, can be drawn to a great extent. In Rupa, almost fifty percent of the male population is into government services. But the number of people engaged in other economic activities like government service and business which include contractual works has been found in all the three villages where the fieldwork had been conducted. This is not the case for males alone; the females are also engaged in the government service and business. It is found that the occupational activities are not gender biased according to the table. Both males and females are engaged in different economic occupations, only that the number of people participating in various economic activities may vary.

In economic activities, it is not found that a definite economic activity or occupations are attached to the class or clan within the society. All the people are engaged in different occupations irrespective of class. The *Chaos* traditionally are said to go and help in their respective *Thong*'s field but not vice-versa. According to this, it can be said that the *Chaos* were engaged as manual labour. But it was not in strict sense as the *Thongs* also engaged in the work together with the *Chaos*. This was a privilege received by the *Thongs* from their *Chaos*. This is the reason that the *Thongs* could cultivate large portion of areas thus producing more in comparison to the *Chaos*. Though this was the truth of the past, now manual labourers are engaged by both the sections of the society. However, the number of labourers varies with the economic condition or we can say with the area of cultivation. Hence, the practice of the *Chaos* working in the *Thong*'s field does not prevail anymore. Now everyone is busy with their respective works to gain comforts and to provide education for their children. This is due to the awareness of the money concept and the essence of money which is getting deep rooted within the mindset of the people of the society.

The traditional agriculture practice has been replaced by modern agricultural methods to compete in the market with a motive to earn good returns of profit. Changes also came in plantation of products and its quantity. Now many people have engaged themselves in cultivation of tomatoes which carries prospects of huge profits. The products grown in the field keep on changing according to the market demand and profit. Introduction of hired labour force brought from outside is a common practice as cultivating of tomatoes is a tedious job. People have to take utmost care of the plants because even if a single plant is infected the whole field gets infected. Cultivators are happy in their earnings but no one is paying any attention towards the hazardous effects of using excess chemicals in fields.

The land can be the criterion which differentiates the sections of the society but cannot be taken for generalisation. It is because there are certain *Thong* families who have lesser land property than some *Chao* families or equivalent to theirs. The other reason is that the land is not controlled by the higher section of the society. As discussed in the previous chapters that the land is divided as individual land, clan land and territorial land, any individual irrespective of the class strata has the right to occupy land for cultivation within the territory. The average number of plots, in general, according to the data collected, combining the three villages i.e., Rupa, Thongre and Jigaon, is four for the *Thongs* and two for the *Chaos*.

However, the number of plots of land varies within the classes but most of the families occupying land fall under the category of 1–5 plots (Table 4.21). But if we go individually, it is found that some *Thong* families have lesser number of plots of land in comparison to some *Chao families* (see Appendix-A). It is also found that no person in the society is landless though they may not have cultivable plot but the plot where the house is built is their own sometimes even with a space for gardening. Here the question of landlessness is in relation to economy that relates to the question of having agricultural land or not, though the family may have domestic land. This happens because of the following reasons:

1. The land inherited gets fragmented due to redistribution among the sons.
2. The people are not occupying new cultivable land as they have to occupy the land which will be far from domestic areas as all the lands in and around the domestic areas are already occupied.

3. The reason for the people not occupying more land for themselves may be because there are lands available for cultivation around the domestic areas are not being cultivated by the owners, on which they could cultivate by making some payments.

From the material life it is difficult to depict the stratification. No division is found in terms of material culture. It is said that the *Thongs* used to construct stone houses. The criteria of stratification according to this was not found during the fieldwork as even the *Thongs* live in the types of houses which are considered to belong to the *Chaos*. It can be argued here that the houses were constructed according to the economic conditions of the people. In construction of a stone house large number of labourers were needed to be employed which required much more expenditure. So those who had the capacity to spend more constructed stone houses (*Dcha yam*), those who had lesser to spend constructed the house made of stone, bamboo and wood (*Pamthing yam*) and those who couldn't afford even that much constructed matted bamboo houses (*Tamplayam*). *Tamplayam* have not been seen during the fieldwork. It shows that the economic conditions of the people have gone a little higher. Regarding the stone house also some broken remains are found in Rupa. *Panthing yam* still can be traced in every village with slight modifications. The roofs have been replaced by tin sheets and few have attached an additional room which is used as the kitchen. People of both the sections and classes were found staying in this kind of houses.

Now with the advancement in the society even the so-called traditional house is disappearing and the modern houses made of bricks and cements are coming up. Here also it is seen that the families who are economically well off construct big reinforced cement concrete (RCC) houses. The houses are equipped with modern luxury items and are architecturally structured. So it is difficult to draw a line of division according to the house types which fits the notion of division that persists in the society.

Even in terms of the dresses and ornaments it is not possible to state that a particular person(s) belongs to the *Thongs* or *Chaos* class. As both the *Thongs* and *Chaos*, use same dress pattern in their day to day life. However, during the *Khiksaba* festival the difference of the classes can be traced according to the clothes one wears. Here it is only in relation to males as the female dresses are same for both the classes. The *Chaos* dress and ornaments are similar to that of their neighboring tribe such as Aka, Bugun, Miji, and Sartang tribes. Reference regarding the inhabitant of *Chaos* in Jerigaon and Khoina can be found in the writing of Sharma (1960: p. 7) also.

A conclusion can be drawn that *Japtang* was accompanied by *Chaos* from here itself but not from Tibet. It can also be concluded that *Thong*'s forefather *Japtang* had married a girl from this area so she follows the same pattern. Even in the use of ornaments there is no taboo hence both the classes have the freedom in wearing the ornaments, if they have the capacity to purchase them. But as the beads or ornaments do not play very important role in the society hence its importance or use is decreasing. In the phase of rapid growth of consumerism, the Sherdukpens are becoming more inclined towards modern market ornaments rather than the traditional varieties.

The social set up which shows the picture of stratification has also ceased to work in that manner. As said, earlier a practise was followed wherein while talking to a *Thong*, a *Chao* did not speak to him having eye to eye contact and maintained a low voice, which is however no longer present in the modern society. In social gatherings also the *Thongs* and *Chaos* are not provided with separate places to sit. Everyone takes part and enjoys the occasions and inter-dine together in the same manner. The taking of the horse rein by the respective *Chaos* for the *Thongs* during their horse ride is not practised anymore. In terms of marriage also, the frequency of inter marriages have shown an increasing rate. In terms of inter tribe marriages the role of mediator (*Achung Jring*) is absent. Other than this, the society accepts women as part of the class where she gets married and is given the same privilege.

In the traditional political system only members from the *Thong* clan represented earlier. This has to be seen through the relationship of the clans. As each clan of *Chaos* is attached with a clan of *Thongs*, a representative was selected from the *Thong* being from the ruler family. And those *Chaos* with their *Thongs* lived in good faith that they (*Thongs*) would represent them (*Chaos*) in the political arena. In the present day political scenario, though traditional political system is still headed by the *Thongs* but members are included from both the classes. The fine or penalties are still imposed by the village council, only that the amount has been raised accordingly. However, the *Kachin* system is still maintained according to the tradition of the society where representative of each clan works in the name of their clan for the society for three years. In the modern political system also all the legislative members who came till date are from Thong clans. It is only in the Panchayat that the *Chaos* are also given a place. Through this one can analyse that the society is still ruled by the *Thong*, be it in the traditional council or in the legislative assembly.

No ceremony, from birth to death, is different among the different classes of people. The only difference that can be traced in the marriage and death ceremony is that during the marriage ritual it is the sister (*mring*) from the attached *Chao* clan who leads the people to receive the bride for a *Thong* from her house. It is to be noted that this does not happen in marriage by capture. However, great changes have been found in the marriage system, such as, in marriage by capture. It is compulsory for a girl to return to her house after three nights which however is not practised now. The girl is not sent back as there is an insecure feeling that the girl may not return after that. These days the youth are opting for love marriage which is not a traditional form of marriage. Whatever may be the form of marriage; the couple is accepted and considered to be husband and wife by the society.

The society practises class endogamy, class exogamy and tribe exogamy. The society is crossing the barriers of class endogamy. Though it is so, but according to the Table 5.2 it is found that Rupa, as an urban area, class endogamy in marriage is given preference. However, the percentage of tribe exogamy has shown a higher rate in comparison to Thongre and Jigaon.

In negotiation marriage, the girl is set off with whatever available products, from the market, by the bride's side depending upon the capacity of the bride's family. This is becoming common within the society as the parents want to send their daughters in marriage with great enthusiasm. During a discussion the general secretary of Women's Welfare Association of Sherdukpen, Rupa giving her personal view, said that she was not in favour of this kind of marriage, where the daughter is set off with expensive gifts, because it looks more like dowry system kind of marriage.

The disposal systems have gone through various stages. In the past the dead bodies were buried in caves (*bo-log*) where the *Thongs* were kept on the upper portions while the *Chaos* in lower. Later when the disposal system changed the *Thongs* were cremated while the *Chaos* were buried. Now the cremation system is open to all according to the religious text. However, one significant cultural practice that still exists is that the touching and carrying of dead body is not done by the *Thongs*. The last rites of the death ceremony for the *Thong* are still performed by the *Chaos*.

In religious life, the Sherdukpens consider themselves as Buddhist and follow the lunar calendar. Even though they are Buddhist by religion but they also maintain the traditional religion by still celebrating the *Khiksaba* festival. This is the festival where every clan of the society participates equally.

In relation to education also it is found that many are pursuing higher studies especially among the *Thongs*. In term of education Rupa is more advanced than Thongre and Jigaon. The reason could be that Rupa, being an urban area the people have the knowledge regarding education and are giving it importance. On comparing the education table of the three villages it is found that the Jigaon people are not giving much importance to education. Though, they are enrolling in schools but mostly study upto primary level.

It can be concluded at least that the notion of stratification is not overtly visible within the society. This is due to the educational system and the market which provides various opportunities to a person irrespective of class background. Though the division from the point of materials life or economic life or religious life cannot be traced but still the notion of classes exist within the society. A *Chao* person may economically go ahead in comparison to a *Thong* and may avail all the modern facilities and comforts like a *Thong*. But in strata within the society the *Chao* will remain a *Chao* and the *Thong* will remain a *Thong*. Discrimination obviously remains but not as much as it was before their exposure to modernity and administrative intervention in post colonial phase.

The picture of stratification exists only in ideological state. The economic activity is open for all. There is no discrimination in land acquisition but the number of plots occupied within the society is in some cases higher among the *Thongs* in comparison to the *Chaos*. Equal penalty or punishment is imposed even to a *Thong* if he is found guilty. By these we can say that the society has transformed a lot and whether this transformation is going to cease here or it will generate another reformed structure within the society remains a question. As Sharma (2010: 34) cited "there is always a striving for equality, and in this process, at times, new forms of inequality may also emerge along with disappearance/weakening of the persisting inequalities".

Endnotes

1. But is a present day Jerigaon inhabited by Sartang tribe, on the way to Nafra.
2. R.K. Thongdok, aged 35.

Appendix-A

Table No. A-1 Familywise possession of land of Rupa village

Sl. No	*Name of family Head*	*Number of plots*
1	Pema Norbu megeji	3
2	Sonam Dorjee Thongchi	3
3	Dorjee Khandu Dingla	2
4	Pema Norbu Thongdok	15
5	Dor Chom Khrime	2
6	Tsering Dorjee Megeji	2
7	Prem Norbu Megeji	2
8	Sang Norbu Mosobi	8
9	Rinchin Dorjee Wangja	3
10	Tenzin Wangja	7
11	Sang Khandu Mosobi	2
12	Rinchin Khandu Khrime	13
13	Sange Lhamu Megeji	1
14	Chom Khrime	2
15	Pema Dorjee Megeji	3
16	Tsering Dorjee Megeji	3
17	Prem Norbu Thongdok	1
18	Bongpu Dorjee Dingla	2
19	Phunchu Wangja	1
20	Kesang Dorjee Dingla	2
21	Dorjee Tsewang Megeji	5 (Joint land)
22	Rinchin Norbu Mosobi	6
23	Tsering Dema Megeji	No cultivable land
24	Tsewang Dorjee Karma	2
25	Dorjee Khandu Megeji	4
26	Don Megeji	3
27	Tsering Norbu Sinchaji	1
28	Wangdi Sinchaji	2

Sl. No	*Name of family Head*	*Number of plots*
29	Kesang Dorjee Thongdok	3
30	Dorjee Khandu Thongdok	3
31	Khandu Thongon	3
32	Sang Dorjee Sinchaji	2
33	Nima Dondu Mijiji	3
34	Dorjee Khandu Sinchaji	3
35	Pema Khandu Dingla	2
36	Asa Mijiji	1
37	Passang Tsering Dingla	1
38	Rinchin Dorjee Megeji	2
39	Dorjee Khandu Wangja	2
40	Norbu Mosobi	No cultivable land
41	Dor Chom Khrime	6
42	Sange Tsering Karma	1
43	Norbu Thongdok	5
44	Pem Dorjee Khrime	1
45	Rinchin Norbu Thongdok	1
46	Passang Khrime	4
47	Rinchin Dotjee Megeji	2
48	Rinchin Dorjee Khrime	20
49	Pema Dorjee Mosobi	1
50	Dorjee Wangdi Karma	3
51	Dorjee Karma	2
52	Tanchom Thongdok	7
53	Rinchin Dorjee Thongdok	11
54	Rinchin Dorjee Mosobi	1
55	Gese Karma	1
56	Sange Thongdok	3
57	Tsering Dorjee Khrime	3
58	Sang Tsering Khrime	6
59	Wangchu Thongdok	15
60	Phurpa Karma	2
61	Sang Khandu Khrime	21
62	Dipu Thongchi	5
63	Rinchin Dorjee Thongon	23

Sl. No	*Name of family Head*	*Number of plots*
64	Tenzin Gombu Khrime	10
65	Dorjee Khandu Thongdok	8
66	Dorjee Khandu Thongdok	4
67	Sang Khandu Mosobi	12
68	Nima Thongchi	5
69	Nana Khrime	5
70	Ashy Dorjee Thongdok	24
71	Namgey Wangmu Thongon	5
72	Sangya Wangja	2
73	Rinchin Dorjee Mosobi	3
74	Rinchin Dorjee Yangfan	4
75	Rinchin Khandu Karma	6
76	Rinchin Dorjee Thongdok	5
77	Kesang Norbu Thongdok	3
78	Netan Dorjee Thongdok	5
79	Pem Norbu Mijiji	2
80	Sang Norbu Thongchi	2
81	Dorjee Khandu Thongdok	24
82	Yese Dondu Thongon	7
83	Tsering Mijiji	2
84	Sang Khandu Thongon	3
85	Dorjee Khandu Thongon	3
86	Pem Chom Thongon	15
87	Dorjee Khandu Mosobi	2
88	Dorjee Khandu Khrime	11
89	Rinchin Dorjee Wangja	5
90	Pema Dorjee Wangja	7
91	Sange tashi Meggeji	1
92	Pem Dorjee Thongdok	3
93	Rinchin Dorjee Thongdok	2
94	Dorjee Khandu Megeji	No cultivable land
95	Dorjee Mijiji	2
96	Dothar Khrime	7
97	Dorjee Khandu Mosobi	1

Source: Fieldwork 2010

Table No. A-2 Familywise possession of land of Thongre village

Sl. No	*Name of family Head*	*Number of plots*
1	Tsering Thongdok	2
2	Dorjee Khandu Sinchaji	5
3	Kesang Dema Khrime	3
4	Dorjee Khandu Thongdok	2
5	Sang Khandu Khrime	4
6	Netan Thongdok	2
7	Leiki Khandu Thongchi	2
8	Wangchu Megeji	2
9	Rinchin Khandu Thongdok	7 (Joint land)
10	Tsering Norbu Thongdok	5
11	Rinchin Thongdok	3
12	Rinchin Norbu Thongchi	4
13	Sang Norbu Thongdok	4
14	Pema Khandu Megeji	4
15	Pema Norbu Megeji	7
16	Pema Khandu Megeji	3
17	Dorjee Khandu Megeji	3
18	Sang Khandu Megeji	3
19	Rinchin Jacho Megeji	1
20	Dorjee khandu thongdok	2
21	Topgey Thongdok	2
22	Dorjee Khandu Megeji	Cultivate on other's land
23	Rinchin Dorjee Khrime	4
24	Nima Thongchi	4
25	Pema Khandu Thongon	6
26	Dorjee Khandu Thongon	3
27	Sang Tsering Megeji	8
28	Chumbi Thongchi	3
29	Pema Tashi Megeji	3
30	Pema Ledo Megeji	3
31	Rinchin Khandu Megeji	7 Joint land
32	Chumbi Thongdok	5
33	Rinchin Khandu Khrime	1
34	Pema Norbu Thongdok	2
35	Dondu Thongon	1

Sl. No	Name of family Head	Number of plots
36	Netan Dorjee Thongchi	2
37	Dorjee Thongon	4
38	Dorjee khandu Thongdok	2
39	Chezom Dema Khrime	3
40	Rinchin Dorjee Thongchi	3
41	Sonam Phunchu Khrime	3
42	Khandu Thongdok	3
43	Khandu Thongdok	2
44	Tsering Norbu Sinchaji	1
45	Rinchin Norbu Khrime	3
46	Rinchin Norbu Megeji	2
47	Gombu Thongdok	2
48	Pema Norbu Thongdok	6
49	Sang Tsering Thongdok	3
50	Topgey Megeji	3
51	Jomu Wangmu Khrime	3
52	Pema Khandu Thongchi	5
53	Karma Jacho Khrime	3
54	Rinchin Dorjee Thongdok	3
55	Pema Wangdi Thongdok	2
56	Chumbi Megeji	2

Source: Fieldwork 2010

Table No. A-3 Familywise possession of land of Jigaon village

Sl. No	Name of family Head	Number of plots
1	Wangmu Thongchi	2
2	Tsering Norbu Sinchaji	4
3	Dorjee Khandu Thongchi	4
4	Phurpa Dorjee Megeji	2
5	Tsering Jangmu Thongchi	2
6	Wangmu Megeji	1
7	Sange Khandu Mosobi	1
8	Sange Tsering Mijiji	1
9	Dorjee Phunchu Thongchi	1
10	Pema Dorjee Dingla	1

Sl. No	Name of family Head	Number of plots
11	Sang Tsering Dingla	1
12	Sang Norbu Dingla	Cultivate on other's land
13	Kesand Tsering Dingla	1
14	Dorjee Yudon Dingla	1
15	Pema Yudon Thongon	2
16	Sange Tsering Mosobi	5
17	Dorjee Dema Thongchi	3
18	Sange Dorjee Thongchi	1
19	Rinchin Phunchu Thongchi	2
20	Leiki Khandu Dingla	1
21	Tenzing Tsering Dingla	2
22	Rinchin Norbu Dingla	Cultivate on other's land
23	Nima Dondu Thongdok	2
24	Tsering Chom Thongdok	2
25	Dorjee Khandu Thongchi	2
26	Pema Dema Megeji	2
27	Netan Dorjee Dingla	1
28	Netan Dorjee Thongdok	1
29	Namje Dema Dingla	1
30	Rinchin Dorjee Thongdok	5
31	Tenzin Thongon	3
32	Sange Tsering Mijiji	2
33	Rinchin Dorjee Dingla	2
34	Dorjee Dema Sinchaji	1
35	Rinchin Khandu Thongchi	2
36	Phurpa Tsering Thongchi	2
37	Sang Chewang Dingla	2
38	Pema Dorjee Thongchi	4
39	Daswa Tsering Thongdok	3
40	Pema Dorjee Thongdok	Cultivate on other's land
41	Pem Norbu Thongchi	2
42	Dorjee Thongchi	2

Sl. No	*Name of family Head*	*Number of plots*
43	Sange Tsering Thongchi	2
44	Yese Dorjee Thongchi	2
45	Pema Khandu Thongchi	4
46	Tenzin Dingla	3
47	Pema Dorjee Sinchaji	1
48	Dorjee lhandu Mijiji	1
49	Dojee Tsewang Dingla	1
50	Lenga Dema Thongdok	1
51	Dorjee Buti Mosobi	2
52	Rinchin Wangdi Thongdok	2

Source: Fieldwork 2010

Appendix-B

Table No. B-1 Clan and age wise occupation for Rupa village

Clan	Age	Main Occupation								Subsidiary Occupation								Dependent			
		Male				Female				Male				Female				Student		Others	
		A	S	B	O	A	S	B	O	A	S	B	O	A	S	B	O	M	F	M	F
THONGDOK	0-5																	1	2	4	3
	6-10																	3	2		
	11-15																	4	4		
	16-20								1					1				3	6		
	21-25	1		1		1			3					3				3	1	2	1
	26-30	3	2	1					3			2		2				1			
	31-35	1	1				1											1			
	36-40		2	1					2	1				2							
	41-45	2		1			1		3		1			2							
	46-50	1	2	1					2	2				2							
	51-55		1	1					3					2							
	56-60		1						2					2							
	61+	3	1	1	1				3												
	Total	**11**	**10**	**7**	**1**	**1**	**2**		**22**	**3**	**1**	**2**		**16**				**16**	**15**	**6**	**4**
KHRIME	0-5																	1	2	3	
	6-10																	2	1		
	11-15																	3	1		
	16-20	3																1	3		1
	21-25		1						1					1				3	1	1	1
	26-30	2	3	1					2					2							
	31-35	1		2					1	1				1							
	36-40		1	1		1	2			1							2				
	41-45		1	1		1			1					1							
	46-50	1	1					1	2					3							
	51-55			2					2	2				1			1				
	56-60								1												
	61+	1		1	1				1					1						2	

Clan	Age	Main Occupation								Subsidiary Occupation								Dependent			
		Male				Female				Male				Female				Student		Others	
		A	S	B	O	A	S	B	O	A	S	B	O	A	S	B	O	M	F	M	F
	Total	**8**	**7**	**8**	**1**	**2**	**2**	**1**	**11**	**4**				**10**			**3**	**10**	**8**	**6**	**2**
THONGON	0-5																	1	1	1	
	6-10																	4	4		
	11-15																		2		
	16-20																		1		
	21-25		2			1	1											1		1	2
	26-30		3				1		3					2					1	1	
	31-35	2	2	1			2														
	36-40	1		1			1			1											
	41-45		2																		
	46-50																				
	51-55								1												
	56-60		1																		
	61+	1		1					2												1
	Total	**4**	**10**	**3**		**1**	**5**		**6**	**1**				**2**				**6**	**9**	**3**	**3**
THONGCHI	0-5																		1	1	1
	6-10																				
	11-15																		3		
	16-20																	1			
	21-25								1										1		
	26-30		1			1															
	31-35	1							1					1							
	36-40																				
	41-45																				
	46-50	1							1					1							
	51-55						1														
	56-60			1						1											
	61+																				
	Total	**2**	**1**	**1**		**1**	**1**		**3**	**1**				**2**				**1**	**5**	**1**	**1**

Clan	Age	Main Occupation								Subsidiary Occupation								Dependent			
		Male				Female				Male				Female				Student		Others	
		A	S	B	O	A	S	B	O	A	S	B	O	A	S	B	O	M	F	M	F
WANGJA	0-5																			3	
	6-10																	4	1		
	11-15																	3	4		
	16-20																		4		
	21-25	1							3					1					1		
	26-30	1	3	2			3			1											
	31-35		1						2					1							
	36-40						1		1					1							
	41-45	1	1										1								
	46-50	1							1					1							
	51-55		1	1					3	1				3							
	56-60	1	1																		
	61+																				1
Total		**5**	**7**	**3**			**4**		**10**	**2**			**1**	**7**				**7**	**10**	**3**	**1**
MOSOBI	0-5																			1	1
	6-10																	2	2		
	11-15																	1	1		
	16-20																	2	4		
	21-25			1			1			1								1		1	
	26-30	1		1					1									1			
	31-35		1	1					2	1				1							
	36-40	1																			
	41-45	1					1		1					1							
	46-50		2						1					1							
	51-55			1					2	1				2							
	56-60	1							1					1							
	61+	2				1															
Total		**6**	**3**	**4**		**1**	**2**		**8**	**3**				**6**				**7**	**7**	**2**	**1**

Clan	*Age*	*Main Occupation*								*Subsidiary Occupation*								*Dependent*			
		Male				*Female*				*Male*				*Female*				*Student*		*Others*	
		A	*S*	*B*	*O*	*A*	*S*	*B*	*O*	*A*	*S*	*B*	*O*	*A*	*S*	*B*	*O*	*M*	*F*	*M*	*F*
	0-5																		1	1	1
	6-10																	1	2		
	11-15																	1	2		
KARMA	16-20																	2	2	1	
	21-25																				
	26-30	1	1						1					1							
	31-35		1						2												
	36-40	2							2					2							
	41-45		1																		
	46-50								1					1							
	51-55	1							1				1	1							
	56-60																				
	61+	1																			
Total		**5**	**3**						**7**				**1**	**5**				**4**	**7**	**2**	**1**
	0-5																				
	6-10																				
	11-15																				
YANGFAN	16-20																				
	21-25																				
	26-30																				
	31-35																				
	36-40																				
	41-45																				
	46-50																				
	51-55	1							1					1							
	56-60																				
	61+																				
Total		**1**							**1**					**1**							

Clan	*Age*	*Main Occupation*								*Subsidiary Occupation*								*Dependent*			
		Male				*Female*				*Male*				*Female*				*Student*		*Others*	
		A	*S*	*B*	*O*	*A*	*S*	*B*	*O*	*A*	*S*	*B*	*O*	*A*	*S*	*B*	*O*	*M*	*F*	*M*	*F*
	0-5																	4	2	3	
	6-10																	2	2		
	11-15																	4	1		
	16-20																	4	1		
MEGEJI	21-25	2	2						2					2				1	3	1	
	26-30		1						5					2						1	
	31-35		2	1					1												
	36-40	3	3				1		3			1		2							
	41-45		1						1												
	46-50		1																		
	51-55		2			1			1					1							
	56-60		1	1						2											
	61+		1						1											1	1
Total		**5**	**14**	**2**		**1**	**1**		**14**	**2**		**1**		**7**				**15**	**9**	**6**	**1**
	0-5																	1		1	
	6-10																	1	3		
	11-15																				
	16-20																	2	1		
DINGLA	21-25	1	1						1					1				1			
	26-30	2							2			1		2							
	31-35																				
	36-40		1																		
	41-45								1					1							
	46-50								1					1							
	51-55	2																			
	56-60																				
	61+																			1	1
Total		**5**	**2**						**5**			**1**		**5**				**5**	**4**	**2**	**1**

Clan	*Age*	*Main Occupation*								*Subsidiary Occupation*								*Dependent*			
		Male				*Female*				*Male*				*Female*				*Student*		*Others*	
		A	*S*	*B*	*O*	*A*	*S*	*B*	*O*	*A*	*S*	*B*	*O*	*A*	*S*	*B*	*O*	*M*	*F*	*M*	*F*
SINCHAJI	0-5																				
	6-10																	3	1		
	11-15																	2	1		
	16-20																	1	3		
	21-25																				
	26-30								2					2							
	31-35								1												
	36-40		4																		
	41-45	1																			
	46-50																				
	51-55																				
	56-60																				
	61+	1																			
	Total	**2**	**4**						**3**					**2**				**6**	**5**		
MIJIJI	0-5																				
	6-10																	1			
	11-15																	1	1		
	16-20																	1	5		
	21-25		1			1													2		
	26-30			1																	
	31-35																				
	36-40		1						1	1				1							
	41-45		1			1			1					1							
	46-50		1																		
	51-55	1							1					1							
	56-60																				
	61+																				
	Total	**1**	**4**	**1**		**2**			**3**	**1**				**3**				**3**	**8**		

Source: Fieldwork 2010

Table No. B-2 Clan and age wise occupation for Thongre village

Clan	*Age*	*Main Occupation*								*Subsidiary Occupation*								*Dependent*			
		Male				*Female*				*Male*				*Female*				*Student*		*Others*	
		A	*S*	*B*	*O*	*A*	*S*	*B*	*O*	*A*	*S*	*B*	*O*	*A*	*S*	*B*	*O*	*M*	*F*	*M*	*F*
THONGDOK	0-5																		5	2	3
	6-10																	2	9	1	1
	11-15																	3	3		
	16-20	1																5	2		
	21-25	2							4					4							
	26-30	5	2						8	1				8							
	31-35	5							1					1							
	36-40	1			1				3	1				3							
	41-45	3	1						1					1							
	46-50	1							2					2							
	51-55	2																			
	56-60	2							1					1							
	61+	2							3					3							
	Total	**24**	**3**		**1**				**23**	**2**				**23**				**10**	**19**	**3**	**4**
KHRIME	0-5																		1	1	1
	6-10																		3		
	11-15																	2	3		
	16-20				1	2													1		
	21-25		1						3					3				1			
	26-30								1					1							
	31-35	4							2					2							
	36-40				1				2	1				2							
	41-45	1		1						1											
	46-50								2					2							
	51-55		1			1															1
	56-60																				2
	61+																				
	Total	**5**	**2**	**1**	**2**	**3**			**10**	**2**				**10**				**3**	**8**	**1**	**4**

Clan	*Age*	*Main Occupation*								*Subsidiary Occupation*								*Dependent*			
		Male				*Female*				*Male*				*Female*				*Student*		*Others*	
		A	*S*	*B*	*O*	*A*	*S*	*B*	*O*	*A*	*S*	*B*	*O*	*A*	*S*	*B*	*O*	*M*	*F*	*M*	*F*
	0-5																	1		1	
	6-10																		2		
T	11-15																	1	1		
H O	16-20	1							1					1				3	1		
N	21-25	1			1				1					1				1	1		
G C	26-30	2							4					4							
H	31-35	2																			
I	36-40																				
	41-45								1					1							
	46-50								1					1							
	51-55	2							1					1							
	56-60	1							1					1							
	61+	1							1					1							
Total		**10**			**1**				**11**					**11**				**6**	**5**	**1**	
	0-5																	1			
T	6-10																	2			
H	11-15																	1	2		
O N	16-20																	1	3		
G	21-25	1																			
O N	26-30	1							1					1							
	31-35																				
	36-40								1					1							
	41-45								2					2							
	46-50	1																			
	51-55	1																			
	56-60																				
	61+	1																			
Total		**5**							**4**					**4**				**5**	**5**		

Clan	Age	Main Occupation								Subsidiary Occupation								Dependent			
		Male				Female				Male				Female				Student		Others	
		A	S	B	O	A	S	B	O	A	S	B	O	A	S	B	O	M	F	M	F
MEGEJI	0-5																		1		5
	6-10																	2			
	11-15																	4	1		
	16-20	2				1			2					2				3	4		
	21-25	2				2			3					3							
	26-30	2							1					1							
	31-35	4							3					3							
	36-40	2	1		1	1			3	2				3							
	41-45	1				1															
	46-50								1					1							
	51-55	1							1					1							
	56-60	1							1					1							
	61+	2							2					1						2	2
	Total	**17**	**1**		**1**	**5**			**17**	**2**				**16**				**9**	**6**	**2**	**7**
SINCHAJI	0-5																		1		
	6-10																				
	11-15																		1		
	16-20																	1	1		
	21-25					2															
	26-30																				
	31-35																				
	36-40																				
	41-45																				
	46-50								1					1							
	51-55	1																			
	56-60																				
	61+	1																			
	Total	**2**				**2**			**1**					**1**				**1**	**3**		

Source: Fieldwork 2010

Table No. B-3 Clan and age wise occupation for Jigaon village

Clan	*Age*	*Main Occupation*								*Subsidiary Occupation*								*Dependent*			
		Male				*Female*				*Male*				*Female*				*Student*		*Others*	
		A	*S*	*B*	*O*	*A*	*S*	*B*	*O*	*A*	*S*	*B*	*O*	*A*	*S*	*B*	*O*	*M*	*F*	*M*	*F*
THONGHI	0-5																	3	2	1	1
	6-10																	3	3		
	11-15																	4	7		
	16-20																	2	5		
	21-25	1	1			2			1					1				1		1	
	26-30	1	1				2		6					7							
	31-35	1	2						1	1				1							
	36-40	2							1					1							
	41-45	1		2					2	2				2							
	46-50	3																			
	51-55								2					2							
	56-60		1	2		1	1		1	3				1							
	61+	1							1					1							
Total		**10**	**5**	**4**		**3**	**3**		**15**	**6**				**16**				**13**	**17**	**2**	**1**
THONGDOK	0-5																			2	
	6-10																	3	1		
	11-15				1													1	2		
	16-20																				
	21-25					1			2					1							
	26-30	1	2						2	1				2							
	31-35	1	1																		
	36-40								1												
	41-45			1																	
	46-50																				
	51-55			1					1					1							
	56-60	1				2			1					1							
	61+			1					1												
Total		**3**	**3**	**3**	**1**	**3**			**8**	**1**				**5**				**4**	**3**	**2**	

Clan	*Age*	*Main Occupation*								*Subsidiary Occupation*								*Dependent*			
		Male				*Female*				*Male*				*Female*				*Student*		*Others*	
		A	*S*	*B*	*O*	*A*	*S*	*B*	*O*	*A*	*S*	*B*	*O*	*A*	*S*	*B*	*O*	*M*	*F*	*M*	*F*
THONGON	0-5																				
	6-10																				
	11-15																				
	16-20	1																1			
	21-25	1			1	1												1			
	26-30					1															
	31-35																				
	36-40																				
	41-45																				
	46-50								1					1							
	51-55																				
	56-60	1							1					1							
	61+																				
Total		**3**			**1**	**2**			**2**					**2**				**2**			
MOSOBI	0-5																			1	
	6-10																	3			
	11-15																				
	16-20																	1	1		
	21-25																		1		
	26-30								1					1							
	31-35	1																			
	36-40																				
	41-45																				
	46-50																				
	51-55	1							1					1							
	56-60																				
	61+	1											1								1
Total		**3**							**2**				**1**	**2**				**4**	**2**	**1**	**1**

Clan	*Age*	*Main Occupation*								*Subsidiary Occupation*								*Dependent*			
		Male				*Female*				*Male*				*Female*				*Student*		*Others*	
		A	*S*	*B*	*O*	*A*	*S*	*B*	*O*	*A*	*S*	*B*	*O*	*A*	*S*	*B*	*O*	*M*	*F*	*M*	*F*
	0-5																			1	
	6-10																				
S	11-15																				
I N	16-20																	1	1		
C	21-25								1												
H A	26-30		1																		
J	31-35								1					1							
I	36-40																				
	41-45	1																			
	46-50	1							1					1							
	51-55																				
	56-60		1																		
	61+	1																			
Total		**3**	**2**						**3**					**2**				**1**	**1**	**1**	
	0-5																	1		1	2
	6-10																				
	11-15																		1		
M E	16-20	1																2			
G	21-25	1							1					1							
E J	26-30					1			1					1							
I	31-35		1																		
	36-40																				
	41-45																				
	46-50								1					1							
	51-55																				
	56-60		1						1	1				1							
	61+					1															
Total		**2**	**2**			**2**			**4**	**1**				**4**				**3**	**1**	**1**	**2**

Clan	*Age*	*Main Occupation*								*Subsidiary Occupation*								*Dependent*			
		Male				*Female*				*Male*				*Female*				*Student*		*Others*	
		A	*S*	*B*	*O*	*A*	*S*	*B*	*O*	*A*	*S*	*B*	*O*	*A*	*S*	*B*	*O*	*M*	*F*	*M*	*F*
	0-5																			1	
	6-10																	2			
	11-15				1													2	1		
MIJIJI	16-20																		1		
	21-25																				
	26-30																				
	31-35	1							2				1	2							
	36-40	1											1								
	41-45			1						1											
	46-50																				
	51-55																				
	56-60																				
	61+																				
Total		**2**		**1**	**1**				**2**	**1**			**2**	**2**				**4**	**2**	**1**	
	0-5																	2	1		1
	6-10																	2	2		
	11-15	1																3	2		
	16-20	1			1				1	1				1				2	2		
DINGLA	21-25	2	1						1					1							
	26-30	2	1		1				3					3							
	31-35	1							1					1							
	36-40	2							1					1							
	41-45	2							2					2							
	46-50	1							2					2							
	51-55								2					2							
	56-60		2																		
	61+	1	1						1					1							1
Total		**13**	**5**		**2**				**14**					**14**				**9**	**7**		**2**

Source: Fieldwork 2010

Appendix-C

Table No. C-1 Clan and age wise educational standard for Rupa village

Clan	*Age*	*Non-Lit*		*Lower Primary*		*Primary*		*Middle*		*Secondary*		*Higher Secondary*		*Graduate and Above*	
		M	*F*	*M*	*F*	*M*	*F*	*M*	*F*	*M*	*F*	*M*	*F*	*M*	*F*
T	0-5				2										
H	6-10			1		2	2								
O	11-15							3	3	1	1				
N	16-20								1	2	2	1	4		
G	21-25	1						1	1	1	2	1	1	3	2
D	26-30					1		2		1	2	1		2	1
O	31-35							1					1	2	
K	36-40		1						1			1		2	
	41-45		1						1	2	1		1	1	
	46-50		1			1	1					3			
	51-55		2							1	1			1	
	56-60		2					1							
	61+	1	4			2		2		1					
Total		**2**	**11**	**1**	**2**	**6**	**3**	**10**	**7**	**9**	**9**	**7**	**7**	**11**	**3**
K	0-5			1	2										
H	6-10					2	1								
R	11-15							2	1	1					
I	16-20						1	1	1	1	1	1	1	1	
M	21-25								1	1	1	3		1	1
E	26-30		1					1		1		1	1	2	1
	31-35		1					1		1				1	
	36-40		1										2	2	
	41-45		1								1	2			
	46-50		1				1		1	1				1	
	51-55					1	1	1							1
	56-60		1												
	61+	3	2							1				1	
Total		**3**	**8**	**1**	**2**	**3**	**4**	**6**	**4**	**7**	**3**	**7**	**4**	**9**	**3**

Clan	*Age*	*Non-Lit*		*Lower Primary*		*Primary*		*Middle*		*Secondary*		*Higher Secondary*		*Graduate and Above*	
		M	*F*	*M*	*F*	*M*	*F*	*M*	*F*	*M*	*F*	*M*	*F*	*M*	*F*
THONGON	0-5			2	1										
	6-10			1	2	3	2								
	11-15						1		1						
	16-20														1
	21-25							1	1	1		1		1	3
	26-30							1	1		1		1	3	2
	31-35					1				1		1	2	2	
	36-40							1				1			1
	41-45													2	
	46-50														
	51-55		1												
	56-60	1	1												
	61+	1	1			1	1								
Total		**2**	**3**	**3**	**3**	**5**	**4**	**3**	**3**	**2**	**1**	**3**	**3**	**8**	**7**
THONGCHI	0-5				1										
	6-10														
	11-15								3						
	16-20											1			
	21-25										1				1
	26-30									1	1				
	31-35						1	1							
	36-40														
	41-45														
	46-50					1	1								
	51-55								1						
	56-60							1							
	61+														
Total					**1**	**1**	**2**	**2**	**4**	**1**	**2**	**1**			**1**

Clan	*Age*	*Non-Lit*		*Lower Primary*		*Primary*		*Middle*		*Secondary*		*Higher Secondary*		*Graduate and Above*	
		M	*F*	*M*	*F*	*M*	*F*	*M*	*F*	*M*	*F*	*M*	*F*	*M*	*F*
	0-5														
	6-10			1		1	1		1						
	11-15							1			1				
MOSOBI	16-20									1	1		1	1	2
	21-25									1		1		1	1
	26-30									1		1	1	1	
	31-35		1					1			1	1			
	36-40					1									
	41-45						1			1	1				
	46-50					1			1					1	
	51-55		2							1					
	56-60		1			1						1			
	61+	1	1												
Total		**1**	**5**	**1**		**4**	**2**	**2**	**2**	**5**	**4**	**4**	**2**	**4**	**3**
	0-5														
	6-10					4	1								
	11-15						1	2	2	1	1				
WANGJA	16-20								1		1				2
	21-25								1	1	1				2
	26-30									3	1		1	3	1
	31-35		1							1	1				
	36-40										1		1		
	41-45	1												1	
	46-50	1							1						
	51-55		2					1	1					1	
	56-60	1								1					
	61+		1												
Total		**3**	**4**			**4**	**2**	**3**	**6**	**7**	**6**		**2**	**5**	**5**

Clan	*Age*	*Non-Lit*		*Lower Primary*		*Primary*		*Middle*		*Secondary*		*Higher Secondary*		*Graduate and Above*	
		M	*F*	*M*	*F*	*M*	*F*	*M*	*F*	*M*	*F*	*M*	*F*	*M*	*F*
KARMA	0-5				1										
	6-10					1	2								
	11-15								1	1	1				
	16-20										1	2			1
	21-25														
	26-30		1					2	1	1					
	31-35										1	1	1		
	36-40								1	1					
	41-45													1	
	46-50	1													
	51-55		1			1									
	56-60														
	61+							1							
Total		**1**	**2**		**1**	**2**	**2**	**3**	**3**	**3**	**3**	**3**	**1**	**1**	**1**
YANGFAN	0-5														
	6-10														
	11-15														
	16-20														
	21-25														
	26-30														
	31-35														
	36-40														
	41-45														
	46-50														
	51-55	1	1												
	56-60														
	61+														
Total		**1**	**1**												

Clan	*Age*	*Non-Lit*		*Lower Primary*		*Primary*		*Middle*		*Secondary*		*Higher Secondary*		*Graduate and Above*	
		M	*F*	*M*	*F*	*M*	*F*	*M*	*F*	*M*	*F*	*M*	*F*	*M*	*F*
MEGEJI	0-5			4	2										
	6-10				1	2	1								
	11-15					1		1		2	1				
	16-20							1		2			1	1	
	21-25						1		1	3	1	4			2
	26-30						1		3		1	1		1	
	31-35									2		1	1		
	36-40	1				1			2			2	1		1
	41-45								1			1			
	46-50							1							
	51-55	1	2					1							
	56-60	1							1					1	
	61+		1			1						1			
Total		**3**	**3**	**4**	**3**	**5**	**3**	**4**	**8**	**9**	**3**	**10**	**3**	**3**	**3**
DINGLA	0-5			1											
	6-10			1	1		2								
	11-15														
	16-20											2	1		
	21-25								1		1		1	1	
	26-30	1							2	1	1				
	31-35														
	36-40							1							
	41-45		1												
	46-50						1								
	51-55					1		1							
	56-60														
	61+	1	1												
Total		**2**	**2**	**2**	**1**	**1**	**3**	**2**	**3**	**1**	**2**	**2**	**2**	**1**	

Clan	*Age*	*Non-Lit*		*Lower Primary*		*Primary*		*Middle*		*Secondary*		*Higher Secondary*		*Graduate and Above*	
		M	*F*	*M*	*F*	*M*	*F*	*M*	*F*	*M*	*F*	*M*	*F*	*M*	*F*
	0-5														
	6-10					3	1								
S I N C H A J I	11-15						1	2							
	16-20								1	1	1		1		
	21-25								1						
	26-30								1		1				
	31-35												1		
	36-40								1	2		1			
	41-45	1													
	46-50														
	51-55														
	56-60														
	61+	1													
Total		**2**				**3**	**2**	**2**	**4**	**3**	**2**	**1**	**2**		
	0-5														
	6-10					1									
M I J I J I	11-15							1	1						
	16-20								2		2	1	1		
	21-25		1					1			1				1
	26-30									1					
	31-35														
	36-40							1	1						
	41-45		1						1			1			
	46-50					1									
	51-55		1			1									
	56-60														
	61+														
Total			**3**			**3**		**3**	**5**	**1**	**3**	**2**	**1**		**1**

Source: Fieldwork 2010

Table No. C-2 Clan and age wise educational standard for Thongre village

Clan	*Age*	*Non-Lit*		*Lower Primary*		*Primary*		*Middle*		*Secondary*		*Higher Secondary*		*Graduate and Above*	
		M	*F*	*M*	*F*	*M*	*F*	*M*	*F*	*M*	*F*	*M*	*F*	*M*	*F*
THONGDOK	0-5				5										
	6-10				1	1	8		1						
	11-15					1	1	2	1		1				
	16-20							2		4			1		1
	21-25		1					1		1	3				
	26-30					1	3	3	1	2	4				
	31-35					1	1	4							
	36-40					1		1	3	1					
	41-45					1	1	1		1				1	
	46-50						1	1	1						
	51-55							2							
	56-60					1	1								
	61+	2	3			1	1								
Total		**2**	**4**		**6**	**8**	**17**	**17**	**7**	**9**	**8**		**1**	**1**	**1**
KHRIME	0-5				1										
	6-10					1	2								
	11-15					1		2	2						
	16-20						1		1	1			1		
	21-25								1	1		1	1		
	26-30												1		
	31-35					1		3			2				
	36-40					1	2								
	41-45									1				1	
	46-50		2												
	51-55		1				1	1							
	56-60		2												
	61+														
Total			**5**		**1**	**4**	**6**	**6**	**4**	**3**	**2**	**1**	**3**	**1**	

Clan	*Age*	*Non-Lit*		*Lower Primary*		*Primary*		*Middle*		*Secondary*		*Higher Secondary*		*Graduate and Above*	
		M	*F*	*M*	*F*	*M*	*F*	*M*	*F*	*M*	*F*	*M*	*F*	*M*	*F*
THONGCHI	0-5			1			1								
	6-10						1								
	11-15							1	1						
	16-20							1	1	2		1	1		
	21-25							1		1	1	1			1
	26-30	1				1	2		2						
	31-35							2							
	36-40														
	41-45						1								
	46-50								1						
	51-55	1	1							1					
	56-60	1	1												
	61+	1	1												
Total		**4**	**3**	**1**		**1**	**5**	**5**	**5**	**4**	**1**	**2**	**1**		**1**
THONGON	0-5			1											
	6-10					2									
	11-15						2	1							
	16-20								1	1	2				
	21-25							1							
	26-30					1			1						
	31-35														
	36-40								1						
	41-45						1		1						
	46-50					1									
	51-55							1							
	56-60														
	61+	1													
Total		**1**		**1**		**4**	**3**	**3**	**4**	**1**	**2**				

Clan	*Age*	*Non-Lit*		*Lower Primary*		*Primary*		*Middle*		*Secondary*		*Higher Secondary*		*Graduate and Above*	
		M	*F*	*M*	*F*	*M*	*F*	*M*	*F*	*M*	*F*	*M*	*F*	*M*	*F*
MEGEJI	0-5														
	6-10					2									
	11-15					2		2	1						
	16-20								1	4	5	1			1
	21-25							1	1		3	1	1		
	26-30					2		1			1				
	31-35					1		3	2		1				
	36-40		1			2	1		2			1			
	41-45								1	1					
	46-50		1												
	51-55		1			1									
	56-60		3												
	61+	3	3							1					
Total		**3**	**9**			**10**	**1**	**7**	**8**	**6**	**10**	**3**	**1**		**1**
SINCHAJI	0-5				1										
	6-10														
	11-15						1								
	16-20									1	1				
	21-25								2						
	26-30														
	31-35														
	36-40														
	41-45														
	46-50		1												
	51-55							1							
	56-60														
	61+	1													
Total		**1**	**1**		**1**		**1**	**1**	**2**	**1**	**1**				

Source: Fieldwork 2010

Table No. C-3 Clan and age wise educational standard for Jigaon village

Clan	*Age*	*Non-Lit*		*Lower Primary*		*Primary*		*Middle*		*Secondary*		*Higher Secondary*		*Graduate and Above*	
		M	*F*	*M*	*F*	*M*	*F*	*M*	*F*	*M*	*F*	*M*	*F*	*M*	*F*
THONGCHI	0-5			3	3										
	6-10					3	2								
	11-15					2	2	1	2	1	3				
	16-20								1		3	2	1		
	21-25								1	2		2	1		1
	26-30		1				2		3			1	2	1	
	31-35						1	2				1			
	36-40		1			1				1					
	41-45		2			1		1		1					
	46-50	1				2									
	51-55		1						1						
	56-60	1	2			1						1	1		
	61+	1	1												
Total		**3**	**8**	**3**	**3**	**10**	**7**	**4**	**8**	**5**	**6**	**7**	**5**	**1**	**1**
THONGDOK	0-5														
	6-10			1		2	1								
	11-15					1	2	1							
	16-20														
	21-25						3								
	26-30					1	1	1		1	1				
	31-35							1						1	
	36-40												1		
	41-45													1	
	46-50														
	51-55								1					1	
	56-60	1	2				1								
	61+		1			1									
Total		**1**	**3**	**1**		**5**	**8**	**3**	**1**	**1**	**1**		**1**	**3**	

Clan	*Age*	*Non-Lit*		*Lower Primary*		*Primary*		*Middle*		*Secondary*		*Higher Secondary*		*Graduate and Above*	
		M	*F*	*M*	*F*	*M*	*F*	*M*	*F*	*M*	*F*	*M*	*F*	*M*	*F*
THONGON	0-5														
	6-10														
	11-15														
	16-20					1		1							
	21-25					1		1	1			1			
	26-30								1						
	31-35														
	36-40														
	41-45														
	46-50		1												
	51-55														
	56-60		1			1									
	61+														
Total			**2**			**3**		**2**	**2**			**1**			
MOSOBI	0-5														
	6-10					3									
	11-15														
	16-20							1	1						
	21-25										1				
	26-30								1						
	31-35											1			
	36-40														
	41-45														
	46-50														
	51-55		1			1									
	56-60														
	61+	1	1												
Total		**1**	**2**			**4**		**1**	**2**		**1**	**2**			

Clan	*Age*	*Non-Lit*		*Lower Primary*		*Primary*		*Middle*		*Secondary*		*Higher Secondary*		*Graduate and Above*	
		M	*F*	*M*	*F*	*M*	*F*	*M*	*F*	*M*	*F*	*M*	*F*	*M*	*F*
SINCHAJI	0-5														
	6-10														
	11-15														
	16-20										1	1			
	21-25						1								
	26-30									1					
	31-35		1												
	36-40														
	41-45					1									
	46-50						1			1					
	51-55														
	56-60							1							
	61+						1								
Total			**1**			**1**	**3**	**1**		**2**	**1**	**1**			
MEGEJI	0-5			1											
	6-10														
	11-15								1						
	16-20							1		1		1			
	21-25							1	1						
	26-30										1		1		
	31-35													1	
	36-40														
	41-45														
	46-50						1								
	51-55														
	56-60		1			1									
	61+		1												
Total			**2**	**1**		**1**	**1**	**2**	**2**	**1**	**1**	**1**	**1**	**1**	

Clan	*Age*	*Non-Lit*		*Lower Primary*		*Primary*		*Middle*		*Secondary*		*Higher Secondary*		*Graduate and Above*	
		M	*F*	*M*	*F*	*M*	*F*	*M*	*F*	*M*	*F*	*M*	*F*	*M*	*F*
	0-5														
	6-10					2									
M	11-15					3			1						
I	16-20												1		
J	21-25														
I	26-30														
J	31-35					1	1		1						
I	36-40	1													
	41-45							1							
	46-50														
	51-55														
	56-60														
	61+														
Total		**1**				**6**	**1**	**1**	**2**				**1**		
	0-5			2											
	6-10			1		6	2								
D	11-15					2	1	2	1						
I	16-20					2			2	1	1	1			
N	21-25					2		2	1						
G	26-30		1			1	1	2	1	1					
L	31-35									1	1				
A	36-40							1	1			1			
	41-45		1						1	1		1			
	46-50		1				1			1					
	51-55		1				1								
	56-60					2									
	61+	1	2			1									
Total		**1**	**6**	**3**		**6**	**6**	**7**	**7**	**5**	**2**	**3**			

Source: Fieldwork 2010

Bibliography

Ali, H. (1974). Elements of Caste Among the Muslims in a District in Southern Bihar, *Man in India*, Vol. 54 (3), pp. 190–212.

Athparia, R.P. (2003). Transformation Among the Noctes of Arunachal Pradesh, Jayanta Sarkar and Jyotirmoy Chakraborty (eds.). *Transition Change and Transformation,* Anthropological Survey of India, Kolkata, pp. 169–191.

Barber, B. (1956). *Social Stratification*, Harcourt, Brace and Company, New York.

Bareh, H.M. (2001). (ed.) *Encyclopaedia of North East India-I: Arunachal Pradesh,* Mittal Publication, New Delhi.

Behura, N.K. (1993). Caste: Hierarchy, Status & Power: A Critique, *Journal of the Indian Anthropological Society*, Vol. 28 (1), pp. 11–22.

Bera, G.K. (2003). The Riangs of Tripura in the Changing Scenario, Jayanta Sarkar and Jyotirmoy Chakraborty (eds.), *Transition Change and Transformation*, Anthropological Survey of India, Kolkata, pp. 139–168.

Berreman, G.D. (1979). *Caste and Other Inequities: Essays on Inequality*, Folklore Institute, Meerut.

Berreman, G.D. (2004). Ethnography: Method and Product, Vinay Kumar Srivastava (ed.). *Methodology and Field Work*, OUP, New Delhi.

Behera, M.C. & Chaudhuri, S.K. (1996). *Indigenous Faith and Practices of the Tribes of Arunachal Pradesh*, Himalayan Publishers, Itanagar.

Beteille, A. (1971). *Caste, Class and Power: Changing Pattern of Stratification in a Tanjore Village,* University of California Press, Berkeley.

Beteille, A. (1972). *Inequality and Social Change,* OUP, Calcutta.

Beteille, A. (1992). *Society and Politics in India: Essay in a Comparative Perspective,* Oxford University Press, New Delhi.

Bhagabati, A.C. (1992). Tribal Transformation in Assam and North-East India: An Appraisal of Emerging Ideological Dimensions, Buddhadeb Chaudhuri (ed.).

Tribal Transformation in India, Vol. 3, Inter-India Publications, New Delhi, pp. 487–509.

Blunt, E.A.H. (1969). *The Caste System of Northern India*, S. Chand & Co., New Delhi.

Borthakur, B.N. (1997). Caste and Social Stratification in Assam, *Man in India,* Vol. 23(3–4), pp. 143–154.

Bose, M.L. (1997). *History of Arunachal Pradesh*, Concept Publishing Company, New Delhi.

Bose, N.K. (1975). *Structure of Hindu Society* (translated from Bengali by Andre Beteille from *Hindu Samajer Garan*, 1949), Orient Longman, Delhi.

Chakraborty, K. (1996). Caste and the Indian Society Overtime: A Review, *The Journal of the Anthropological Survey of India,* Vol. 45(1), pp. 35–49.

Chakravarti, N.K. (1989). Origin of Caste (Jati) System in India; A Comprehensive Theory, *Human Science*, Vol. 38 (1), pp. 1–13.

Chakravarty, L.N. (1973). *Glimpses of the Early History of Arunachal*, Directorate of Research, Govt. of Arunachal Pradesh, Itanagar.

Chatterjee, S. (1991). *A Comprehensive History of Arunachal Pradesh*, Prabartak Printing Halftone Ltd., Calcutta.

Chattopadhyay, G. (1966). Caste and Class in West Bengal, *Journal of Indian Anthropological Society*, Vol. 1, pp. 185–190.

Chaudhuri, M. (1998). Among My Own in Another Culture: Meeting the Asian Indian Americans, Meenakshi Thapan (ed.). *Anthropological Journeys: Reflections on Fieldwork,* Orient Longman, New Delhi, pp. 188–216.

Chaudhuri, S.K. (2003). The Mans of Garo Hills: A Study on Change, Jayanta Sarkar and Jyotirmoy Chakraborty (ed.), *Transition Change and Transformation*, Anthropological Survey of India, Kolkata, pp. 216–227.

Chauhan, S.K. (1980). *Caste Status and Power: Social Stratification in Assam*, Classical Publishing Company, New Delhi.

Clifford, J. & Marcus George (1986). *Writing Culture: The Poetics and Politics of* (ed.). *Ethnography,* University of California Press, Berkeley.

Choudhury, S.D. (1996). (ed.). *Gazetteers of India, Arunachal Pradesh*: *East Kameng, West Kameng and Tawang District*, Government of Arunachal Pradesh, Shillong.

Chowdhury, J.N. (1976). Evidence of Caste-Like Features in Some Arunachal Tribes, *Resarun*, Vol. 75, Directorate of Research, Govt. of Arunachal Pradesh, Shillong.

Danda, A.K. (1986). Forms and Nature of Stratification in a West Bengal Village, *Human Science,* Vol. 35(1), pp. 1–19.

Danda, A.K. & Mandal, P. (1997). Creation Myth from North East India. Manis K. Raha (eds.) *North East India: The Human Interface*, Gyan Publishing House, New Delhi.

Dirk, N.B. (2001). *Caste of Mind: Colonialism and the Making of Modern India*, Permanent Black, New Delhi.

Das, T.C. (2005). Nature and Extent of Social Change in Tribal Society in Eastern India, Pariyan M. Chacko (ed.). *Tribal Communities and Social Change,* Sage Publications, New Delhi, pp. 97–113.

Das, V. (1998). Anthropological Knowledge, Alterity and the Autobiographical Voice, Meenakshi Thapan (ed.). *Anthropological Journeys: Reflection on Fieldwork*, Orient Longman, New Delhi, pp. 41–53.

Dasgupta, S., Hennesey, S. & Mukhopadhyay, R.S. (2000). Class, Caste and Agrarian Structure in West Bengal, *Man in India*, Vol. 80 (1&2), pp. 31–55.

Debnath, D. (1998). Dynamism of Caste System in Rajasthan, *The Eastern Anthropologist*, Vol. 51(4), pp. 363–372.

Debnath, D. (1995). Hierarchies within Hierarchy: Some Observations on Caste System in Rajasthan, *Indian Anthropologist*, Vol. 25(1), pp. 23–30.

Deliege, R. (1980). Division and Hierarchy Among the Bhils, *Man in India* Vol. 60(1&2), pp. 43–58.

Dey, K. (2004). Class Structure in a Tribal Village: Aspects of Change and Continuity with Reference to Impact of Modern Education, T. Mibang and M.C. Behera (ed.), *Dynamics of Tribal Villages in Arunachal Pradesh: Emerging Realities*, Mittal Publication, New Delhi, pp. 44–56.

Deogaonkar, S.G. (2005). The Changing Scenario in the PTGS from Vidarbha: Some Observation on Madia-Gonds and Kolams; Sarit K. Chaudhuri and Sucheta S. Chaudhuri (eds.), *Primitive Tribes in Contemporary India: Concept, Ethnography and Demography*, Vol. 1, Mittal Publications, New Delhi, pp. 269–276.

Deuri, R.K. (1977). A Note on Some Popular Sherdukpen Traditions about their Conversion from Animism to Buddhism, *Resarun* Vol. 2(1), Research Department, Arunachal Pradesh, Shillong, pp. 24–27.

Deuri, R.K. (1983). *Festivals of Kameng*, Directorate of Research, Shillong, pp. 1–6.

Duarah, D.K. (1990). Foods habit of the tribes of Arunachal Pradesh, P.C. Dutta and D.K. Duarah (eds.) *Aspects of Culture and Customs of Arunachal Pradesh*, Directorate of Research, Itanagar, pp. 83–92

Dubey, S.M. (1972). Class, Stratification, Mobility: Some Theoretical Issues, *The North Eastern Research Bulletin*, Vol. 3, pp. 1–19.

Dutta, P. (1990). *The Wanchos*, Directorate of Research, Govt. of Arunachal Pradesh, Itanagar.

Dutta, P. (2005). *Nokte Chieftainship*, Himalaya Publications, New Delhi.

Elwin, V. (1957). *A Philosophy for NEFA,* Directorate of Research, Govt. of Arunachal Pradesh, Itanagar.

Elwin, V. (1958). *Myth of The North-East Frontier of India*, Directorate of Research, Govt. of Arunachal Pradesh, Itanagar.

Firth, R. (1959). *Social Change in Tikopia,* George Allen & Unwin Ltd., London.

Ganszle, M. (2003/2004). Introduction: Representing Local Histories in the Himalayas, *European Bulletin of Himalaya Research* 25/26, pp. 7–14.

Ghosh, A. & Soni, L. (1990). Stratification and Social Change Among the Tribes of Central India, *Man and Life,* Vol. 16(1&2), pp. 43–58.

Ghurye, G.S. (1957). *Caste and Class in India,* Popular Book Depot, Bombay.

Goswami, M.C. (1990). *The People of Arunachal Pradesh: A Physical Survey*, Directorate of Research, Itanagar, pp. 11–46.

Gowloog, R.R. (2001). Social Organisation and Change Among the Lepchas of Sikkim, Sarthak Sengupta (ed.). *Tribes of Eastern Himalayas*, Mittal Publication, New Delhi, pp. 47–54.

Grewal, D.S. (1997). *Tribes of Arunachal Pradesh, Identity, Culture and Languages*, Vol-II, South Asian Publication, Delhi.

Gupta, D. (1991). (ed.). *Social Stratification,* Oxford University Press, New Delhi.

Haimendorf, C.V.F. (1984). *The Sherpas Transformed: Social Change in a Buddhist Society of Nepal*, New Delhi.

Haimendorf (1962). *The Apatanis and their Neighbours: A Primitive Society of Eastern Himalayas*, Routledge, New York.

Haimendorf, C.V.F. (1989). *Tribes of India: The Struggle for Survival,* OUP, New Delhi.

Hazra, M. (2003). Transformation in Economy and Social Change: A Case Study of the Gujjar of Himachal Pradesh, Jayanta Sarkar and Jyotirmoy Chakraborty (eds.). *Transition Change and Transformation*, Anthropological Survey of India, Kolkata, pp. 59–71.

Hutton, J.H. (1951). *Caste in India: Its Nature, Function and Origin*, Oxford University Press, New Delhi.

Jaer, O. (1997). Caste and Class in Karchana, *The Eastern Anthropologist*, Vol. 50: (3&4), pp. 395–414.

Jain, R.K. (1967). Social Stratification and Political Process, *Journal of the Indian Anthropological Society*, Vol. 2, pp. 69–73.

Jatso, U. (2003). *The History of the Sherdukpen Monpas*, Nobel Publishers Pvt. Ltd., New Delhi.

Kassbaum, G. (1974). A Survey of Caste and Occupational Mobility in a Small City in India, *Man in India,* Vol. 54(4), pp. 253–270.

Kloos, P. (2004). Restudies in Anthropology, Vinay Kumar Srivastava (ed.), *Methodology and Fieldwork,* Oxford University Press, New Delhi.

Koley, R.N. (1999). Tribal Village Council of A.P.: Sherdukpen, B.B. Pandey, D.K. Duarah and N. Sarkar (ed.) *Tribal Village Council of Arunachal*

Pradesh, Directorate of Research, Govt. of Arunachal Pradesh, Itanagar, pp. 13–39.

Kri, S. (2010). (ed.). *State Gazetteer of Arunachal Pradesh Vol-I*, Government of Arunachal Pradesh, Itanagar.

Kumar, S. (2002). Caste Mobility and Political Process: A Case of the Jatavs of Abupur, *Man in India*, Vol. 82(1&2), pp. 101–115.

Lambek, M. (2002). (ed.) *A Reader in the Anthropology of Religion*, Blackwell Publishing Ltd., U.K.

Leach, E. (1964). *Political System of Highland Burma*, Atlone Press, London.

MacIver, R.M. & Page, C.H. (1998). *Society: An Introductory Analysis*, Macmillan India Limited, New Delhi.

Mackenzie, A. (1979). *The North East Frontier of India*, Mittal Publication, New Delhi, pp. 15–20.

Madan, T.N. (1998). Discovering Anthropology: A Personal Narrative, Meenakshi Thapan (ed.) *Anthropological Journeys: Reflection on Fieldwork,* Orient Longman, New Delhi, pp. 143–162.

Mahapatra, L.K. (1997). Social Change in Tribal Society in Eastern India-Supplement to Professor Tarak Chandra Das' Analysis 1961, *Journal of Indian Anthropological Society*, Vol. 32 (3), pp. 197–205.

Mair, L. (1972). *An Introduction To Social Anthroppology*, Oxford University Press, New Delhi.

Mann, R.S. (2004). *Social Change and Social Research: An Indian Perspective*, Concept Publishing Company, New Delhi.

Marcus, G. & Fischer, M. (1986). *Anthropology as Cultural Critique*, University of Chicago Press, Chicago.

Mascarenhaskeyes, S. (2004). The Native Anthropologist: Constraints and Strategies in Research, Vinay Kumar Srivastava (ed.) *Methodology and Fieldwork*, Oxford University Press, New Delhi.

Mathur, P.R.G. (1998). Social Stratification Among the Muslims in Kerela, *The Journal of the Anthropological Survey of India,* Vol. 47(3), pp. 39–64.

Mibang, T. (1994). Social Change in Arunachal Pradesh (The Minyongs) 1947–1989, Omsons Publication, New Delhi.

Misra, K.K. (1998). The Emerging Pattern of Stratification Among the Khamptis of Arunachal Pradesh, *The Journal of the Anthropological Survey of India,* Vol. 47(1), pp. 1–24.

Misra, P.K. (1997). Tribes-Caste: A Non-Issue, *Journal of the Indian Anthropological Society*, Vol. 12(2), pp. 137–150.

Megejee, R. (2006). Marriage Rules, Practices and Emotions in Sherdukpen Marriage Ceremony, Tamo Mibang and M.C. Behera (ed.) *Marriage and Culture:*

Reflections from Tribal Societies of Arunachal Pradesh, Mittal Publications, New Delhi, pp. 299–310.

Merrill, F. E. (1962). *An Introduction to Sociology: Society and Culture*, Prentice Hall, New Jersey.

Mohidden, M.A. & Ramana, G.V. (2003). Transformation in Economy, Socio-Religious Practices and Political Organisation of the Chenchus, Jayanta Sarkar and Jyotirmoy Chakraborty (eds.) *Transition Change and Transformation*, Anthropological Survey of India, Kolkata, pp. 72–92.

Mondal, S.R. (2006). Social and Cultural Dynamics of Indigenous People, *The Eastern Anthropologist*, Vol. 59(2), pp. 229–238.

Mookherjee, H. (1967). Caste Ranking & Brahmanical Doctrines in a West Bengal, *Journal of the Indian Anthropological Society*, Vol. 2(2), pp. 175–181.

Mookherjee, H. & Dasgupta, S. (1970). Caste, Status and Ritual Observances in a West Bengal Village, *Man in India*, Vol. 50(4), pp. 390–402.

Mukhopadhyay, R. (1997). Caste, Kinship and Agrarian Structure: Case Study of Three Types of Village in Hooghly District, *Man in India*, Vol. 77(1), pp. 35–49.

Narayan, K. (1998). How 'Native' is a native anthropologist? Meenakshi Thapan (ed.) *Anthropological Journeys: Reflections on Fieldwork*, Orient Longman, New Delhi, pp. 163–187.

Obeyesekere, G. (2004). The First Inter-Subjectivity: The Anthropologist and the Native, Vinay Kumar Srivastava (ed.) *Methodology and Fieldwork*, Oxford University Press, New Delhi.

Palakshappa, T.C. (1978). *Tibetan in India: A Case Study of Mundgod Tibetans*, Sterling Publishers, New Delhi.

Patel, A. (1997). Caste in Changing Society: A Study of Kolis of South Gujarat, Ghanshyam Shah (ed.) *Social Transformation in India*, Vol. I, Rawat Publications, New Delhi, pp. 324–338.

Prasad, R.R. (1989). *Bhotia Tribals of India: Dynamics of Economic Transformation*, Gyan Publishing House, New Delhi.

Raatan, T. (2004). *Encyclopaedia of North-East India*, Vol. 2, Kalpaz Publication, New Delhi.

Roy, S. (1960). *Aspect of Padam-Minyong Culture*, Directorate of Research, Arunachal Pradesh, Itanagar.

Sachchidananda (1988). *Social Change in Village India*, Concept Publishing Company, New Delhi.

Sahay, M. (2003). Pao Identity and Transformation, Jayanta Sarkar and Jyotirmoy Chakraborty (ed.) *Transition Change and Transformation*, Anthropological Survey of India, Kolkata, pp. 381–393.

Sarkar, J. (1987). *Society, Culture and Ecological Adaptation Among Three Tribes of Arunachal Pradesh*, Anthropological Survey of India, Ministry of Human Resource Development, Department of Culture, Govt. of India.

Sarkar, J. (2003). Transition, Change and Transformation: Impacting the Tribes in India- An Introduction, Jayanta Sarkar and Jyotirmoy Chakraborty (ed.) *Transition Change and Transformation*, Anthropological Survey of India, Kolkata, pp. 1–8.

Sarkar, N. (1990). Minor Religious Structures of the Monpas & Sherdukpens, P.C. Dutta and D.K. Duarah (eds.) *Aspect of Culture and Customs of Arunachal Pradesh*, Directorate of Research, Government of Arunachal Pradesh, Itanagar, pp. 150–154.

Sathyanarayanan, C.R. (2003). The Todas of Nilgiris: A Study on their Transition, Jayanta Sarkar and Jyotirmoy Chakraborty (eds.) *Transition Change and Transformation*, Anthropological Survey of India, Kolkata, pp. 9–36.

Sen, S. (1986). *Arunachal Pradesh and the Tribes Select Bibliography*, Gyan Publishing House, Delhi.

Shah, B.V. (2005). Educational and Social Change Among Tribal in India, Pariyaram, M. Chocko (ed.) *Tribal Communities and Social Change*, Sage Publications, New Delhi, pp. 114–133.

Shalins, M.D. (1958). *Social Stratification in Polynesia*, University of Washington Press, Seattle.

Sharma, A.K. (1985). *Social Inequality and Demographic Process*, Mittal Publication, New Delhi.

Sharma, K.L. (1970). Changing Class Stratification in Rural Rajasthan, *Man in India*, Vol. 50(3), pp. 257–268.

Sharma, K.L. (1997). *Social Stratification in India: Issues and Themes*, Sage Publication, New Delhi.

Sharma, K.L. (2007). *Indian Social Structure and Change*, Rawat Publications, Jaipur.

Sharma, K.L. (2010). *Perspectives on Social Stratification*, Rawat Publications, Jaipur.

Sharma, R.R.P. (1960). *The Sherdukpens*, Directorate of Research, Govt. of Arunachal Pradesh, Itanagar.

Singh, A.K. (1993). *Tribes and Tribal Life*, Sarup & Son, New Delhi, pp. 324–338.

Singh, J.P. (2000). Buddhist Folk Tradition and the History of the Sherdukpens, S. Dutta (ed.) *Studies in the History, Economy and Culture of Arunachal Pradesh*, Itanagar, pp. 435–443.

Sills, D.L. (1972). *International Encyclopedia of the Social Sciences*, Vol. 15, 16 & 17, The Macmillan Company and the Free Press, New York.

Singh, K.S. (1995). (ed.) *People of India: Arunachal Pradesh* Vol. 14, Anthropological Survey of India, Calcutta, pp. 288–292.

Sinha, A.K. (1992). Changing Dimension of Tribal Economy in Chotanagpur with Special Reference to their Problems Among the Korwas Tribes, B. Chaudhuri (ed.) '*Tribal Transformation in India*, Socio-Economic & Ecological Development, Vol. 2, Inter India Publication, New Delhi, pp. 162–175.

Srinivas, M.N. (1962). *Caste in Modern India*, Media Promoters & Publishers Pvt. Ltd., Bombay.

Srinivas, M.N. (1966). *Social Change in Modern India,* Orient Longman Pvt. Ltd., New Delhi.

Srinivas, M.N. (1977). *Caste: Its Twentieth Century Avatar,* Penguin Books, New Delhi.

Srinivas, M.N. (1997). Changing Values in India Today, Ghanshyam Shah (ed.) *Social Transformation in India* Vol. 1, Rawat Publications, Jaipur, pp. 55–76.

Srinivas, M.N. (2004). The Insider Versus the Outsider in the Study of Culture, Vinay Kumar Srivastava (ed.), *Methodology and Fieldwork*, Oxford University Press, New Delhi.

Srivastava, S.L. (1970). Stratification and Etiquette in Village Communities, *Man in India*, Vol. 50(3), pp. 269–279.

Thakur, A.K. (1998). Evolution of Social Stratification in Arunachal Pradesh, *Journal of North East Indian Council for Social Science Research*, Vol. 22(1), pp. 46–53.

Thakur, A.K. (1998). State Formation in Arunachal Pradesh, *NEHU Journal of Social Sciences and Humanities*, Vol. 1(1), pp. 73–87.

Thapan, M. (1998). Rethinking Anthropology Anew, Meenakshi Thapan (ed.) *Anthropological Journeys: Reflection on Fieldwork*, Orient Longman, New Delhi, pp. 1–37.

Index